Mac Application Development by Example Beginner's Guide

A comprehensive and practical guide, for absolute beginners, to developing your own App for Mac OS X

Robert Wiebe

BIRMINGHAM - MUMBAI

Mac Application Development by Example Beginner's Guide

First published: December 2012

Production Reference: 1141212

Published by Packt Publishing Ltd.
Livery Place
35 Livery Street
Birmingham B3 2PB, UK.

ISBN 978-1-84969-382-0

www.packtpub.com

Cover Image by J.Blaminsky (milak6@wp.pl)

Credits

Author
Robert Wiebe

Reviewers
Luca Bernardi
John Dumais
Dominik Jaworek
Jamie B. McHardy

Acquisition Editor
James Keane

Lead Technical Editor
Ankita Shashi

Technical Editor
Sharvari Baet

Project Coordinator
Amey Sawant

Proofreader
Steve Maguire

Indexer
Monica Ajmera Mehta

Production Coordinator
Nilesh R. Mohite

Cover Work
Nilesh R. Mohite

About the Author

Robert Wiebe was born in 1961. He has more than 30 years experience designing, implementing, and testing software. He wrote his first App in 1979, as a high school student, using 6502 assembler code on an Ohio Scientific C2-4P computer with 8k RAM. More recently, he has focused on developing games and utilities for Mac OS X.

His interests include a vintage computer collection which includes many pre-IBM PC era microcomputers; Apple Macintosh computers starting with the SE/30 running Mac OS 7 through to the Macbook Pro running Mac OS X that he uses today.

He has developed many popular Mac OS X Apps including ShredIt X, NetShred X, Music Man, iVCD, and many more.

He has experience developing software in a number of industries, including mining, finance, and communications. He has worked for a number of employers including Motorola as a Senior Systems Architect developing two-way wireless data systems and Infowave Software as the Software Development Manager for their Imaging Division. After working for other people's companies, he founded his own companies, Mireth Technology and Burningthumb Software, which are his primary interests today.

He is also the author of *Unity iOS Essential* book (ISBN 978-1-849691-82-6).

I would like to thank my son, Abram, who is a beginning Mac OS X programmer himself, for always asking questions. I would also like to thank my wife, Donna, for not only encouraging me but also for making it possible for me to pursue the things I want to do. And finally, I would like to thank my daughter, Amanda, who keeps me focused on the things that really matter in life.

About the Reviewers

Luca Bernardi is from Milan, Italy. He is 25 years old, has a degree in Computer Science and he is currently pursuing a Master's Degree in Software Development and Design. Luca is a passion-driven iOS engineer and a mobile enthusiast, has developed applications that have been awarded as Apple's App of the Week and top selling app. When he's not programming he really enjoys learning new things, reading books, and sports such as basketball, snowboarding, and running.

> I want to thank my family, Matilde, Claudio, Veronica and Adread who have always supported me, giving me everything I need to follow my passions. To my father, Giorgio, who passed away when I was a child, who gave me my first computer, an Apple II, and taught me to always follow my passion. To my amazing girlfriend, Veronica, who always has a smile for me.

John Dumais has over 25 years of experience developing system and circuit simulation software on a wide variety of platforms, including Mac OS X. He has been using Objective-C since StepStone originally introduced it. Most recently, the reviewer has been developing system monitoring and control software for iOS devices.

The other book he has reviewed is:

http://books.google.com/books/about/Visual_Programming_With_HP_VEE.html?id=1JRQPgAACAAJ

Dominik Jaworek is an experienced SW professional living in Vancouver Area, British Columbia, with his wife and two kids.

He has been working in mobile SW area for more than 14 years experiencing all aspects of Software Engineering, starting from development through business analysis, product management and R&D management. He has also been involved in accessibility technologies and solutions, and participated and presented in the CSUN 2001 conference.

Dominik loves the outdoors and he tries to take every opportunity for trips and hikes with his family. Also he has always been fascinated with and interested in cars so it's no surprise that with his engineering soul he is an avid motorsports fan.

Jamie B. McHardy is originally from the Isle of Man. He has worked in the mobile telecommunications domain for over a decade. He has developed embedded middleware used in millions of devices globally on technologies ranging from communication protocols to audio playback to digital security. Now based in Vancouver, Canada, he is father to one, has a passion for General Aviation and is due to wed his beautiful fiancé in the summer of '13.

www.PacktPub.com

Support files, eBooks, discount offers and more

You might want to visit www.PacktPub.com for support files and downloads related to your book.

Did you know that Packt offers eBook versions of every book published, with PDF and ePub files available? You can upgrade to the eBook version at www.PacktPub.com and as a print book customer, you are entitled to a discount on the eBook copy. Get in touch with us at service@packtpub.com for more details.

At www.PacktPub.com, you can also read a collection of free technical articles, sign up for a range of free newsletters and receive exclusive discounts and offers on Packt books and eBooks.

http://PacktLib.PacktPub.com

Do you need instant solutions to your IT questions? PacktLib is Packt's online digital book library. Here, you can access, read and search across Packt's entire library of books.

Why Subscribe?

- Fully searchable across every book published by Packt
- Copy and paste, print and bookmark content
- On demand and accessible via web browser

Free Access for Packt account holders

If you have an account with Packt at www.PacktPub.com, you can use this to access PacktLib today and view nine entirely free books. Simply use your login credentials for immediate access.

Table of Contents

Preface

Apple is taking the world by storm. Their market share is growing faster than the industry average and has been for years. So, it's never been more important to have the ability to develop an App for Mac OS X. Whether it's a System Preference, a business app that accesses information in the Cloud, or an application that uses a multi-touch trackpad or uses a camera, you will need a solid foundation in app development to get the job done.

Mac Application Development by Example takes you through all the aspects of using the Xcode development tool to produce complete working apps that cover a broad range of topics. This comprehensive book on developing applications covers everything a beginner needs to know and demonstrates the concepts using examples that take advantage of some of the most interesting hardware and software features available.

You will discover the fundamental aspects of OS X development while investigating innovative platform features to create a final product that takes advantage of some of the unique aspects of OS X.

You will learn how to use Xcode tools to create and share Mac OS X Apps and explore numerous OS X features including iCloud, multi-touch trackpad, and the iSight camera.

Using fundamental development concepts and innovative platform features, this book provides you with an illustrated and annotated guide to bring your ideas to life!

What this book covers

Chapter 1, Our First Program – SimpleCalc, covers how to get up and running with the Xcode Integrated Development Environment (IDE). We create an App icon, a user interface, implement the App behavior, and build and run the App with Xcode.

Chapter 2, Debugger – Finding and Fixing Problems, covers the concept of debugging our program code. We learn how to explore our program code when the debugger is invoked, how to change the values of our variables with the debugger, and how to use the debugger to find and fix problems in our program.

Chapter 3, System Preferences – NewDefaults, covers creating our own System Preference plugin and learning how to run command-line tools from within the System Preference to customize the behavior of the Mac OS X Finder.

Chapter 4, Business Application – Global Currency Converter, covers how to get publicly-available data from the Internet and use it to create a currency converter. We will download an XML file from the Internet and extract the information that we need from it into our program. We learn how to access the Internet using a background thread so that our user interface does not freeze while we wait for the XML file to download. Finally, we learn how to use pop-up menus, table views, and how to perform arithmetic operations on an array of numbers.

Chapter 5, Personal Information – Numbers in the iCloud, how to take your data and store it on the Internet using Cloud services Cloud services. Cloud services are popping up everywhere. We learn about Apple's iCloud and how to store and retrieve information from the iCloud servers. Along the way, we learn how to implement two table views in the same window and how to implement a toolbar.

Chapter 6, Painting – Multi-finger Paint, covers multi-touch. Mobile computing has introduced a new way of interacting with computer touches and gestures. Laptop and desktop computing have adopted this trend through the use of multi-touch trackpads. In this chapter, we learn about multi-touch, including how to handle multi-touch and gesture events. We also learn how to use the 2D drawing features of Mac OS X to draw into custom views.

Chapter 7, Capturing Still Images – iSight iMage cApture App, covers how to use the Image Kit Framework to capture and manipulate still Images using the iSight camera.

Chapter 8, Video Recording – iSight Recorder, covers capturing videos. While capturing still images is nice, capturing movies is better. In this chapter, we learn how to use Quicktime Kit Capture to preview Video and Audio, to capture still frames, and to record movies using the iSight camera.

Chapter 9, Video Recording – Full Screen iSight Recorder, covers how to convert a windowed App to a full screen App. We'll learn how to convert our iSight Recorder App to a full screen App, including enhancing the user interface, giving the screen an illusion of depth, and implementing the animations used to enter and exit full screen.

Chapter 10, Sharing our App with others – Becoming a Mac developer. Now that we know how to create Mac OS X Apps, we'll want to share them. This chapter explores both the free and paid Apple developer programs - describing the features of each as well as explaining how to join them and why you might want to. It also explains code signing - what it is and how to do it. Then we'll be able to share our Mac Apps and have them interact nicely with modern security software like Gatekeeper on Mac OS X 10.8.

What you need for this book

You need a Mac OS X computer capable of running Mac OS X 10.7 or later. Some App features require Mac OS X 10.8. You also need to install Xcode Version 4 from the Mac OS X App store. Xcode is a free download.

Who this book is for

This book is for people who are programming beginners and have a great idea for a Mac OS X app and need to get started.

Conventions

In this book, you will find a number of styles of text that distinguish between different kinds of information. Here are some examples of these styles, and an explanation of their meaning.

Code words in text are shown as follows: "In the file named BTSAppDelegate.h use the #import directive to import the <QTKit/QTKit.h> file so that the QTKit interface objects can be referenced."

A block of code is set as follows:

```
// Define two local variables
// that will contain the results
// of various operations
BOOL l_success = NO;
NSError* l_error;
```

When we wish to draw your attention to a particular part of a code block, the relevant lines or items are set in bold:

```
// Define two local variables
// that will contain the results
// of various operations
BOOL l_success = NO;
NSError* l_error;
```

New terms and **important words** are shown in bold. Words that you see on the screen, in menus or dialog boxes for example, appear in the text like this: "When we click the **Next** button, Xcode will ask us to select options for our new project".

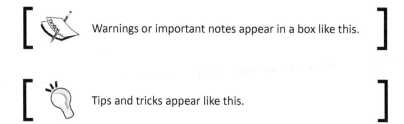

Warnings or important notes appear in a box like this.

Tips and tricks appear like this.

Reader feedback

Feedback from our readers is always welcome. Let us know what you think about this book—what you liked or may have disliked. Reader feedback is important for us to develop titles that you really get the most out of.

To send us general feedback, simply send an e-mail to feedback@packtpub.com, and mention the book title through the subject of your message.

If there is a topic that you have expertise in and you are interested in either writing or contributing to a book, see our author guide on www.packtpub.com/authors.

Customer support

Now that you are the proud owner of a Packt book, we have a number of things to help you to get the most from your purchase.

Downloading the example code

You can download the example code files for all Packt books you have purchased from your account at http://www.packtpub.com. If you purchased this book elsewhere, you can visit http://www.packtpub.com/support and register to have the files e-mailed directly to you.

Errata

Although we have taken every care to ensure the accuracy of our content, mistakes do happen. If you find a mistake in one of our books—maybe a mistake in the text or the code—we would be grateful if you would report this to us. By doing so, you can save other readers from frustration and help us improve subsequent versions of this book. If you find any errata, please report them by visiting http://www.packtpub.com/support, selecting your book, clicking on the **errata submission form** link, and entering the details of your errata. Once your errata are verified, your submission will be accepted and the errata will be uploaded to our website, or added to any list of existing errata, under the Errata section of that title.

Piracy

Piracy of copyright material on the Internet is an ongoing problem across all media. At Packt, we take the protection of our copyright and licenses very seriously. If you come across any illegal copies of our works, in any form, on the Internet, please provide us with the location address or website name immediately so that we can pursue a remedy.

Please contact us at copyright@packtpub.com with a link to the suspected pirated material.

We appreciate your help in protecting our authors, and our ability to bring you valuable content.

Questions

You can contact us at questions@packtpub.com if you are having a problem with any aspect of the book, and we will do our best to address it.

1

Our First Program – SimpleCalc

*This chapter will walk us through the steps needed to set up Xcode as well as the development of the **SimpleCalc** App. SimpleCalc will allow us to take two numbers and perform addition, subtraction, multiplication, and division. This App is intentionally kept simple because we have many things to learn about how to develop Apps in this chapter.*

In this chapter, we shall learn the following:

- Installing the Xcode App
- Creating a new Xcode project
- Configuring an Xcode project
- Creating an App Icon
- Configuring an Xcode target
- Creating a user interface
- Implementing a Mac OS X App behavior
- Building and running a Mac OS X program

Locating developer tools

Before we start to develop our first Mac OS X program, we need to locate the tools needed to create programs. There are several different choices for software development on Mac OS X and the tools that we will select depend on the programming environment that we want to use. Because we want to write our programs using the native Objective-C programming language and the Cocoa frameworks we are going to use Apple's free **Integrated Development Environment (IDE)**, called Xcode.

The code in this book has been developed and tested with Xcode 4.3.

Cocoa frameworks

The Cocoa frameworks consist of libraries, **Application Programming Interfaces (APIs)**, and runtimes that form the development layer for all of Mac OS X. By developing with Cocoa, we will be creating applications the same way Mac OS X itself is created. Our application will automatically inherit the behavior and appearances of Mac OS X. Using Cocoa with Xcode IDE is the best way to create native Mac applications.

Time for action - Installing the Xcode App

For Mac OS X, Apple provides the Xcode IDE for free in the Mac OS X App store. We are going to install the Xcode IDE so that we can start making our first App. To do this, we need to follow these steps:

1. Access the Mac App store by clicking on the Apple menu and selecting **App Store**.
2. Search the **App Store** to locate the Xcode App.
3. Install the Xcode App from the App store.

What just happened?

Because Apple distributes Xcode through the Mac App store, we were able to find and install developer tools in the same way we would find any App that is available in the store.

Working with projects

When we want to build a Mac OS X App, we need to first create an Xcode project. The Xcode project is the place that we keep all of the parts (code, icons, user interface, and images) that Xcode will put together to build our App.

Time for action - creating the SimpleCalc Xcode project

Now that we have installed Xcode, we can start using it to write our own Mac OS X App. Let's get started:

1. To create a new Xcode project, launch the Xcode App and click the button titled **Create a new Xcode project** on the **Welcome to Xcode** window as shown in the following screenshot:

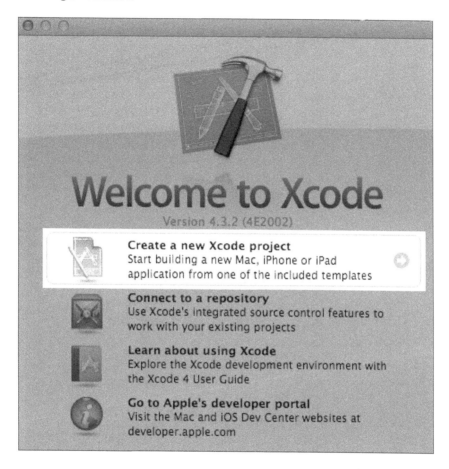

2. When Xcode asks us to select a template, select **Application** under **Mac OS X** and **Cocoa Application** as the template. Then, click on the **Next** button.

3. When we click the **Next** button, Xcode will ask us to select options for our new project. The options that we need to select are as follows:

Option	Value	Description
Product Name	SimpleCalc	The product name will be the name of your App program file that shows up in the Mac OS X Finder.
Company Identifier	com.yourdomain	The company identifier needs to be unique and typically uses the reverse domain notation. It can be anything but you should use a company identifier that will not conflict with an existing company. If you don't have an Internet domain name you can acquire one new or you can use *com.yourlastname.first* name.
Class Prefix	Your Initials (For consistency, throughout this book we will use BTS but when you develop your own code you should use your own initials)	The class prefix is used to make sure any program classes that you create do not have the same name as any program classes that some-one else may create.

4. Finally, there are some checkboxes at the bottom of the options screen. The only one that needs to be checked is the option titled **Use Automatic Reference Counting**. This setting permits Xcode to automatically manage the memory that our program uses and helps keep programing simple because we do not need to think about destroying objects that our program creates. This checkbox, along with the rest of our settings, is shown in the following screenshot:

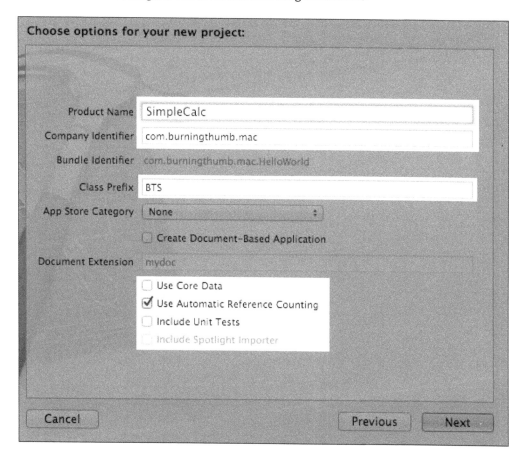

5. Click on the **Next** button and Xcode will ask us where we want to save the new project that we are creating. While we can save projects anywhere that we like, a good place may be a new folder called `projects` in our `Documents` folder. Whatever we decide, when we have navigated to that folder, we need to click on the **Create** button as shown in the following screenshot:

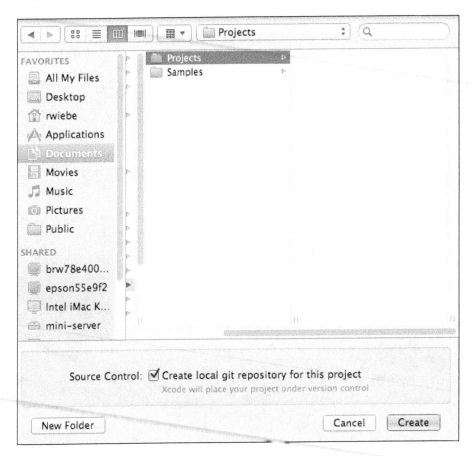

Xcode automatically creates project subfolders

We do not need to create a subfolder in the projects folder because Xcode will do that automatically using our product name. If we look for our project folder in the **Finder**, after Xcode has created it, we will find it in `projects/SimpleCalc`.

What just happened?

When we clicked on the **Create** button, Xcode created the new project from the template that we chose and displayed its main interface window.

Don't Panic

The main Xcode window can be quite overwhelming. The following screenshot shows the entire interface simply to give us an idea of its scope. We don't need to understand all of the sections or be intimidated by Xcode's main window. As we get deeper into programming, we will learn more about each part of the window.

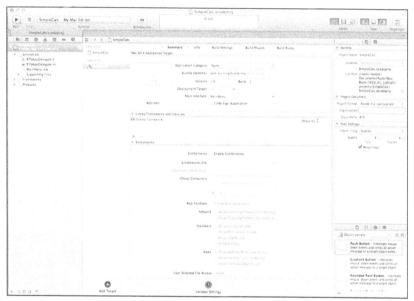

As we progress in our App development and become more familiar with Xcode, we will become comfortable with the contents of this interface. Xcode's interface is very similar to iTunes. It contains the following:

- A control area along the top where we can build and run ("play") or stop our App
- A navigation area on the left where we can select different components of our project to inspect
- An editing area in the center where we can modify different components that were selected in the navigation area
- A utilities area on the right where we can inspect and change attributes of selected items

It is a good idea to take some time now to become familiar with the meaning of each of the little icons for the navigator section of the Xcode view, which appear across the top of the navigation area on the left-hand side of the window. The following table gives descriptions of these icons:

Icon	Description
	Shows the project navigator, which lists all of the files in this project
	Shows the symbol navigator, which lists all of the symbols (method names, property names, and so on) in this project
	Shows the search navigator, which lists all of the search results for anything that we want to search for in the project
	Shows the issue navigator, which lists all of the issues (typically error or warning)
	Shows the debug navigator, which lists all of the App threads and symbols if a debug session is active
	Shows the breakpoint navigator, which lists all of the places we want the App to stop at so that we can inspect its state during an active debug session
	Shows the log navigator, which lists a log of the different activities that we have performed

Xcode will sometimes change the selected navigator based on actions that we perform or events that occur. It is useful to know that we can always switch back to the navigator that we want to see by clicking on the appropriate icon.

Understanding the Xcode project template

When we used Xcode to create a new project from a template, Xcode did a lot of things behind the scenes that we need to understand. The best way to understand what Xcode did is to look at the contents of the project navigator.

Time for action – examine the items in the project navigator

1. In Xcode, open the **SimpleCalc** project.

2. Click on the disclosure triangles beside each folder icon in the project navigator to reveal all of the items that Xcode created as shown in the following screenshot:

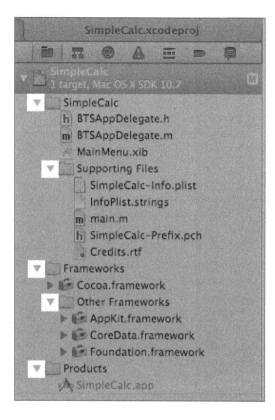

3. We don't, yet, need to understand everything that the Xcode template has done for us, but it is important to understand each of the main types of files in these folders. The file type is determined by the file extension (`.h`, `.m`, `.app`, and so on).

What just happened?

We examined the contents of the Xcode project template and gained a better understanding of the different types of files that are needed to create a Mac OS X App. While it is not important, yet, to understand each of the different file types in detail, it is important to have an overview of all of the different components that are needed to create a Mac OS X App. As we develop our own Apps, we will acquire a much better understanding of these files and their contents.

Each file type is explained in the following table:

Extension	Description
.h	A program header file is used to separate the interface from the implementation. It defines what can be done but not how it is done.
.m	A program implementation file. It defines how things are done..
.xib	An Interface Builder file. It defines what the program interface, including windows, buttons, text fields, and so on will look like.
.plist	A property list. It contains a list of keys and corresponding values. The Info.plist includes important App information (like App name, App version, App copyright, and so on.)
.strings	A list of strings that are localizable (translated into other languages). The InfoPlist.strings file contains localized versions of some of the strings found in the Info.plist file.
.pch	A precompiled header file. When we build our program the files are compiled into a single runnable file. Because compiling takes time, the compiler will precompile the .h files and save them in the .pch file. This is used to make building the App faster.
.rtf	A rich text formatted file. Rich text, differs from standard text, in that it can contain things like bold, italics, and embedded images. The Credits.rtf file is automatically displayed by the standard About window for our App.
.framework	A framework is a bundle (and a bundle is just a folder that looks like a file) that contains .h, .xib, and library files. Frameworks are provided by Apple to perform common functions (like displaying windows) so that we don't need to write that program code ourselves.
.app	An app is a bundle that contains everything our App needs to run.

Configuring an Xcode project

There are a lot of different things that we can configure in an Xcode project. As we create different projects, we will look at different aspects of what can be configured. For our SimpleCalc App, we are going to consider which the version of Mac OS X that we want the App to run which icon that we want the App to display.

By default, Xcode will configure our project to run only on the latest version of Mac OS X with the generic App Icon. Sometimes we may want our project to run on an earlier version of Mac OS X. For example, if we want to give our software to someone with an older computer or if we want to put our software in the Mac App store. This setting is called the Mac OS X deployment target.

We will always want to assign an icon to our App so that we can easily identify our App on the Mac desktop. This setting is called the **App Icon**.

Time for action - configuring the SimpleCalc Xcode project

To change the Mac OS X deployment target for our project we need to do the following:

1. In the project navigator, click the folder icon to show the project navigator.

2. In the project navigator, click on the very top item, just under the icons, named **SimpleCalc**.

3. Under **PROJECT**, click on **SimpleCalc**.

4. Under **Deployment Target**, click on the drop-down menu beside **Mac OS X Deployment Target** and select the oldest version of Mac OS X on which we want our App to run as shown in the following screenshot:

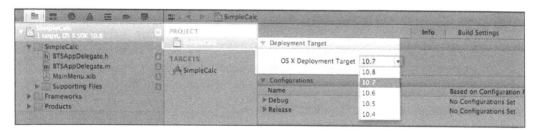

5. Change **TARGETS** setting for the **Organization** of the **Project Document** to our name or the name of our company as shown in the following screenshot:

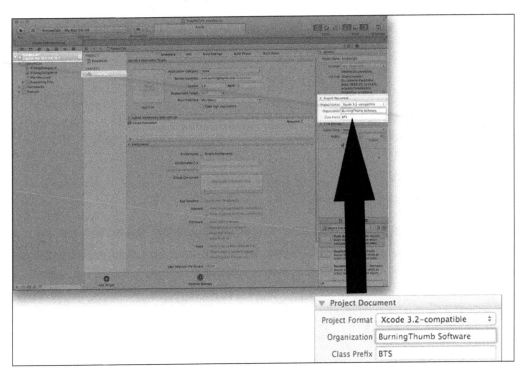

6. Before we continue to configure our Xcode target, we need to take a small detour and create an App Icon. We are going to need our App Icon as part of the process of configuring an Xcode target.

7. The first thing we need to do is create the icon. We can do this in any image editing program, from Illustrator, to Photoshop, to Gimp. The program that we use does not matter. What matters is that the image has a transparent background and that the image size is 512 x 512 pixels. We need to export our image in PNG format and it may look like the following image, which has been created in Photoshop Elements:

Apple recommends we create App Icon images in a variety of different sizes ranging from 16 x 16 to 1024 x 1024. If we were building an App to deploy in the App Store, we would create more than a single 512 x 512 icon but for our SimpleCalc App a single icon is all we need.

8. Once we have the image that we want to use as our icon, we need to save it in a folder named `SimpleCalc.iconset` with the name `icon_512x512.png`.

 The filename must be exact. If you name it anything other than `icon_512x512.png` the icon will not be correctly updated and you will see a generic icon instead of your App Icon.

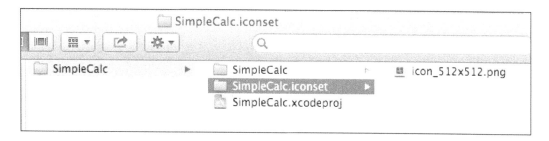

9. Once we have our PNG image saved in the `iconset` folder, we simply drag that folder to the App Icon section of our project target and Xcode will automatically convert it to a suitable `.icns` file as shown in the following screenshot:

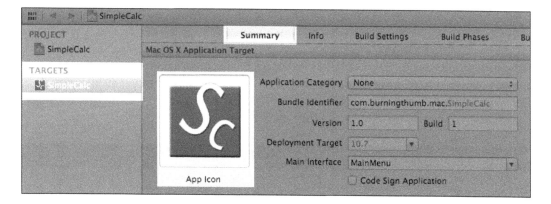

10. Because we have not provided all the required image sizes, Xcode will warn us that some image sizes are missing. For the purposes of our **SimpleCalc** App we can ignore these warnings but if we planned to deploy our App to the Mac OS X App Store we would create a PNG file for each required icon size and place it in our `iconset` folder prior to dragging the folder in to the **App Icon** section of the **Target** as shown in the following screenshot:

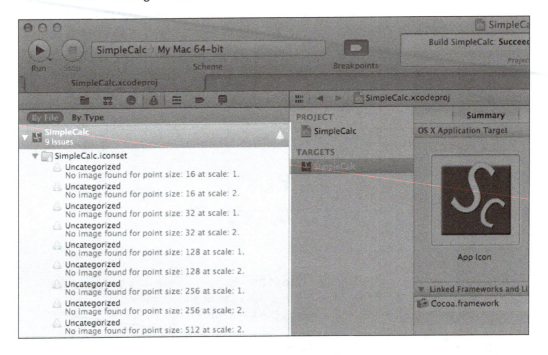

What just happened?

When we set up the Deployment Target and App Icon, we made changes to our Xcode project. Xcode will use those changes and apply them to the App when we build it so that the App is ready to run on the versions of Mac OS X that we need and the Finder will display our unique icon to identify our App on the desktop.

Have a go hero – make your own icon

Create your own 512 x 512 bitmapped image, save it in `.png` format, and put it in the `iconset` folder for the SimpleCalc App. You can use any image editing software that you like. You may want to create all of the required image sizes so that you don't get warnings from Xcode. The following screenshot shows the images of all required sizes present in the **SimpleCals.iconset** folder:

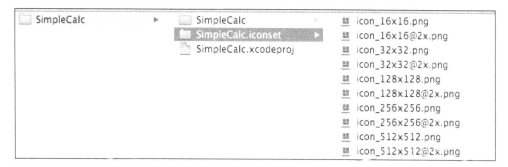

If you need a free bitmap editor take a look at Gimp for Mac OS X:

```
http://www.gimp.org/downloads/
```

Running an App

When we use an Xcode template to create an App, Xcode creates a project that will build a fully functional App. The App will display a menu bar, display a window, allow us to drag the window around and even present an **About** box when the **About** menu item is selected. An Xcode template is the perfect starting point for any App.

Time for action – run the SimpleCalc App

To run the SimpleCalc App that Xcode created from its template do the following steps:

1. In the main Xcode window, click on the **Run** button as shown in the following screenshot:

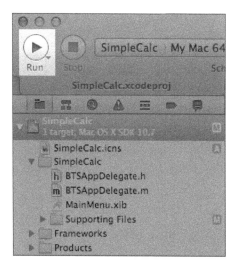

2. If we watch the Xcode status panel after clicking the **Run** button, we will (very briefly) see some messages that indicate Xcode is building our App as shown in the following screenshot:

3. After the building of the App is complete, the **SimpleCalc** App will display its menu bar and main window. When the **SimpleCalc** App is running we can drag its main window around, click on its menus, display the **About** window, and quit the App by selecting **Quit SimpleCalc** from the App's menu as shown in the following screenshot:

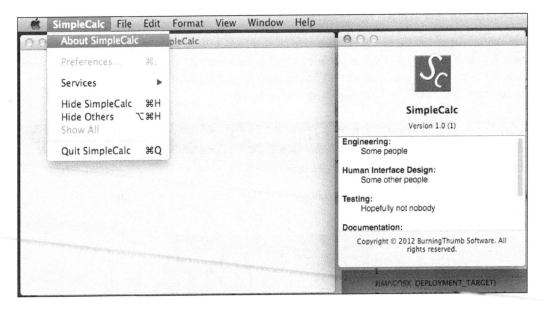

What just happened?

Xcode created a fully functional App from its template and we were able to build and run the App. When the App was running, we were able to use its menu and move around its windows, and quit from the App back to Xcode.

Customizing an Xcode template's interface

When we create a project from an Xcode template, the resulting App needs to be customized to provide the interface that we want in our App. So as soon as we have created the basic project we need to make our interface changes.

 Because the sample program code used in this and the next section is both short and concise, the explanation of the code is included in the code as comments rather than using descriptive text surrounding the code. We can identify comments in the program code by looking for the // characters that start each line or the /* and */ characters that surround a block of comments in the code. We need to become comfortable with reading program code and distinguishing the comments in the code, from the code.

The way that we implement our features is to open the files created from the template and change their contents to include the new program code that implements the behaviors that we want to add.

Time for action – creating the SimpleCalc interface

1. Open the `SimpleCalc` project in Xcode.

2. Click on the item named `BTSAppDelegate.h` and add the highlighted new interface `@property` definitions and the button action interface definition for the SimpleCalc App. Notice they are placed in the template code after the `window` property and before the `@end` statement as shown in the following code snippet:

```
@interface BTSAppDelegate : NSObject <NSApplicationDelegate>

@property (assign) IBOutlet NSWindow *window;

/*
    Create the user interface elements
 */

// Buttons
@property (assign) IBOutlet NSButton *mAdd;
@property (assign) IBOutlet NSButton *mSubtract;
@property (assign) IBOutlet NSButton *mMutliply;
@property (assign) IBOutlet NSButton *mDivide;

// Text Fields
@property (assign) IBOutlet NSTextField *mValue1;
@property (assign) IBOutlet NSTextField *mValue2;
@property (assign) IBOutlet NSTextField *mResult;
```

```
/*
 Create the App interface for the buttons
 */

- (IBAction)myButtonAction:(id)sender;

@end
```

Click on the item named **BTSAppDelegate.m** and add the highlighted new interface `@synthesize` definitions and the button action implementation for the SimpleCalc App.

3. Again notice the position of the code after the `@implementation` keyword and before the `@end` keyword as shown in the following code snippet:

```
@implementation BTSAppDelegate

/*
 Create the user interface setter and getter functions
 */

// Buttons
@synthesize mAdd;
@synthesize mSubtract;
@synthesize mMutliply;
@synthesize mDivide;

// Text Fields
@synthesize mValue1;
@synthesize mValue2;
@synthesize mResult;

- (void)applicationDidFinishLaunching:(NSNotification *)
aNotification
{
    // Insert code here to initialize your application
}

/*
 Create the App implementation for the buttons
 */

- (IBAction)myButtonAction:(id)sender;
{
    // For now, just beep
    NSBeep();
}

@end
```

4. Click on the item named **MainMenu.xib**.

5. Click the Show Document Outline button as shown in the following screenshot:

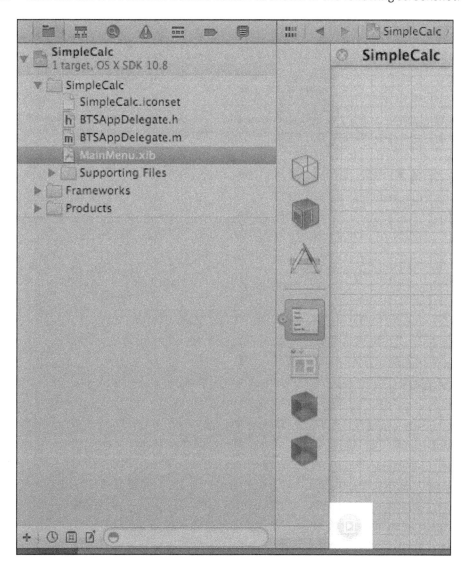

6. Click on the **Window - SimpleCalc** tab in **Objects** to display the App window as shown in the following screenshot:

7. Locate the **Object Library** option and scroll to find the **Square Button** shape as shown in the following screenshot:

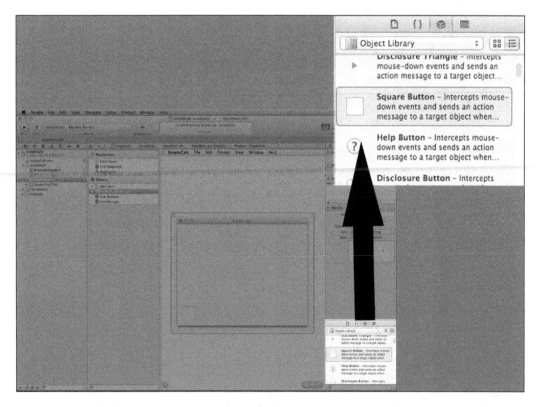

8. Click and drag a **Square Button** shape from the **Object Library** to the **SimpleCalc** window. Then drag three more buttons and place them beside the first button to form a row of buttons. Finally, resize the window so that it fits the four buttons as shown in the following screenshot:

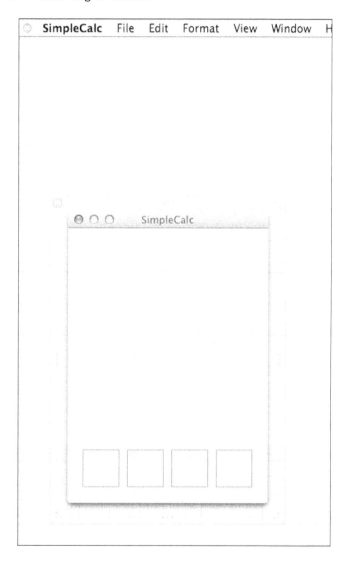

9. Double-click on the buttons one at a time and type the labels +, -, ÷, x respectively.

To enter the ÷ character, hold down the *option* key while pressing / on the keyboard.

10. You will end up with something that looks like the following screenshot:

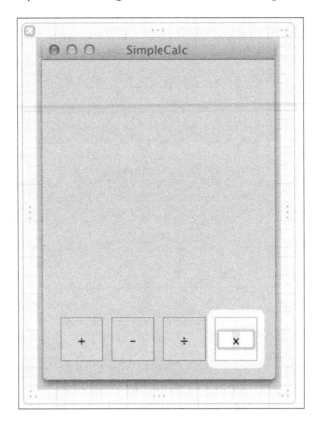

11. Locate the **Object Library** and scroll to find the **Text Field** option.

12. Drag two **Text Field** objects into the **SimpleCalc** window, and place them one below the other.

13. Locate the **Object Library** and scroll to find the **Horizontal Line** option.

14. Drag a **Horizontal Line** into the **SimpleCalc** window and position it below the two **Text Field** objects.

15. Locate the **Text Field** object in the **Object Library** and drag a third **Text Field** into the **SimpleCalc** window.

16. Click and drag to select all the **Square Button** objects and drag them up below the third **Text Field**.

17. Resize the **SimpleCalc** window to fit the **Text Field** and **Square Button** objects. After you are done, you will have something like the following screenshot:

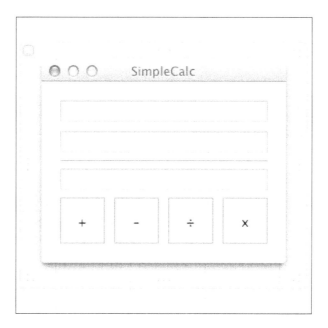

18. Because we don't want our calculator window to change size, we need to set constraints. Click on the **SimpleCalc** window to select it, select **Show the size inspector** in the inspector pane, and under **Constraints**, enable both the **Minimum Size** and **Maximum Size** options as shown in the following screenshot:

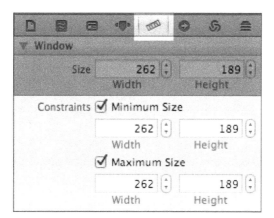

19. Right-click (or if you don't have a three-button mouse, hold down the *Ctrl* key and left click) on the **+** button and drag it to the **App Delegate** object as shown in the following screenshot:

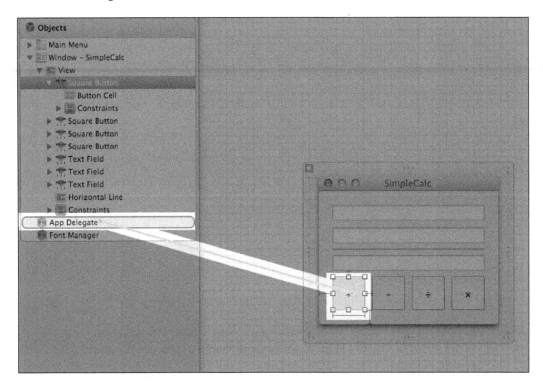

20. When the **App Delegate** object highlights, release the mouse button and select **myButtonAction** from the **Received Actions** selection pane as shown in the following screenshot:

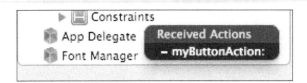

21. Repeat the process to connect the remaining three buttons to the **– myButtonAction** method.

22. Right-click (or if you don't have a three-button mouse, hold down the *Ctrl* key and left click) on the **App Delegate** object and drag until the first **Text Field** is highlighted as shown in the following screenshot:

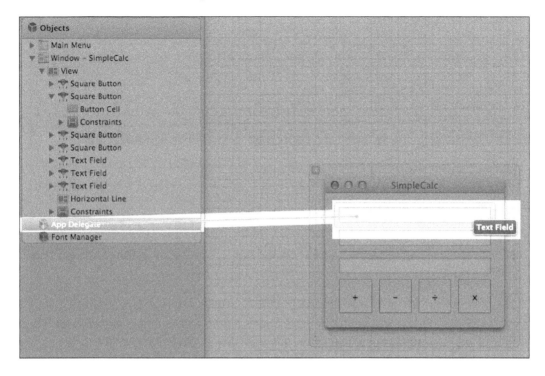

23. Release the mouse button and select **mValue1** from the **Outlets** selection pane as shown in the following screenshot:

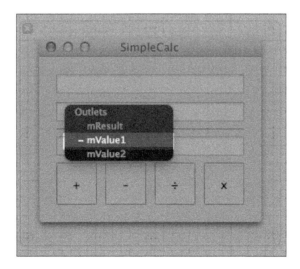

24. Repeat these steps to connect **mValue2** to the second **Text Field** and **mResult** to the third **Text Field**.

What just happened?

We created the interface for our **SimpleCalc** App and connected the interface to the program code for our App. We also connected the **App Delegate** object to the **Text Fields** in the interface. Now when we run **SimpleCalc** we see the new interface and when we click any of the buttons we hear a system beep.

Customizing an Xcode template's implementation

When we create a project from an Xcode template, the resulting App needs to be customized to provide the behavior that we want in our App. So as soon as we have created the basic project we need to make our behavior changes.

Time for action – implement the SimpleCalc behavior

The following steps will help us implement the SimpleCalc behavior:

1. Open the `SimpleCalc` project in Xcode.

2. Click on the item named `BTSAppDelegate.m` and add an implementation for the `myButtonAction:` method. The code that we need to add is as follows:

```
/*
 Create the App implementation for the buttons
 */

- (IBAction)myButtonAction:(id)a_sender;
{
    // For now, just beep
    // Comment out the beep, we don't need it
    // NSBeep();

    // Get the button title (+, -, x, or ÷) to
    // determine which operation the App will
    // preform
    NSString *l_operation = [a_sender title];

    // Get a double precision number from the
    // first text field
    double l_value1 = [mValue1 doubleValue];
```

```
// Get a double precision number from the
// second text field
double l_value2 = [mValue2 doubleValue];

// Create a double precision variable to
// hold the result of l_value1 <op> l_value2
double l_result;

// If the operation was addition, then
// add the two values
if ([@"+" isEqual: l_operation])
{
    l_result = l_value1 + l_value2;
}
// If the operation was subtraction, then
// subtract the two values
else if ([@"-" isEqual: l_operation])
{
    l_result = l_value1 - l_value2;
}
// If the operation was multiplication, then
// multiply the two values
else if ([@"x" isEqual: l_operation])
{
    l_result = l_value1 * l_value2;
}
// The operation must have been division, so
// divide the first value by the second value
else
{
    l_result = l_value1 / l_value2;
}

// Set the result text field to the result
[mResult setDoubleValue:l_result];
}
```

Downloading the example code

You can download the example code files for all Packt books you have purchased from your account at http://www.packtpub.com . If you purchased this book elsewhere, you can visit http://www.packtpub.com/ support and register to have the files e-mailed directly to you.

What just happened?

We created and implemented the behavior for our **SimpleCalc** App (including removing the beep). Now when we run **SimpleCalc** we can enter two numbers and press one of the operation buttons to see the result as shown in the following screenshot:

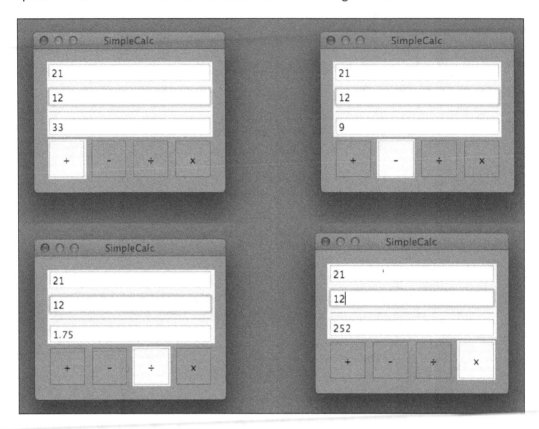

Building an App

Once we can successfully run our App from Xcode and it is doing everything that we want it to do, it's time to build our App as a standalone package that we can install in our Applications folder.

Time for action – building and installing the SimpleCalc App

Let's learn how to build and install the SimpleCalc app:

1. Open the SimpleCalc project in Xcode.

2. Under the **Product** menu, select **Clean**.

3. Under the **Product** menu, select **Edit Scheme**.

4. In the scheme editing panel, select **Run SimpleCalc.app**, click on the pop-up menu for **Build Configuration** and select **Release**. Then click on the **OK** button as shown in the following screenshot:

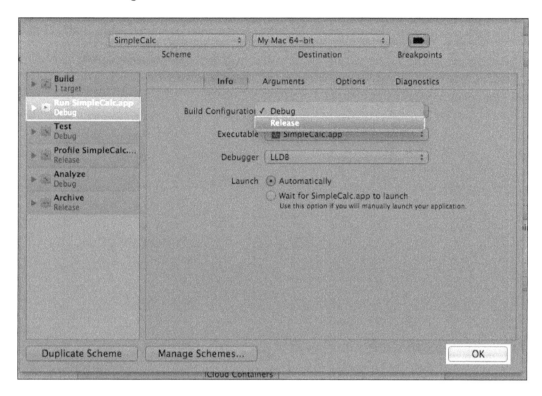

5. From the **Product** menu, select **Build For** and select **Running** as seen in the following screenshot:

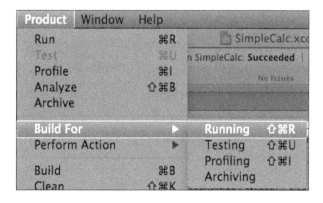

6. In the **Project Navigator**, right-click (or hold down the *Ctrl* key on the keyboard and left click if you don't have a three button mouse) on **SimpleCalc.app** and select **Show in Finder** as shown in the following screenshot:

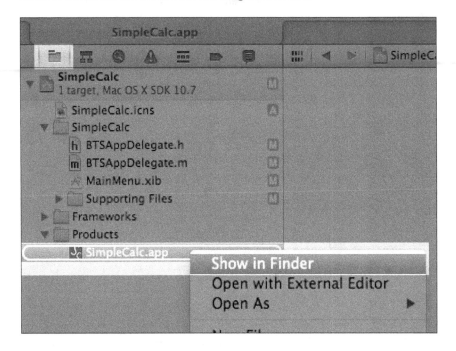

What just happened?

We built a standalone Mac OS X App that we can copy from the `Release` folder to our `Applications` folder and double-click to run just like any standard Mac OS X App as shown in the following screenshot:

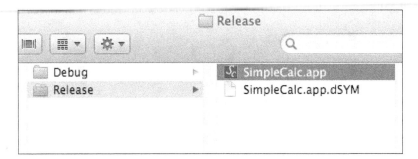

Summary

In this chapter, we have covered everything that we need to know to develop Mac OS X Apps.

Specifically, we covered how to install the Xcode IDE from the Mac App store and how to create a new Xcode project from a template. We then identified the different types of files needed to create a Mac OS X App. Then we customized the Xcode template and created a new icon for our App. Finally we created the user interface and actions for our App so that we could build it for installation into the `Applications` folder.

Now that we've learned how to develop a basic Mac OS X App, we need to take a small diversion in our route to learn what to do when the unexpected happens and the debugger appears when least expected – which is the topic of the next chapter.

2
Debugger – Finding and Fixing Problems

*This book is not about finding and fixing problems – known as **debugging**. However, sometimes the debugging tool can appear unexpectedly or our App will not do what we want and we may want to see the debugging tool. So it's important to be able to recognize the debugger and figure out what to do next. Knowing how to respond to the unexpected appearance of the debugger and knowing how to use the debugger to figure out why our App is not behaving correctly can really make our lives easier.*

In this chapter, we shall learn the following:

◆ Recognizing the Debug area in Xcode

◆ What kind of problems can result in the Debug area appearing and Xcode showing us the problem

◆ Examining program variables in the debugger

◆ What kinds of common problems can result in the Debug area appearing or unexpected App behavior without Xcode showing us the problem

◆ How to interpret what the debugger is trying to tell us and getting Xcode to show us the problem

The Debug area in Xcode

The main Xcode window is split into panes. Typically, when we launch Xcode, the Debug area is not visible. We can either wait for the debugger to appear on its own, which it will due to some program errors, or we can show the debugger area manually and familiarize ourselves with where the Debug area will appear in Xcode.

Time for action – displaying the Debug area in Xcode

If we want to manually display the debugger area in Xcode, we can do so by clicking the correct icon in the Xcode toolbar. The setting is on a per project basis so if we display the debugger area in one project it will not be visible in another project, unless we also make it visible in the second project.

1. In the Xcode project window toolbar, locate the **Hide or show the Debug area** button in the **View** tools as shown in the following screenshot:

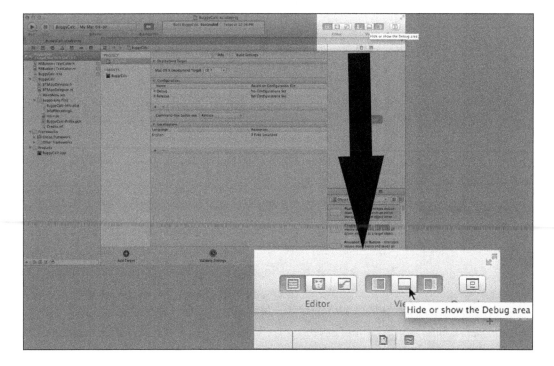

2. Click the **Hide or show the Debug area** button in the **View** tools to reveal the Debug area as shown in the following screenshot:

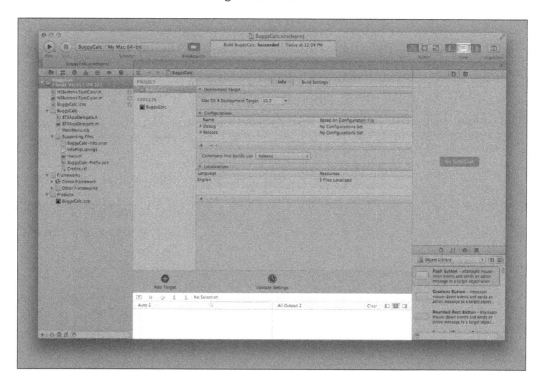

What just happened?

By manually displaying the Debug area we can see where it will appear in the Xcode window. If we are running our App and Xcode ever brings itself forward, in front of our App, we should look in the Debug area to see if our App has an error that has caused the debugger to take control.

The Debug area appears on its own

There are a few kinds of programming errors that will cause the Debug area to be displayed. These problems are critical errors such as trying to access memory that does not belong to your program, dividing integer values by zero, or trying to access objects that have been released or garbage collected (dangling pointers).

Time for action - integer division by zero

We can make a small change to the SimpleCalc program to demonstrate an integer division by zero that results in the Debug area appearing while the program is running.

1. Create a new Xcode project (we can follow the steps given in *Chapter 1, Our First Program – SimpleCalc*) but call it `BuggyCalc` instead of `SimpleCalc`. Other than the App name being **BuggyCalc**, all the steps are the same as was done for SimpleCalc.

> The complete project for **BuggyCalc** is included in the downloadable content for this book so if you don't want to create **BuggyCalc** yourself, you can just download the project and open it in Xcode.

2. In **BuggyCalc**, select the filename **BTSAppDelegate.m** and add the following line of code that uses the compiler directive `#define` to create a symbol named `D_SHOW_DIVIDEBYZERO_BUG` with a value of `1`:

```
#define D_SHOW_DIVIDEBYZERO_BUG 1
```

> If you are using the pre-built project, locate the line of code that defines the symbol and change its value from `0` to `1`.

The following screenshot shows what the program source code will look like in Xcode after the `#define` has been added:

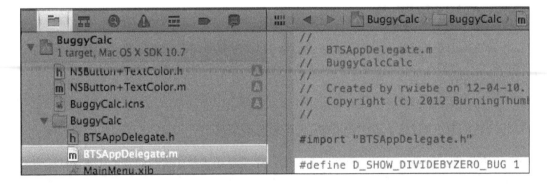

3. Still in the file named **BTSAppDelegate.m**, locate the lines of the program that declare `l_value1` and `l_value2` as `double` precision numbers and change the program code to declare the variables as `int` when the `D_SHOWDIVIDEBYZERO_BUG` symbol is equal to `1`.

If you are using the prebuilt project, locate the lines of code and make sure they match the following lines of code:

```
// Get a double precision number from the
// first text field
// To make this buggy we use int instead of double
#if D_SHOW_DIVIDEBYZERO_BUG
    int l_value1 = [mValue1 doubleValue];
#else
    double l_value1 = [mValue1 doubleValue];
#endif


// Get a double precision number from the
// second text field
// To make this buggy we use int instead of double
#if D_SHOW_DIVIDEBYZERO_BUG
    int l_value2 = [mValue2 doubleValue];
#else
    double l_value2 = [mValue2 doubleValue];
#endif
```

 This is called **conditional compilation**. It allows us to change our program behavior based on a defined value. If the value of the symbol is not zero, the program code between the #if and #else directives will be used. If the value of the symbol is zero, the program code between the #else and the #endif directives will be used. It is a very convenient way to demonstrate different program code because we can simply change the value of the symbol and re-run the program to see the variation in behavior.

4. If the Debug area is visible in Xcode, click on the **Hide or show the Debug area** button to hide the Debug area.

5. Click on the **Run** button to run **BuggyCalc** in **Xcode**.

6. When **BuggyCalc** launches, don't enter any values in the text fields, and press the **+, -, ÷,** and **x** buttons in that order.

7. When we click on **+**, and **-**, the **BuggyCalc** app behaves as expected and displays the result **0**. When we click on ÷ something unexpected happens. Xcode brings itself forward and shows us our program code (focused on the specific line of offending code) in the Xcode file browser. Xcode also automatically shows us the Debug area and something else we have not seen before, the Debug navigator (see the following screenshot for reference).

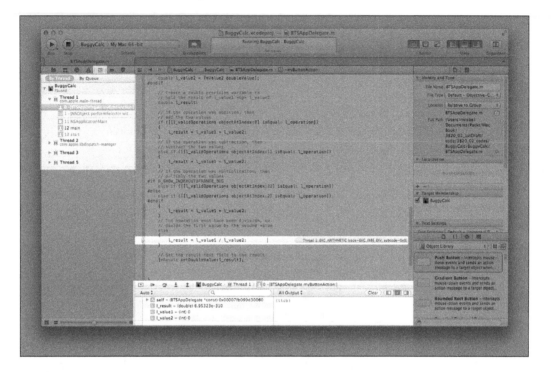

What just happened?

Because division by zero (or an invalid memory reference) is a serious programming error that would result in a crash, Xcode instead traps the App in the debugger and presents it to us so that we can fix the error.

If we hadn't been expecting this it could have been quite distressing to see our App disappear and be replaced by Xcode displaying these never before seen panels. Instead, we know from what Xcode is showing us that something is wrong with the highlighted line of program code and we can fix it.

Examining variable values in the debugger

Sometimes, when our App ends up in the debugger, we need to look at the values of the variables to determine what is wrong. Once we can see the value that a variable contains the reason for the program problem becomes obvious.

Time for action – examining a variable value

Since **BuggyCalc** has crashed, and Xcode has brought itself to the foreground with the Debug area displayed, we can take this opportunity to look at some of the information that is available in the debugger:

1. Look more closely at the Debug area. You will see it has two panes. On the left-hand side is the variable view and on the right-hand side is the console as shown in the following screenshot:

2. By looking in the variable view, we can see the actual values that are in our variables when the program ended up in the debugger.

3. Drag the top of the Debug area up, to make the view larger.

4. Click on the disclosure triangle beside **self** to display all the member variables for our **AppDelegate** as shown in the following screenshot:

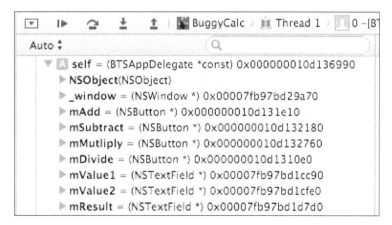

What just happened?

When our App was stopped in the debugger we were able to examine the values of variables in the buttonAction: method that were causing the problems. We were also able to examine the variables for the **AppDelegate**.

There are a lot of other things we could use the debugger for but they are beyond the scope of this book. All we really want to do here is make sure we are familiar with the debugger and know what to do when it shows up.

To continue writing Apps, we can press the stop button in Xcode and go back to look at our program code.

In this case, fixing the bug is as easy as changing the value for the symbol D_SHOW_DIVIDEBYZERO_BUG from 1 to 0.

Unexpected App behavior – no debugger?

There are many more programming errors that will cause the App to behave in an unexpected way but the Debug area will not be displayed. These problems are for less critical errors. Less critical errors include things such as:

◆ Including a parameter in a known message but with an invalid value

◆ Sending a message to an object that does not know how to handle that message

Time for action – index out of range

We can make a small change to the SimpleCalc program to demonstrate an index out of range that will cause our **BuggyCalc** App to misbehave, but will not automatically display the Debug area. For this type of error, we can create something called a breakpoint, which will force the Debug area to appear when the error occurs.

1. In **BuggyCalc**, select the filename BTSAppDelegate.m and set the value of D_SHOW_DIVIDEBYZERO_BUG to 0.

2. Add one line of code that uses the compiler directive #define to create a symbol named D_SHOW_INDEXOUTOFRANGE_BUG with a value of 1 as shown in the following code snippet:

```
#define D_SHOW_DIVIDEBYZERO_BUG 0
#define D_SHOW_INDEXOUTOFRANGE_BUG 1
```

3. Locate the - `(IBAction)myButtonAction:(id)a_sender` method and add the following lines of code, to create an array of operators, in the method. These should be the first lines of code in the implementation:

```
// Use an array to hold the valid operations
NSArray *l_validOperations = [NSArray arrayWithObjects: @"+",
                                                        @"-",
                                                        @"x",
                                                        @"÷",
                                                        nil];
```

The following screenshot shows what the program code will look like in Xcode after you make this change:

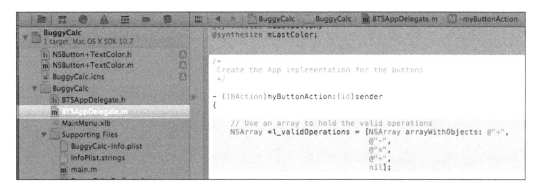

4. Change the code that calculates the result so that rather than comparing to literal string values, it compares to the strings stored at different locations in the new array:

```
// If the operation was addition, then
// add the two values
if ([[l_validOperations objectAtIndex:0]
     isEqual: l_operation])
{
    l_result = l_value1 + l_value2;
}
// If the operation was subtraction, then
// subtract the two values
else if ([[l_validOperations objectAtIndex:1]
          isEqual: l_operation])
{
    l_result = l_value1 - l_value2;
}
```

```
        // If the operation was multiplication, then
        // multiply the two values
#if D_SHOW_INDEXOUTOFRANGE_BUG
        else if ([[l_validOperations objectAtIndex:22]
                    isEqual: l_operation])
#else
        else if ([[l_validOperations objectAtIndex:2]
                    isEqual: l_operation])
#endif
        {
            l_result = l_value1 * l_value2;
        }
        // The operation must have been division, so
        // divide the first value by the second value
        else
        {
            l_result = l_value1 / l_value2;
        }
```

5. Click on the **Run** button to execute **BuggyCalc**.

6. Enter two numbers, for example, 15 and 3.

7. Click on the **+**, **-**, **÷**, and **x** buttons.

What just happened?

When we click on **+** and **-**, **BuggyCalc** works, but when we click on **÷** and **x**, **BuggyCalc** does not work. Instead, Xcode displays the Debug area but does not come to the foreground and does not locate the line of code that is causing the problem as shown in the following screenshot:

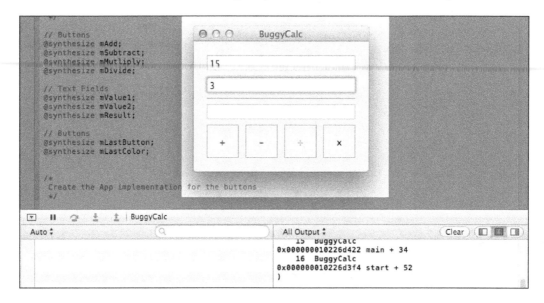

If we switch to Xcode and expand the Debug area, we can see that there is a very cryptic message being displayed in the console pane of the Debug area (see the following screenshot for reference). This console message provides a lot of clues and with some greater understanding would lead us to the programming error but wouldn't it be nice if we could get Xcode to bring up the Debug area and point us directly at the line in the program that is causing the problem? Of course it would be, and we will see how that is accomplished in the next section.

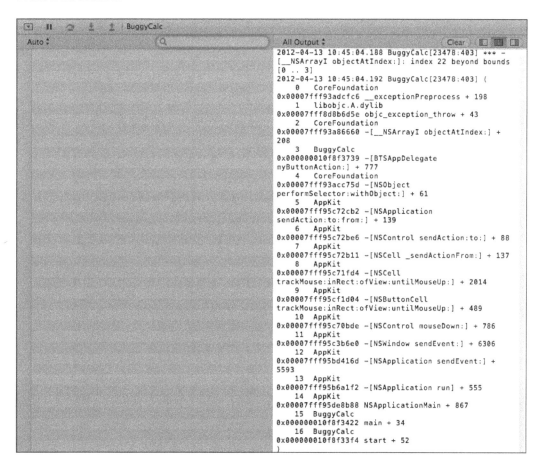

Using breakpoints to get more information from Xcode

When our App does not behave as expected, and we see console messages in the Debug area we can use something called a breakpoint to cause Xcode to reveal the line at which our program code caused the problem. Once we have identified the exact location and cause of the problem, it becomes much easier to fix Apps that do not behave as expected.

Time for action – set a breakpoint

We can add a breakpoint to the **BuggyCalc** App to cause Xcode to identify the exact line of program code that is causing the index out of range error.

1. In **BuggyCalc**, select the filename `BTSAppDelegate.m` and make sure the value of `D_SHOW_DIVIDEBYZERO_BUG` is 0 and the value of `D_SHOW_INDEXOUTOFRANGE_BUG` is 1.

2. In the Xcode navigator pane, click on the icon to **Show the Breakpoint navigator** as shown in the following screenshot:

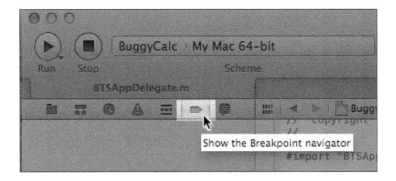

3. In the Xcode navigator pane, click on the **+** icon and select the menu item titled **Add ExceptionBreakpoint...** as shown in the following screenshot:

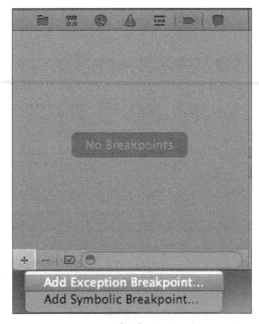

4. In the Xcode navigator pane, on the breakpoint options window, select **Done** to accept the default settings for the exception breakpoint as shown in the following screenshot:

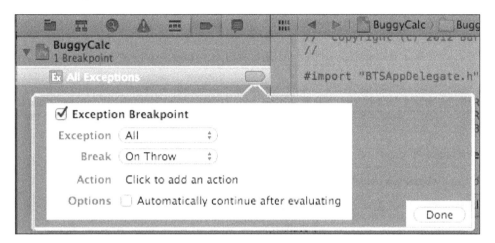

5. Click on the **Run** icon again to launch **BuggyCalc**.
6. Click on the ÷ button.

What just happened?

When we clicked on ÷ our program misbehaved, just as before, but this time Xcode became the foreground App and indicated the exact line in our program source code where the problem was caused as shown in the following screenshot:

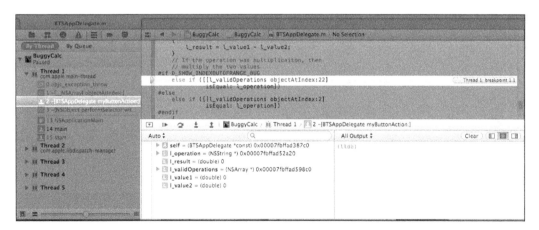

Summary

In this chapter, we have learned to both recognize the debugger and recognize when our App is not behaving, so that if the debugger appears or our App misbehaves we know how to find and fix the problem. We know that as beginning programmers, we don't need to know everything about the debugger but we do need to be able to recognize when the debugger shows up and how it can be used to help us identify the problem with our program code.

Specifically, we covered how to recognize when the debugger appears on its own and how to force our App into the debugger if it is not behaving correctly. We also covered how the debugger can be used to look at the values of our variables.

Now that we've learned how to recognize the debugger, we can take a look at a more advanced programming topic and learn how to build our own System Preference – which is the topic of the next chapter.

3
System Preferences – NewDefaults

*This chapter will walk us through the steps needed to create a System Preference pane. A **System Preference**, rather than being a standalone double-clickable App, is a plugin or bundle, that can be loaded by the System Preferences App to display our own system preference.*

The System Preference that we implement in this chapter is going to use an NSTask object to run a command-line tool as a separate process from within the preference pane. While we will not go into the intricate details of how NSTask runs and communicates with external processes, it is a topic that you may wish to investigate further.

In this chapter, we shall learn the following:

- Creating preference panes
- The 64-bit transition and how it affects our preference pane
- Creating a preference pane project in Xcode
- Configuring a preference pane project in Xcode
- Sudden termination
- Customizing a bundle project to implement new behavior
- Running command-line tools from a Cocoa program

Understanding preference panes

Typically, when we write an App for Mac OS X, we expect it to be something that is placed in the `Applications` folder that the user double-clicks to launch and use. But that is not the only kind of App that we can develop.

We can also develop a plugin that rather than being installed in the `Applications` folder and double-clicked, is installed in the `PreferencePanes` folder and loaded by the System Preferences when the user clicks on its icon in the System Preferences.

This is commonly referred to as a plug-in because there is a special set of rules that the App must follow in order to interact with the preferences framework.

 While we are going to build a preference pane and install it in the **System Preferences** it is also possible to use preference panes in an Apps preferences and provide an Apps preference panel that is similar in style to the **System Preferences**.

When our preference pane is installed, it will appear in the **Other** section of the **System Preferences**.

The transition to 64 bit from 32 bit

In a nutshell, desktop computer operating systems (Mac, Windows, and Linux) are in transition from 32 bit to 64 bit so that computer hardware can support more than 4 GB of **Random Access Memory (RAM)**.

For Mac OS X, the transitionary version of the OS happens to be Mac OS X 10.7. This means that as of Mac OS X 10.7 there is still support for 32-bit Apps and 32-bit System Preferences (that is, those that are limited to 4 GB of memory) but that Apple want developers to switch to 64-bit Apps and System Preferences because future versions of Mac OS X will not support the 32-bit versions.

While many developers need to go through a transition, because they have existing program code or because they want to continue to support older 32-bit systems for some time to come, we are not going to consider the 32-bit issue (other than this mention of it) so everything that we develop will be 64 bit.

We need to be aware of this because it is possible that if we try to share our 64-bit System Preference with someone who is still using a 32-bit system, it will not work.

Creating an Xcode preference pane project

When we want to build a Mac OS X preference pane, we need to first create an Xcode project. The Xcode project is the place where we keep all of the parts (code, icons, user interface, and images) that Xcode will put together to build our preference pane.

Time for action – creating the NewDefaults Xcode project

We begin the process by using Xcode to create a new project for the preference pane that we want to create:

1. To create a new Xcode project, Launch the Xcode App. If you have any projects open from a previous chapter, close them.

2. If you don't see the **Welcome to Xcode** window, then select **Welcome to Xcode** from the **Window** menu.

3. Click on the button titled **Create a new Xcode project** on the **Welcome to Xcode** window.

4. When Xcode asks to choose a template, select **System Plug-in** under **Mac OS X** and **Preference Pane** as the template. Then click on the **Next** button as shown in the following screenshot:

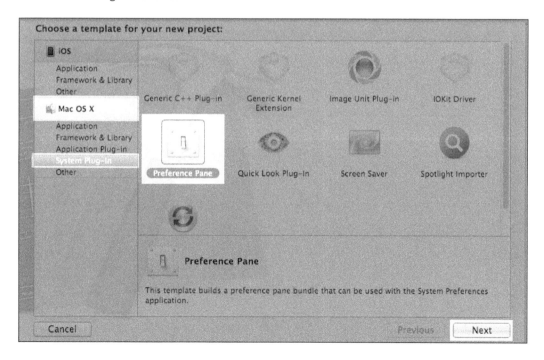

5. When we click on the **Next** button, Xcode will ask us to choose options for our new project. Update the options shown in the following table:

Option	Value	Description
Product Name	`NewDefaults`	The product name will be the name of our preference pane that shows up in the System Preferences.
Company Identifier	`com.yourdomain`	The company identifier needs to be unique and typically uses the reverse domain notation. It can be anything but you should not use a company identifier that will not conflict with an existing company. If you don't have an Internet domain name you can acquire one new or you can use *com.yourlastname.first name*.

The following screenshot shows what it looks like in Xcode after we set the new project options:

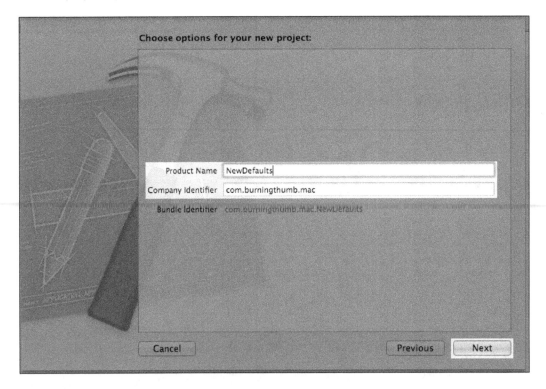

6. Once we have selected our options, click on the **Next** button and Xcode will ask us where we want to save the new project that we are creating. While we can save projects anywhere that we like, a good place may be a new folder called `projects` in our `Documents` folder. Whatever we decide, when we have navigated to that folder, we need to click on the **Create** button.

7. When Xcode creates the project for us it will open in the standard Xcode project window. When we examine the items in the project navigator we notice it looks very similar to an App with the exception that the icon is a `.tiff` file and product is a `.prefPane` file instead of a `.App`. The file extensions `.tiff` and `.prefPane` are explained in the following table:

Extension	Description
`.tiff`	A **Tagged Image File Format** (**tiff**). The `NewDefaults.tiff` file is the icon that will be displayed by the System Preferences.
`.prefPane`	A Preference pane. The `NewDefaults.prefPane` is the product of the build rather than an App.

8. We are going to build the project right away to demonstrate that similar to an App Xcode has created a fully functional System Preference for us from its template. From the **Product** menu, select **Build**.

9. When Xcode finishes building the project, locate **NewDefaults.prefPane** in the **Products** section of the project navigator and right-click on it (or hold down the *Ctrl* key on the keyboard and left-click if you don't have a three-button mouse) and select **Show in Finder** from the pop-up menu as shown in the following screenshot:

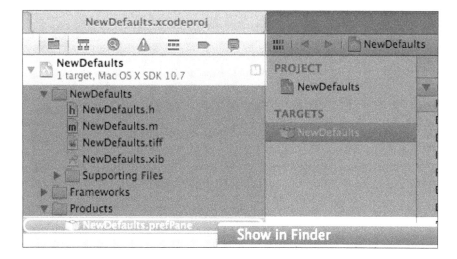

10. When Xcode shows **NewDefaults.prefPane** in the Finder, double-click on it to automatically launch the **System Preferences** window. The **System Preferences** will ask us how we want to install the preference pane. Click on the **Install** button to install the **NewDefaults** preference pane just for this user as shown in the following screenshot:

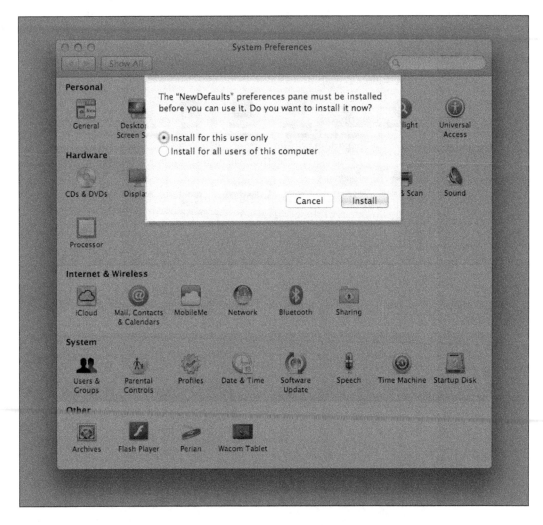

11. The **System Preferences** will display our new, empty preference pane. We need to click on the **Show All** button to return to the full list of **System Preferences**.

What just happened?

We created, built, and installed a brand new preference pane using the Xcode template. While this System Preference does not provide our specific features, yet, the template does provide us with a fully working program that we can now customize to perform the specific functions that we want to do. In the following screenshot, the icon displayed by our preference pane is the default icon from the `.tiff` file:

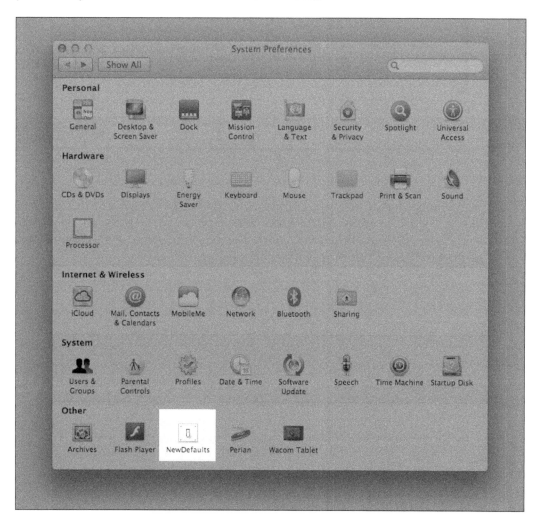

Configuring an Xcode preference pane project

There are two things that we want to configure on our preference pane target in Xcode:

◆ The icon

◆ The human readable copyright string to reflect our name

 By default, the Xcode preference panes template uses a 32 x 32 pixel TIFF file for the icon that is displayed in the System Preferences. Instead of creating an `iconset` folder with a series of PNG images, we need to use our image editing program to export a single TIFF file to be used as the icon.

Time for action – customizing the icon and copyright

We need to update the preference pane to use our custom icon and change the copyright information to indicate who developed the software. Let's begin by following the given steps:

1. To delete the default icon, in the Xcode project navigator, right-click on the `NewDefaults.tiff` file and then press the *Delete* key on the keyboard. When Xcode asks if we want to move the file to the trash or only remove the reference to it, select **Move to Trash** as shown in the following screenshot:

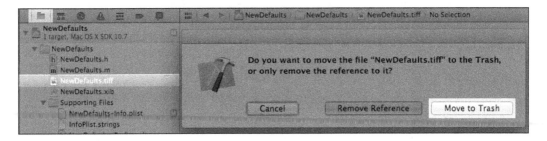

2. Use any imaging editing application to create a new icon image and export it as a TIFF file.

3. Drag the new TIFF icon file into the Xcode project navigator. When Xcode asks us to **Choose options for adding these files**, click on the **Finish** button to accept the default options.

4. Change the **TARGETS** setting for **NewDefaults** so that the **Preference Pane icon file** in the **Info** section is named **NewDefaults** with no extension (that is delete the `.tiff` extension) as shown in the following screenshot:

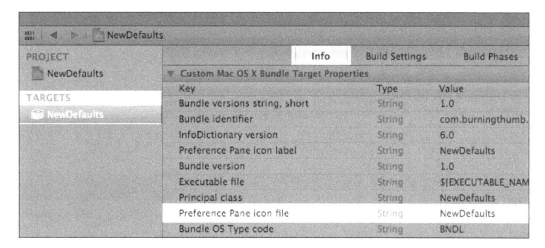

5. Change the **TARGETS** setting for **NewDefaults** so that the **Copyright (human-readable)** section in the **Info** section uses our name or our company's name as shown in the following screenshot:

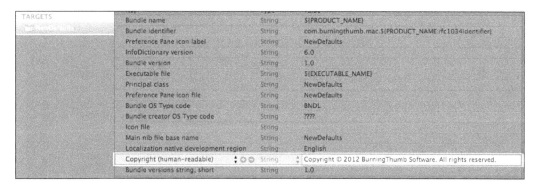

6. Under the **Product** menu, select **Clean**.

7. Under the **Product** menu, select **Build**.

8. In the Project Navigator, under **Products**, right-click on **NewDefaults.prefPane** and select **Show in Finder** from the pop-up menu.

9. In the Finder, double-click on **NewDefaults.prefsPane**.

10. When the **System Preferences** is launched, it will display a sheet that asks **The preference pane you are installing is already installed. Do you want to replace the existing preference pane?**, click on the button titled **Replace**.

What just happened?

We changed the preference pane project template to use our custom icon and to use our name or company's name in the copyright string. Now when the System Preferences are displayed, we will see our custom icon as shown in the following screenshot:

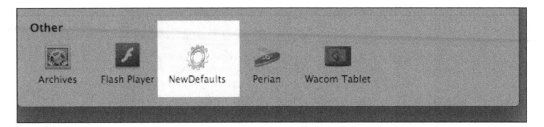

Have a go hero – making our own icon

Instead of creating an icon set, we need to create a single TIFF file to be used as the icon for our System Preference. This is similar to how an icon set was created but this time we need to use our image editing app to export a TIFF file. Do that now and add a custom icon to the **NewDefaults** System Preference.

Customizing the preference pane template interface

The user interface for a preference pane is customized in exactly the same way as the interface would be customized for an App. We create **@property** declarations for **IBOutlet** objects and connect them in the .xib file to the **Graphical User Interface (GUI)** objects.

Before we start building our interface, we need to decide what our preference pane is going to do. After thinking about it we decide that our **NewDefaults** will include the following:

- Enabling and disabling Launchpad fading
- Showing and hiding hidden files in the Finder
- Showing and hiding the Library folder in the current user's home folder

We further decide that our user interface will be a series of checkboxes that can be used to enable or disable these new behaviors.

Time for action – creating the NewDefaults interface

We shall now create the interface by implementing the program code in the file named NewDefaults.h in our Xcode project:

1. Open the **NewDefaults** project in Xcode.

2. Click on the item named NewDefaults.h and add a new interface definition and the button action interface definition for the preference pane as shown in the following program code:

```
#import <PreferencePanes/PreferencePanes.h>

@interface NewDefaults : NSPreferencePane
{

/*
   Create the user interface elements
 */

// Buttons - A Check Box is a button
IBOutlet NSButton*    enableHiddenFilesCheckbox;
IBOutlet NSButton*    enableLaunchpadFadeCheckbox;
IBOutlet NSButton*    enableHomeLibraryCheckbox;

}

- (void)mainViewDidLoad;

/*
   Create the Preference Pane interface for the buttons
 */

- (IBAction)myButtonAction:(id)sender;
```

 Notice that we are not going to use the @property and @synthesize keywords to declare our interface elements. This means that Xcode is not going to create accessor methods for us automatically. It also means we need to include the { and } characters to wrap our instance variable declarations.

3. Click on the item named **NewDefaults.m** and add a new implementation section for the preference pane as shown in the following program code:

```
@implementation NewDefaults

/*
   Create the user interface setter and getter functions
 */

// In this example we are not using setter and getter
// functions so there is nothing to do here

/*
   Create the App implementation for the buttons
 */

- (IBAction)myButtonAction:(id)sender;
{
    // For now, just beep
    NSBeep();
}

- (void)mainViewDidLoad
{
}
```

4. Click on the item named **NewDefaults.xib** and then click on the window **PrefPane** in **Objects** to display the Preference Pane window.

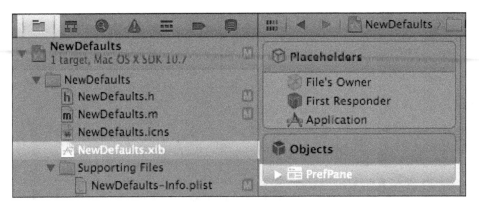

5. Locate the **Object Library** and scroll down to find the **Check Box** option as shown in the following figure:

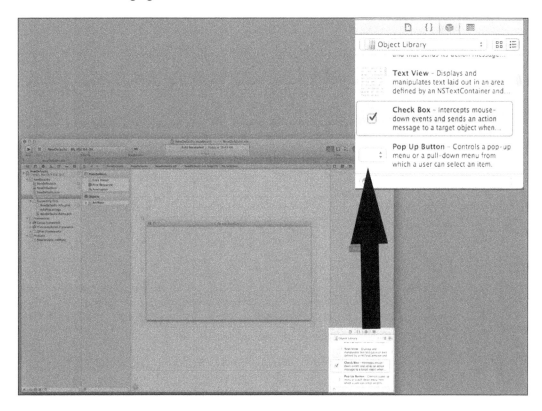

6. Click-and-drag a **Check Box** from the **Object Library** to the **PrefPane** window. Then drag two more checkboxes and place them below the first checkbox to form a column of buttons.

7. Double-click on each button and rename them as follows:

- ❏ Enable Launchpad Fading

- ❏ Show Hidden Files in Finder

- ❏ Show ~/Library Folder

8. Resize the window so that it fits the checkboxes as shown in the following screenshot:

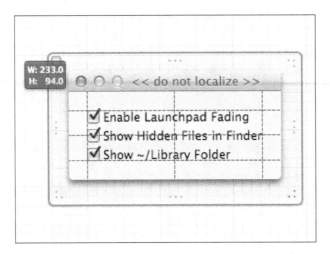

 Before we can connect the buttons to the **NewDefaults** preference pane, we need to establish a relationship between the **NewDefaults** custom class and the file's owner. This step is essential if we are to successfully connect our user interface elements to our preference pane program code.

9. Under **Placeholders**, click on the **File's Owner**.

10. In the **Utilities** pane, under **Custom Class**, enter **NewDefaults** as the class name as shown in the following screenshot:

11. Right-click on the **[] Enable Launchpad fading** checkbox (or if you don't have a three-button mouse, hold down the *Ctrl* key and left-click) and drag it to the **Files Owner** as shown in the following screenshot:

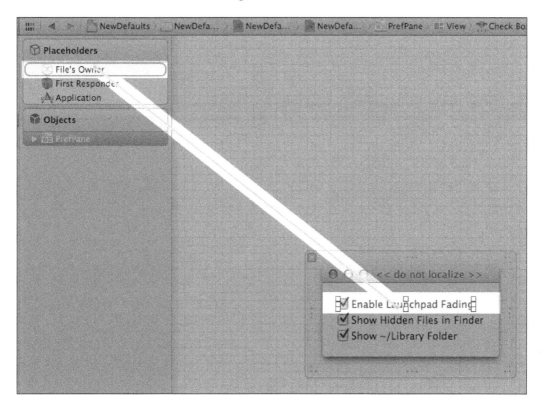

12. When the **File's Owner** object highlights, release the mouse button and select **myButtonAction** from the **Received Actions** selection pane as shown in the following screenshot:

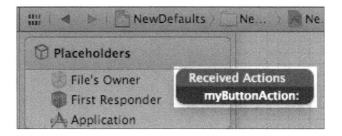

13. Repeat the process to connect the remaining two checkboxes to the – `myButtonAction` method.

14. Right-click on the **File's Owner** object (or if you don't have a three-button mouse, hold down the *Ctrl* key and left-click) and drag it until the **[] Enable Launchpad Fading** checkbox is highlighted as shown in the following screenshot:

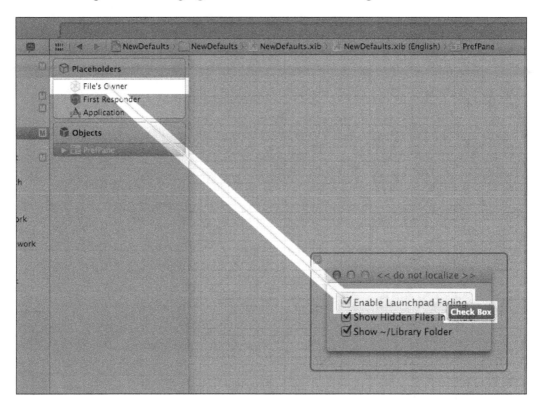

15. Release the mouse button and select **enableLaunchpadFadeCheckbox** from the **Outlets** selection pane as shown in the following screenshot:

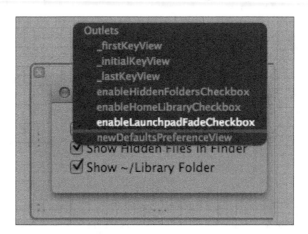

16. Repeat the previous two steps to connect the **File's Owner** to the **enableHiddenFilesCheckbox** and **enableHomeLibraryCheckbox** items in the **Outlets**.

What just happened?

We created the interface for our **NewDefaults** preference pane and connected the interface to the program code for our preference pane. We also connected the **File's Owner** object to the **Check Box** items in the interface. Now, when we build and install the **NewDefaults** preference pane in the **System Preferences**, we see the new interface and when we click any of the checkboxes we hear a system beep.

Customizing the preference pane Xcode template's .h implementation

Similar to creating an App, the preference pane Xcode template needs to be customized to implement our new behavior. We will start completing the interface definition in the NewDefaults.h file.

Time for action – completing the NewDefaults.h interface definition

Now that we have created a basic "stub" interface that Xcode will build successfully, we need to go back and fill in the final details to complete our interface definition:

1. Open the **NewDefaults** project in Xcode.

> Often when we are developing program code it needs to contain literal values – for example, a number or strings. Rather than using literal values in the body of our code, we will define symbols in our .h file and then use those symbols in the body of our program code.

2. Click on the NewDefaults.h file and add the following code to define the literal values that we are going to be using in the body of our code. Now is a good time to read the comments in the program code (the lines that start with //) that precede each #define so that we know what each defined symbol represents.

#define SYMBOL LiteralValue

The #define compiler directive allows us to define SYMBOLS that we can use in the body of our code. When we build our code, the preprocessor will replace each SYMBOL with the corresponding LiteralValue before compiling our program code. By convention, we use an uppercase letter D as the first character of any defined symbol and separate the words with the _ character with the exception of defined symbols that will be used as keys to retrieve dictionary values, in the case of a dictionary key, by convention, we start the symbol with the lowercase letter k and use CamelCase for the symbol name.

```
//
//  NewDefaults.h
//  NewDefaults
//
//  Created by rwiebe on 12-04-16.
//  Copyright (c) 2012 BurningThumb Software. All rights reserved.
//

#import <PreferencePanes/PreferencePanes.h>

// Define the path to the Library folder
// in the users home folder
#define D_HOME_LIBRARY_PATH @"~/Library"

// Define the path to the defaults command
#define D_DEFAULTS_PATH @"/usr/bin/defaults"

// Define the read command
#define D_READ_COMMAND  @"read"

// Define the Finders domain
#define D_DOMAIN_FINDER @"com.apple.finder"

// Define the Docks domain
#define D_DOMAIN_DOCK @"com.apple.dock"

// Define the defaults command to show
// hidden files in the Finder
#define D_DEFAULTS_SHOW_FILES \
    "defaults write com.apple.finder AppleShowAllFiles YES"

// Define the defaults command to hide
// hidden files in the Finder
#define D_DEFAULTS_HIDE_FILES \
    "defaults write com.apple.finder AppleShowAllFiles NO"

// Define the defaults command to delete
// the Finder hidden files key
```

```
#define D_DEFAULTS_DEL_HIDE_FILES \
    "defaults delete com.apple.finder AppleShowAllFiles"

// Define the defaults commands to enable
// Launchpad fading
#define D_DEFAULTS_DEL_SHOW_DURATION \
    "defaults delete com.apple.dock springboard-show-duration"
#define D_DEFAULTS_DEL_HIDE_DURATION \
    "defaults delete com.apple.dock springboard-hide-duration"

// Define the defaults commands to disable
// Launchpad fading
#define D_DEFAULTS_SHOW_DURATION_0 \
    "defaults write com.apple.dock \
    springboard-show-duration -int 0"
#define D_DEFAULTS_HIDE_DURATION_0 \
    "defaults write com.apple.dock \
    springboard-hide-duration -int 0"

// Define the command to restart
// the Finder
#define D_RESTART_FINDER "killall Finder"

// Define the command to restart
// the Dock
#define D_RESTART_DOCK "killall Dock"

// Define the key to show / hide hidden files
#define kHiddenFileKey @"AppleShowAllFiles"

// Define the key to disable Launchpad fading
#define kSpringboardShowTime @"springboard-show-duration"
#define kSpringboardHideTime @"springboard-hide-duration"

// Define a string equal to YES
#define D_YES @"YES"
```

Note that some of our defined literal values start with the @" characters and some start with just a " character. This is an important distinction. Those that start with an @ are literal NSString objects and those that do not are character arrays. This is important because some of the literals will be used where NSString objects are required and others will be used where character arrays are required. Pay very close attention to where (and where not) the @ characters belong. This is important because some methods require string objects, and some methods require character arrays and our program code will not work if we pass one where the other is expected.

3. One of the things that we are going to do in our preference pane is execute the command-line utility `defaults` for the `read` option from within our program (there is no need to launch the Terminal App and type command when we can hide them behind our GUI). When we ask `defaults` to `read` a value from a domain for a key, we need a way to return that value back into our program code. We don't know exactly how we are going to do that, yet, but we do know how we want to do it. We will return the value as an `NSString` object and we will pass in the domain and key that we want to read as `NSString` objects. Since we know how we want to do it, we can add the interface definition to our `NewDefaults.h` file as shown in the following program code:

```
/*
    Define the interface to a method that will use
    the defaults command to retrieve a domain
    defaults value for a key
 */

- (NSString *) readDefaults: (NSString *)a_domain
                     forKey: (NSString *)a_key;
```

What just happened?

We implemented the interface for our **NewDefaults** preference pane by defining the symbols and methods that we believe we will need to complete the functions we want to implement.

Customizing the preference pane Xcode template's .m implementation

Now that we have defined the interface (what we want to do) for our preference pane we need to implement the methods (how we will do it) to perform the functions. We need to complete the implementation in the `NewDefaults.m` file.

Time for action – completing the NewDefaults.m implementation

Now that we have created a basic "stub" implementation that builds, we need to go back and fill in the final details to complete our interface definition:

1. Implement the `readDefaults:forKey` method: This method will allow us to get the results from the defaults command-line tool returned to our preference pane.

2. Implement the `didSelect` delegate method: This method is called automatically by the System Preferences whenever our preference pane is selected.

3. Implement the `myButtonAction` method: This method is called whenever one of our checkboxes is clicked.

What just happened?

Once we have implemented those three methods, we will have a working preference pane that we can install in the System Preference.

Implementing the readDefaults:forKey: method

We need to complete the implementation in the NewDefaults.m file for the method readDefaults:forKey:. This method will execute the command-line tool defaults read for an arbitrary domain and key and return the results (or Nil if there are no results) as an NSString object.

Time for action – writing the readDefaults:forKey: program code

Now we can jump in and write the program code to implement this method as follows:

1. Start by putting a comment in the NewDefaults.m file that describes the method in plain English:

```
/*
    This method will execute the command line tool defaults
    to read a value from a domain for a specific key

    Input:
        a_domain - a reverse domain id for the defaults to read
        a_key - a key value to read

    Output:
        Either the string value of the result or Nil if there
        is no value to return.
*/
```

> It's always a good idea to explain our methods using this kind of plain English comment block.

2. The method needs to match the interface from the .h file. So now we can add the function body to the .m file. Note the opening and closing braces that delimit the start and the end of the method. The implementation of the method will appear between these braces as shown in the following code snippet:

```
- (NSString *) readDefaults: (NSString *)a_domain
                     forKey: (NSString *)a_key
{

}
```

3. Enter the code, following the opening brace, to declare an NSString object. This object will hold the result that is returned by the method as shown in the following code snippet:

```
// Create a string reference to hold the result
NSString *l_result;
```

Notice that when we create a new variable that is local to a method (which means not visible outside this method) we use the prefix l_ (lowercase letter l and underscore), which means *local*. By using this naming convention, we can tell the scope (what parts of our program code can access a value) of a variable by its name. Similarly the arguments passed in to our method are prefixed by a_ to make it clear they are passed in as *arguments* to the method. It is good programing practice to adopt a naming convention that allows the reader of the code to identify the scope of a variable by its name.

4. Next declare a new NSTask object, allocate it (this allocates the memory needed for the object), and initialize it (this sets the values in the memory to the default values for a new NSTask). An NSTask object is what we use to create a task without the need to type the command into the Terminal App.

```
// Create and initialize a new task
NSTask *l_readTask = [[NSTask alloc] init];
```

5. When an NSTask is created and initialized, it does not know what command it is supposed to execute. We need to tell the NSTask object that it will execute the defaults command, which is stored on our computer in the file at the location /usr/bin/defaults. We have already defined this path as an NSString literal named D_DEFAULTS_PATH in our interface so we can use the literal in the body of our program code.

```
// Assign the launch path for the task
[l_readTask setLaunchPath:D_DEFAULTS_PATH];
```

If we cannot remember the value for a defined symbol, we can highlight the symbol in the editor pane and then right-click on it. From the pop-up menu, we can select **Jump to Definition** and Xcode will show us where the symbol is defined so that we can see its value.

6. To read a value, the `defaults` command takes three arguments. They are: `read`, some domain, and some key. We have already defined a symbol that is the `NSString` literal `@"read"` and called it `D_READ_COMMAND`. The domain and key are being passed in to our method as the arguments `a_domain` and `a_read`. So we can use the defined symbol and the two arguments to create an `NSArray` and then set the arguments of the `NSTask` to that `NSArray` object as shown in the following code snippet:

```
// Create an array with the read command
// and the domain and key values
NSArray *l_arguments =
[NSArray arrayWithObjects:  D_READ_COMMAND,
 a_domain,
 a_key,
 nil];

// Assign the argument array to the NSTask
[l_readTask setArguments:l_arguments];
```

7. Now we need a way to get the results of running the command as an `NSTask` object back into our program so that we can return the `NSString` object from our new method. The results from an `NSTask` object are obtained using something called `NSPipe`. When we have an `NSPipe` object, we can read and write to it as if it was a file using an `NSFilehandle` object. Because we only want to read the results of the read command, we need the `fileHandleForReading` from the NSPipe as shown in the following code snippet:

```
// Create a new pipe to read the results
// of the command
NSPipe *l_pipe = [NSPipe pipe];

// Assign the read pipe to the NSTask
[l_readTask setStandardOutput:l_pipe];

// Retrieve the pipe's fileHandleForReading
NSFileHandle *l_file = [l_pipe fileHandleForReading];
```

 All of these references to read should not be confused. The read command for defaults, and the pipe from which we read are two independent and unrelated things that just both happen to use the word read. It's a common theme in computers for the same word to refer to different things. It's just something we need to get used to seeing.

8. Finally, we can launch the NSTask. This is the point in our program code when the independent process will run.

```
// Launch the Task
[l_readTask launch];

// Release the Task - this is not needed on
// Mac OS X 10.7 but is also harmless
[l_readTask release];
```

> Since we are using Mac OS X 10.7 the System Preferences use automatic garbage collection and so we don't need to release the NSTask object. If we wanted to run on an earlier version of Mac OS X, we would need to be much more careful with memory management and would also release the NSTask object at this time to free up the memory that had been allocated for it when we created it.

9. Now, we can read the response from the NSTask object using the NSFileHandle object. When we read the response it will come back as an immutable (unchangeable) NSData object. Because we want to modify the data, specifically to remove the trailing newline character, we create a mutable (changeable) copy of the NSData object. As a result, we will actually end up with an NSMutableData object.

```
// Read all the output data from the Task
// and create a mutable copy
// The NSTask will exit when done
NSMutableData *l_data =
    [[l_file readDataToEndOfFile] mutableCopy];
```

Immutable and Mutable

All NS objects are immutable (unchangeable) unless they contain Mutable in their name. If they are immutable, we can make copies of them but we cannot change them. Most of the time it's fine to have immutable objects, but sometimes we need the mutable variant. We can obtain mutable objects by sending the mutableCopy message to the immutable object. Because we want to trim the newline character off the data we will receive, by using the setLength: method, we need a mutable copy of the data.

10. Now that we have the results from running the task we can inspect them. It turns out that if we use `defaults` to read a value for a domain with a key and the value does not exist we will get nothing back. Our data will be empty. If our data is empty, rather than returning an empty `NSString` we want to return no object at all. The way we return no object, as opposed to an empty object is by using the special keyword `Nil` as follows:

```
// If the NSTask ended but returned
// nothing, then return a Nil
if (0 == [l_data length])
{
    return Nil;
}
```

11. On the other hand, if the defaults command found a value for the domain and key it will return the data but with a newline character appended to the end. Since we don't want the extra newline character, we trim the returned data by 1 character. This is why we needed mutable, instead of immutable data.

```
// The defaults command will append a newline (\n)
// character to its output.  This trims that
// character off so that it is not included in
// the returned value
[l_data setLength:[l_data length] - 1];
```

12. Finally, we need to take the characters from the `NSData` object and convert them to a UTF8 encoded NSString and return that as the result of our method as follows:

```
// Create a new string from the remaining
// returned data
l_result = [[NSString alloc] initWithData:l_data

encoding:NSUTF8StringEncoding];

// Return the final string
return l_result;
```

What just happened?

The method has been implemented and now we can go on to implement the `didSelect` delegate method, which will use the `readDefaults:forKey:` method to display the correct settings for our preference pane checkboxes.

Implementing the didSelect: method

We need to complete the implementation in the `NewDefaults.m` file for the method `didSelect:`. This method will be called by the System Preferences each time we select our preference pane. It needs to determine the current defaults settings and set the values of the checkboxes in the GUI to match the current settings.

Time for action – writing the didSelect: program code

Once more we can jump right in and start writing the program code for this method as follows:

1. Start by putting a comment in the `NewDefaults.m` file that describes the method in plain English as follows:

```
/*
    The didSelect delegate method is called whenever
    the Preference Pane is displayed, even if the
    System Preferences were not quit and relaunched
*/
```

2. The method needs to match the interface from the `NSPreferencePane.h` file because it is a delegate method defined in that file as follows:

```
- (void) didSelect
{

}
```

3. Using the `readDefaults:forKey:` method get the current value for the Finder's hidden files key as an `NSString` object:

```
// Read the current setting for
// Showing Hidden files in he Finder
NSString *l_showHiddenFile = [self readDefaults: D_DOMAIN_
FINDER forKey:kHiddenFileKey];
```

4. Using the `readDefaults:forKey:` method gets the current value for the Docks springboard hide and springboard show keys as `NSString` objects as shown in the following code snippet:

```
// Read the current setting for
// Disabling launchpad fading
NSString *l_launchpadFadeOut =
    [self readDefaults: D_DOMAIN_DOCK
                forKey:kSpringboardHideTime];
NSString *l_launchpadFadeIn =
    [self readDefaults: D_DOMAIN_DOCK
      forKey:kSpringboardShowTime];
```

5. Assume, for now, that all of the checkboxes in the GUI should be unchecked.

```
// Assume everything is off, later we will
// turn the correct things back on
[enableHiddenFilesCheckbox setState: NSOffState];
[enableLaunchpadFadeCheckbox setState: NSOffState];
[enableHomeLibraryCheckbox setState: NSOffState];
```

6. If the Finder flag to show hidden files was found, and if it is equal to the value YES then the checkbox needs to be enabled. Otherwise we are going to delete the setting, which effectively will remove a value of NO from the settings as follows:

```
// If the show hidden files value was found
if (l_showHiddenFile)
{
    // If the show hidden files value is YES
    if ([D_YES isEqual: l_showHiddenFile])
    {
        // Turn the check box on in the
        // interface
        [enableHiddenFilesCheckbox setState: NSOnState];
    }
    else
    {
        // Execute the system command to delete
        // the setting
        system(D_DEFAULTS_DEL_HIDE_FILES);
    }
}
```

7. If values were found for both springboard settings, and those values are both not zero, or if no values were found, then the checkbox needs to be enabled because no value is the same as NSOffState.

```
// If both launchpad values were found
if ((l_launchpadFadeOut) &&(l_launchpadFadeIn))
{
    // If either launchpad values is not equal to 0
    if ((0 != [l_launchpadFadeOut integerValue]) ||
        (0 != [l_launchpadFadeIn integerValue]))
    {
        // Turn the check box on in the
        // interface
        [enableLaunchpadFadeCheckbox setState: NSOnState];
    }
}
```

```
    else
    {
        // Turn the check box on in the
        // interface
        [enableLaunchpadFadeCheckbox setState: NSOnState];
    }
```

8. The setting to hide or show the `Library` folder in the current user's home folder does not use our `readDefaults:forKey:` method. Instead, on Mac OS X 10.6 and later, we can use a file URL to query the `isHidden` setting. So the first thing we need to do is create a URL object for the `~/Library` file path.

```
    // Create a URL object that references the
    // Library file in the users home directory
    NSURL *l_url = [NSURL fileURLWithPath:    [D_HOME_LIBRARY_PATH
stringByExpandingTildeInPath]];
```

9. We also need to declare an `NSNumber` `*` to store the return value from the method that gets the value for the `isHidden` key as follows:

```
    // Define a NSNumber pointer to hod the result
    // of the getResourceValue method
    NSNumber  *l_isHidden;
```

10. Now we can invoke the `getResourceValue:forKey:error:` method on the NSURL object to get the actual value of the `isHidden` attribute for the folder.

```
    // Get the value of the IsHidden attribute
    BOOL l_result = [l_url getResourceValue:&l_isHidden
forKey:NSURLIsHiddenKey error:Nil];
```

11. And finally, if there was no error, and the `isHidden` attribute is set to `NO` then the checkbox needs to be enabled as follows:

```
    // If a value was returned
    if (l_result)
    {
        // If the returned value was NO
        if (NO == [l_isHidden boolValue])
        {
            // Turn the check box on in the
            // interface
            [enableHomeLibraryCheckbox setState: NSOnState];
        }
    }
```

What just happened?

The method has been implemented and now when our preference pane is selected in the System Preferences, the checkboxes in our GUI will reflect the current state of the system. We can go on to implement the `myButtonAction:` method which will be called whenever one of the checkboxes in our GUI is clicked as shown in the following screenshot:

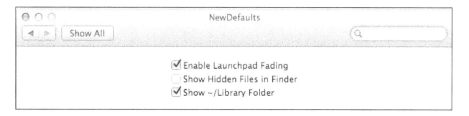

Implementing themyButtonAction: method

We need to complete the implementation in the `NewDefaults.m` file for the `myButtonAction:` method. This method will be invoked each time one of the checkboxes in our GUI is clicked. It needs to determine the current state of the checkbox and change the system settings to match the checkbox.

Time for action – writing the myButtonAction: program code

We previously implemented this method as a stub that called `NSBeep()`. Now, we need to remove that call to the `NSBeep()` function and implement the final working program code as follows:

1. Start by putting a comment in the `NewDefaults.m` file that describes the method in plain English as follows:

    ```
    /*
        Create the Preference Pane implementation for when
        a checkbox is clicked this method is called with the
        sender equal to the check box that invoked it
    */
    ```

2. The method needs to match the interface from the `.h` file. So now we can add the function body to the `.m` file as follows:

    ```
    - (IBAction)myButtonAction:(id)sender;
    {


    }
    ```

3. Mac OS X 10.7 introduced a new feature called *Sudden Termination*. This feature is used to inform the Mac OS when it is safe to kill, rather than gracefully quit from our App (System Preferences is an App). Because we are about to enter a critical part of code, we are going to tell the Mac OS that it is not safe to kill the System Preferences – essentially disabling Sudden Termination as follows:

```
// Disable sudden termination, it is not
// safe to kill the System Preferences
[[NSProcessInfo processInfo] disableSuddenTermination];
```

4. If the **Show ~/Library** checkbox was clicked then we need to set the attribute, using an NSURL object, on the folder. This is done by creating an NSURL object from the NSString object @"~/Library" after expanding the ~ to /User/username and then using the NSURL method setResourceValue:forKey:error to set the isHidden file attribute based on the state of the checkbox as follows:

```
// Was the Show ~/Library Folder button pressed?
if (YES == [sender isEqual: enableHomeLibraryCheckbox])
{
    // Get a URL reference to the file
    NSURL *l_url =
     [NSURL fileURLWithPath:
      [D_HOME_LIBRARY_PATH stringByExpandingTildeInPath]];

    // If the checkbox is ON (checked) then
    if (NSOnState == [sender state])
    {
        // Set the URL IsHidden value to NO
        // This makes the folder Visible in the Finder
        [l_url setResourceValue:
         [NSNumber numberWithBool:NO]
                        forKey:NSURLIsHiddenKey
                        error:Nil];
    }
    // else the checkbox is OFF (unchecked)
    else
    {
        // Set the URL IsHidden value to YES
        // This makes the folder Invisible in the Finder
        [l_url setResourceValue:
         [NSNumber numberWithBool:YES]
                        forKey:NSURLIsHiddenKey
                        error:Nil];
    }
}
```

5. If the **Show Hidden Files in Finder** checkbox was ticked then we need to set the attribute, using the `defaults` command-line tool (this time to `write` instead of `read`). In order for the change to take effect we also need to kill the Finder (it will automatically restart). Because we don't need any information back from the commands that we issue, we don't need a method that runs an `NSTask` and uses a pipe to read the results. We can simply use the `system()` function to execute the commands based on the state of the checkbox as follows:

```
// Was the Show Hidden Files in Finder button pressed?
if (YES == [sender isEqual: enableHiddenFilesCheckbox])
{
    // If the checkbox is ON (checked) then
    if (NSOnState == [sender state])
    {
        // Execute the command to enable showing hidden files
        system(D_DEFAULTS_SHOW_FILES);
    }
    // else the checkbox is OFF (unchecked) then
    else
    {
        // Execute the command to disable showing hidden files
        system(D_DEFAULTS_HIDE_FILES);
    }

    // Execute the system command to restart the Finder
    system(D_RESTART_FINDER);
}
```

6. If the **Enable Launchpad Fading** checkbox was ticked earlier then we need to set the attribute, using the defaults command-line tool. In order for the change to take effect we also need to kill the Dock (it will automatically restart). Note that we execute two system commands to accomplish the change in the settings.

```
// Was the Enable Launchpad fading button pressed?
if (YES == [sender isEqual: enableLaunchpadFadeCheckbox])
{
    // If the checkbox is ON (checked) then
    if (NSOnState == [sender state])
    {
        // Execute the commands to enable fading
        system(D_DEFAULTS_DEL_SHOW_DURATION);
        system(D_DEFAULTS_DEL_HIDE_DURATION);
    }
    else
    {
        // Execute the commands to disable fading
        system(D_DEFAULTS_SHOW_DURATION_0);
```

```
            system(D_DEFAULTS_HIDE_DURATION_0);
    }

    // Execute the system command to restart the Finder
    system(D_RESTART_DOCK);
}
```

7. Finally, now that our critical updates are done, we can re-enable Sudden Termination as follows:

```
// Enable sudden termination, it is
// safe to kill the System Preferences
[[NSProcessInfo processInfo] enableSuddenTermination];
```

What just happened?

The method has been implemented and now when one of the checkboxes in our preference pane GUI is selected we will set the value of the system default to match its setting.

Have a go hero – adding some warning text

Our program code is a bit aggressive in that it will kill the Finder or the Dock when the user clicks the checkbox. It's always a good idea to add some warning text when a program is going to do something like that. Open the xib file in project builder and add some text to warn the user that changing the settings will result in the Finder and Dock being killed so they should do so with caution.

Summary

In this chapter, we have discovered how to create a preference pane and integrate it into the System Preferences.

Specifically, we covered how a preference pane is similar to, and different from, an App. We continued by discussing some key aspects of Mac OS X 10.7 (the 64-bit transition and Sudden Termination) that affect preference pane development. We then covered how to customize an Xcode project template including creating a new icon for a Mac OS X preference pane. Finally, we covered how to execute terminal commands from inside our program code including how to retrieve values from terminal commands and use them inside our program code.

Now that we've learned how to develop a System Preference, we are going to turn our attention to another aspect of programming which is business applications. We are going to look at how we can retrieve information from the Internet and use it to satisfy a common need in the business world, the conversion of monies between different currencies – which is the topic of the next chapter.

4
Business Application – Global Currency Converter

This chapter will walk us through the steps needed to create a Business App that converts a value from one currency to a list of other currencies. In order to do the conversion, our App will need to download a list of currency conversion rates from the Internet.

In this chapter, we shall learn the following:

- What is an XML file?
- Downloading an XML file from the Internet
- Parsing an XML file to extract the information that we need
- Using a background thread so that we don't tie up the main user interface
- Managing a pop-up menu
- Managing a table view
- Performing arithmetic operations using an array of values

Designing the GUI for global currency converter

Our currency converter App is going to download a list of currencies and exchange rates from the Internet. Once the currencies and exchange rates have been downloaded, the App will allow the user to enter a number and specify which currency that number is in by selecting from a pop-up menu. Once the user selects the currency from the menu, so that our App knows which currency that number is in, our App will convert the number to all of the other possible currencies and display the results in a table. Our GUI will look similar to the following screenshot:

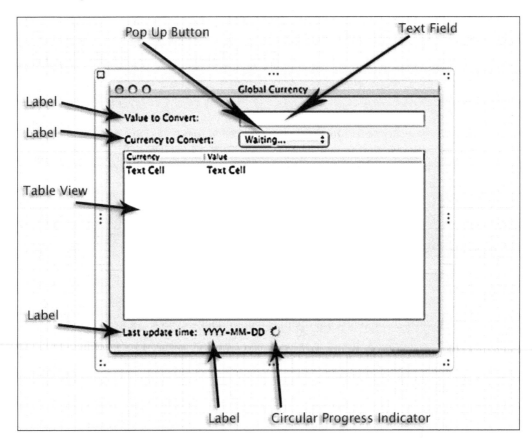

Time for action – creating our project and GUI

We are going to start by creating a new project and designing the .xib file to match our GUI design. Once we have the interface laid out, we will continue to implement the App.

1. To create a new Xcode project, launch the Xcode App.

2. Close any projects open from previous chapters.

3. If the **Welcome to Xcode** window isn't displayed, then select **Welcome to Xcode** from the **Window** menu.

4. Click on the **Create a new Xcode project** button on the **Welcome to Xcode** window.

5. When Xcode asks to select a template, select **Application** under **Mac OS X** and **Cocoa Application** as the template. Then, click on the **Next** button.

6. When the **Next** button, is clicked Xcode will ask us to select options for our new project. The options that we need to select are as follows:

Option	Value
Product Name	Global Currency
Company Identifier	com.yourdomain
Class Prefix	Your Initials (for consistency we use BTS throughout this book)

7. Enable the **Use Automatic Reference Counting** option by checking its checkbox.

8. Click on the **Next** button, locate the project's folder, and click on the **Create** button.

9. After Xcode creates the new project, click on the file named `MainMenu.xib` in the project navigator.

10. Using our GUI design, drag the following items from the **Objects** library into the **Global Currency** window, then rename and position them to match the design as given in the following table:

Object Kind	Value
Label	`Value to convert`
Label	`Currency to convert`
Label	`Last update time:`
Label	`YYYY-MM-DD`
Text Field	
Pop Up Button	`One item named Waiting...`
Table View	Two columns titled `Currency` and `Value`
Circular Progress Indicator	

What just happened?

We created our Xcode project and designed our user interface using Interface Builder. Now, when we click on the **Run** button our project displays our interface.

We have previously examined how to configure Xcode projects and create icons for our Apps. Now is a good time to configure the **Project Document Organization** and create an icon for the **Global Currency** App.

Connecting the GUI to program elements

Now that we have created the GUI in Interface Builder, we need to connect the elements to variables defined in our App Delegate so that we can update the GUI from inside our program code. We will always need these references to GUI elements in our program.

Time for action – connecting the App Delegate to the GUI

Since we have already created the `.xib` file, we just need to add the reference in to our App Delegate and then connect them to our GUI.

1. In Xcode, click on the file named **BTSAppDelegate.h** in the project navigator and add the following properties:

```
/*
    Define the GUI elements
 */

@property (assign) IBOutlet NSTextField *mLastUpdateTimeTextField;
@property (assign) IBOutlet NSProgressIndicator
*mLastUpdateTimeProgressIndicator;
@property (assign) IBOutlet NSTextField *mValueToConvertTextField;
@property (assign) IBOutlet NSPopUpButton
*mCurrencyToConvertPopUp;
@property (assign) IBOutlet NSTableView
*mConvertedCurrencyTableView;
```

> Note that the outlets are declared as assign rather than weak. Typically under **Automatic Reference Counting (ARC)** they would be weak (since they are owned by their super view) but we can also declare them `assign` if we want to be compatible with earlier OS versions that don't support ARC.

2. Click on the file named **BTSAppDelegate.m** in the project navigator and add the following lines of code to synthesize the properties:

```
/*
    Define the GUI elements
 */
```

```
@synthesize mLastUpdateTimeTextField;
@synthesize mLastUpdateTimeProgressIndicator;
@synthesize mValueToConvertTextField;
@synthesize mCurrencyToConvertPopUp;
@synthesize mConvertedCurrencyTableView;
```

3. Click on the file named **MainMenu.xib**.

4. Right-click on the App Delegate object and drag to the GUI elements. Connect them as shown in the following screenshot:

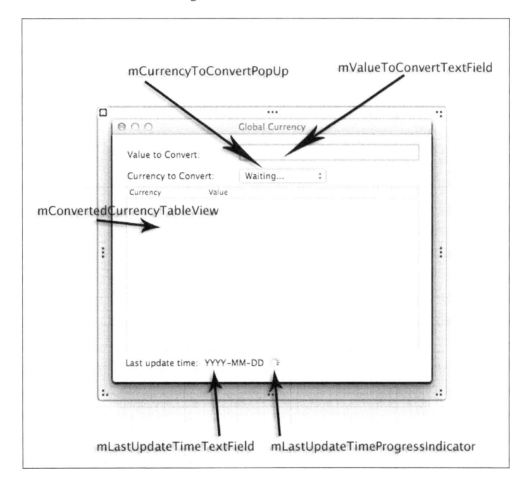

What just happened?

We created and synthesized the properties for the Global Currency GUI. Now our program code can modify the GUI elements. If we run the program now it will display our GUI but will not yet populate it with any values.

What is an XML file?

Since the list of currency exchange rates that we want to download from the Internet is provided as an XML file, it's a good idea if we have an understanding of just what an XML file is in general terms.

So let's take a step back and first answer the question, for what is XML an abbreviation? **XML** is an abbreviation for **eXtensible Markup Language**. As its name implies, XML is an evolution of something even simpler known as a **Markup Language**.

Essentially a Markup Language allows us to embed tags, using whatever syntax is used by the language, into a document and have those tags interpreted as formatting rather than content. A good example is bold text or a font. Somehow within our document we need to indicate that some text is in bold face or that some text is in a different font. We need to indicate both the attribute type and its span.

Markup Languages have been used on computers since the days of mainframes. Apps like Microsoft Word or Word Perfect originally had their own proprietary Markup Languages with their own formats and syntax, but now they use XML instead.

What distinguishes XML from other markup languages is that it is:

◆ Royalty-free
◆ An open standard
◆ Human readable
◆ Extensible

Format of the XML file we will download

Since XML is so widely used, it is quite easy to find resources on the Internet that provide us with data we can incorporate into our App. While there are several choices for exchange rates, we have decided to use the list of exchange rates provided by the European Central Bank. These exchange rates are updated daily and can be found at the following URL:

```
http://www.ecb.int/stats/eurofxref/eurofxref-daily.xml
```

Time for action – downloading an XML file

We can easily use a web browser to download the XML file from the Internet.

1. Launch a web browser that is capable of displaying XML files. This can be Google Chrome or Firefox but it cannot be Safari because Safari will not, by default, display raw XML files (and, as such, is not the best web browser for App developers).

2. Enter the URL for the XML file.

What just happened?

The web browser downloaded and displayed the XML file. Because we carefully selected a web browser that understands XML, we are able to examine the structure of the XML file and locate the information that we want to extract from it.

It's a good thing that XML files are human readable!

```
▼<gesmes:Envelope xmlns:gesmes="http://www.gesmes.org/xml/2002-08-01"
 xmlns="http://www.ecb.int/vocabulary/2002-08-01/eurofxref">
    <gesmes:subject>Reference rates</gesmes:subject>
  ▼<gesmes:Sender>
      <gesmes:name>European Central Bank</gesmes:name>
    </gesmes:Sender>
  ▼<Cube>
    ▼<Cube time="2012-04-24">
        <Cube currency="USD" rate="1.3161"/>
        <Cube currency="JPY" rate="106.87"/>
        <Cube currency="BGN" rate="1.9558"/>
        <Cube currency="CZK" rate="24.997"/>
        <Cube currency="DKK" rate="7.4402"/>
        <Cube currency="GBP" rate="0.81540"/>
        <Cube currency="HUF" rate="297.69"/>
        <Cube currency="LTL" rate="3.4528"/>
        <Cube currency="LVL" rate="0.6993"/>
        <Cube currency="PLN" rate="4.2003"/>
        <Cube currency="RON" rate="4.3818"/>
        <Cube currency="SEK" rate="8.8880"/>
        <Cube currency="CHF" rate="1.2021"/>
        <Cube currency="NOK" rate="7.5565"/>
        <Cube currency="HRK" rate="7.5375"/>
        <Cube currency="RUB" rate="38.6550"/>
        <Cube currency="TRY" rate="2.3510"/>
        <Cube currency="AUD" rate="1.2775"/>
        <Cube currency="BRL" rate="2.4729"/>
        <Cube currency="CAD" rate="1.3020"/>
        <Cube currency="CNY" rate="8.2979"/>
        <Cube currency="HKD" rate="10.2141"/>
        <Cube currency="IDR" rate="12095.57"/>
        <Cube currency="ILS" rate="4.9450"/>
        <Cube currency="INR" rate="69.3260"/>
        <Cube currency="KRW" rate="1500.43"/>
        <Cube currency="MXN" rate="17.2850"/>
        <Cube currency="MYR" rate="4.0335"/>
        <Cube currency="NZD" rate="1.6170"/>
        <Cube currency="PHP" rate="56.235"/>
        <Cube currency="SGD" rate="1.6417"/>
        <Cube currency="THB" rate="40.746"/>
        <Cube currency="ZAR" rate="10.2770"/>
      </Cube>
    </Cube>
  </gesmes:Envelope>
```

XML Trees

XML documents are arranged in trees. A **tree** is very similar to a filesystem and we can think of each element in the tree as a folder. As we navigate down the tree we can think of it as opening the next folder (in XML terminology these are called **nodes**). As we navigate downwards, we may also find named attributes. We can access the named attributes to extract the information that we need from XML files.

Parsing an XML document

Now that we have examined the XML file in a web browser, we need to download it into our App and parse it to extract the information that we need. Specifically, we are looking for the following:

◆ The last update time
◆ The list of currency codes and exchange rates

By looking at the XML Tree, and noting the position of the disclosure triangles, we can determine the paths to the information that we want to access. It becomes clear that the path to the last update time is as follows:

```
/gesmes:Envelope/Cube/Cube
```

And the path to the exchange rates is as follows:

```
/gesmes:Envelope/Cube/Cube/Cube
```

When we extract the exchange rate information we are going to save it in something called an NSDictionary. Actually we will use the mutable variant, NSMutableDictionary, since we want to modify the object instance.

A **dictionary** is an object that allows us to use one object as a key and a second object as a value that corresponds to that key (this is called a **key->value pair**).

In this instance, we will use the currency code as the key and the exchange rate for that currency code as the value. We will use NSString objects for both the key and the value but we should remember that we can use other kinds of objects as either a key or value.

NSDictionary objects make a private copy of the key object so there is a limitation that only objects that support copying can be used as keys. If we need to overcome this limitation, we can use an NSMapTable but since our keys will be NSString objects this is not an issue and NSDictionary objects work just fine in most cases.

Sometimes, we want to examine all the keys in a dictionary object. To get an NSArray (or a list) of all the keys, we can send the `allKeys` message to an NSDictionary (or NSMutableDictionary) object.

In any case, the important thing to remember is that whenever we are using a dictionary we will use a key to set or to get its corresponding value.

Time for action – parsing the XML Document

Once our program has retrieved the raw XML file, we need to examine it and extract the information of interest. This is called **parsing** the file.

1. In Xcode, click on the file named BTSAppDelegate.h in the project navigator and add the following defines that will be used to extract information from the XML file after it is downloaded:

```
/*
    Global Currency defines
 */

// The European Central Bank exchange rate XML File
#define D_ECB_RATES_URL @"http://www.ecb.int/stats/eurofxref/
eurofxref-daily.xml"

// The path to the last update time in the XML tree
#define D_XML_PATH_TIME @"/gesmes:Envelope/Cube/Cube"

// The path to the exchange rates in the XML tree
#define D_XML_PATH_RATES @"/gesmes:Envelope/Cube/Cube/Cube"

// The popup menu title
#define D_SELECT_CURRENCY @"Select Currency"

 // The keys for the XML attributes
#define kTimeKey @"time"
#define kCurrencyKey @"currency"
#define kRateKey @"rate"
```

2. Add the Member variables to BTSAppDelegate.h. These class members will be used to store the NSString object for the last update date and the NSMutableDictionary object for the exchange rates for various currencies. We add them as properties because we want the compiler to automatically create the setter and getter methods.

```
/*
 Define the Member elements
 */

@property (strong)  NSString *mLastUpdateTime;
@property (strong)  NSMutableDictionary *mCurrencyRates;
```

@property (strong)

Notice the @property declaration for mLastUpdateTime and
mCurrencyRates is strong rather than assign. This is required
because our project uses **Automatic Reference Counting (ARC)**. Because
ARC is going to manage our program's object lifetime use, we need to tell
ARC that we want to retain a copy of these objects. If we fail to provide
this hint, then ARC will release the objects as soon as we create them
(this means their retain count will be zero and they will be deallocated at
an unknown time in the future by the memory manager), which would
leave us with what is known as a **dangling pointer** that will cause our
program to randomly crash based on how often memory is cleaned up.

3. Synthesize the setter and getter methods in the file named BTSAppDelegate.h
   as follows:

```
/*
    Define the Member elements
 */


@synthesize mLastUpdateTime;
@synthesize mCurrencyRates;
```

4. Add the method definition for getExchangeRatesFromECB: to
   BTSAppDelegate.h. We will need to implement this new method to retrieve the
   XML file from the Internet and parse it into our member variable.

```
/*
    Methods we need to implement
 */


// Define the method to get the exchange
// rates and parse them.  It takes an object
// as an argument because it will be run on
// a background NSThread
- (void) getExchangeRatesFromECB: (id)a_object;
```

5. Add the method implementation for getExchangeRatesFromECB: to
   BTSAppDelegate.m as follows:

```
/*
This method will download the XML file from
the European Central Bank and parse it into
member variables.

Input:
a_object - the protocol for NSThread requires
```

```
        this method to take an arbitrary
        object as an argument.  It will
        not be used.
```

```
Output:
As a side effect, the member variables mLastUpdateTime
and mCurrencyRates will be populated.
*/
```

```
- (void) getExchangeRatesFromECB: (id)a_object
{

}
```

6. Add the following code inside the implementation block to create a new NSURL object from the string that we defined as the URL to the XML file at the ECB:

```
// Create a URL object using a string
NSURL *l_URL = [NSURL URLWithString: D_ECB_RATES_URL];
```

7. Continue by adding the following code to create an NSXMLDocument and initialize it with the contents of the URL. This code will automatically do all the network access needed to access the Internet and download the file:

```
// Create an XML Document object and
// initialize it with the contents of the URL
// This downloads the contents of the URL
// from the internet
NSXMLDocument * l_xmlDocument = [[NSXMLDocument alloc]
                           initWithContentsOfURL:l_URL
                          options:NSXMLDocumentTidyXML
                           error: Nil];
```

8. Continue by adding the code to extract the last update time from the retrieved XML document object. Note that the following code only runs if the XML document was successfully retrieved:

```
// If the XML document was
// successfully retrieved we
// can parse it
if (l_xmlDocument)
{

    // Declare an array object that we
    // can use to examine nodes
    NSArray *l_nodes;
```

```
// Create an array of nodes at the path
// where we can find the time attribute
l_nodes = [l_xmlDocument
            nodesForXPath:D_XML_PATH_TIME error:Nil];

// Extract the time attribute from the node
mLastUpdateTime =
  [[[l_nodes objectAtIndex:0]
    attributeForName: kTimeKey] stringValue];
```

9. Continue by adding the code to extract the exchange rates from the XML document. Note that this ends the *if* condition and the program code that follows this will be executed in the cases where downloading the XML document was both successful and unsuccessful. Also notice the use of a new object, NSXMLElement, which is used to extract the currency and rate properties from each XML node found at the D_XML_PATH_RATES in the XML document.

```
// Create an array of nodes at the path
// where we can find the currency and rate
// attributes
l_nodes = [l_xmlDocument
            nodesForXPath:D_XML_PATH_RATES error:Nil];

// Declare some working variables
NSString *l_currency;
NSString *l_rate;
NSXMLElement *l_element;

// Loop over all the currency and rate nodes
// and look at each element
for (l_element in l_nodes)
{
    // Extract the currency attribute into a NSString
      l_currency = [[l_element attributeForName:
                      kCurrencyKey] stringValue];

    // Extract the rate attribute into a NSString
      l_rate = [[l_element attributeForName: kRateKey]
                stringValue];

    // Add the rate to the mutable NSDictionary using
    // the currency as the dictionary key
    [mCurrencyRates setObject:l_rate
                    forKey:l_currency];
    }
}
```

10. Finally, finish the method implementation by adding the code to invoke another method, which is used to update the GUI. Note that the new method is invoked on the main thread. This is done because operations that affect the GUI should be done on the main thread.

```
// Because this method will execute on a
// background thread we need to invoke
// another method, on the main thread, to
// update the GUI
[self
performSelectorOnMainThread:@selector(populateGUIOnMainThread:)
withObject:nil waitUntilDone:NO];
```

11. We need to implement the method `populateGUIOnMainThread:` by entering the following code:

```
- (void) populateGUIOnMainThread: (id) a_object
{
    // If the last update time is nil its because
    // the XML file could not be retrieved or
    // parsed so there is nothing to
    // display
    if (mLastUpdateTime)
    {
        // Display the time in the GUI
        [mLastUpdateTimeTextField setStringValue:mLastUpdateTime];

        // Remove everything from the Pop Up Menu
        [mCurrencyToConvertPopUp removeAllItems];

        // Add an item "Select Currency" to the Pop Up menu
        [mCurrencyToConvertPopUp addItemWithTitle:D_SELECT_
CURRENCY];

        // The currency rates returned in the XML
        // file are not sorted.  Create a new NSArray
        // sorted in alphabetical order
        NSArray *l_sortedKeys = [[mCurrencyRates allKeys]
            sortedArrayUsingSelector:@selector(compare:)];

        // Add the currencies to the Pop Up Menu
        [mCurrencyToConvertPopUp addItemsWithTitles: l_
sortedKeys];
    }

    // Stop animating the progress indicator.
    // Animation was started just before the
    // background thread to download the XML file
    // was invoked
    [mLastUpdateTimeProgressIndicator stopAnimation:self];
}
```

What just happened?

We implemented the program code that will download and parse the XML file from the ECB website. Because accessing the Internet and parsing an XML file can be a time consuming operation, we decided to implement the method such that it could run in the background. We did this using a background thread but we really didn't explain what threads are.

A **thread** is an independent unit of program execution. Much in the same way as we can have several Apps that run independently on our computer, we can have different units of program execution running independently inside of an App.

The main thread controls the event processing (mouse, keyboard, and so on) and the GUI. If the main thread gets busy doing a time consuming task that prevents events from being processed, then the Mac OS will display the spinning multicolored cursor and the App will be marked as not responding.

So in order to keep the user experience pleasant, we take time consuming tasks and place them on a second, or background thread. This allows the main thread to continue executing, processing events, and be responsive to the user. In fact the user can even quit from the App, if so desired, while the background thread is running and the Mac OS will kill the background thread and clean up after it.

How to invoke a background thread

If we run our App now, we will notice that the XML file is not downloaded, the progress indicator does not spin, and the GUI is not updated!

This is because we implemented the program code to do all those things but we didn't implement the code to invoke the background thread. So that will be our next step.

Time for action – invoking a background thread

Starting and invoking methods on separate execution threads is made easy in Objective-C if we use NSThread objects.

> **1.** In Xcode, click on the file named BTSAppDelegate.m in the project navigator and locate the method named applicationDidFinishLaunching:.

2. There is one small piece of housekeeping that needs to be done. We created a member variable (mCurrencyRates) to reference our list of currencies and exchange rates but we never created the object. We need to create the object before we can add anything to it. Add the following line of code to create the NSMutableDictionary object:

```
- (void)applicationDidFinishLaunching:(NSNotification *)
aNotification
{
    // Insert code here to initialize your application

    // Create a mutable NSDictionary so that we can
    // save the exchange rate information
    mCurrencyRates = [[NSMutableDictionary alloc] init];
```

3. After that bit of housekeeping, add the following code to change the circular progress indicator properties so that it will not be displayed if it is not spinning. Then, start it spinning:

```
    // Modify the Progress Indicator
    // so that it is not visible when
    // it is not animating
    [mLastUpdateTimeProgressIndicator
     setDisplayedWhenStopped:NO];

    // Start the Progress Indicator spinning
    // It will spin until the XML file is
    // downloaded and parsed.  It should be
    // very brief
    [mLastUpdateTimeProgressIndicator
     startAnimation:self];
```

4. Finally, we need to create our background NSThread object and have it execute the method named getExchangeRatesFromECB:. Add the following code to start the background thread:

```
    // Start the background thread to download
    // the XML file
    [NSThread detachNewThreadSelector:@selector(getExchangeRatesFr
omECB:)
                    toTarget:self withObject:nil];
```

What just happened?

We implemented the code to invoke the background thread and now if we run our App we should see that both the last update time and the pop-up menu are populated.

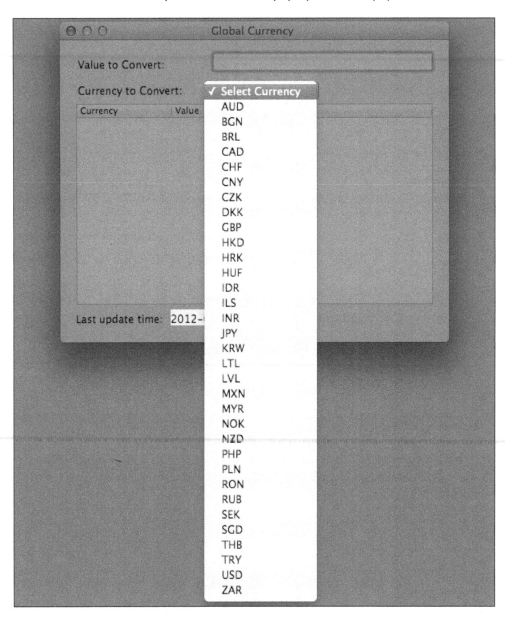

Managing a pop-up menu

The two major components of our user interface are the pop-up menu and the table view. In this section, we are going to look at the pop-up menu in more detail.

After the XML document was parsed, our App updated the contents of the pop-up menu by removing all existing menu items, adding a new menu item using the NSString constant @"Select Currency", and adding all the currency codes to the menu from a sorted NSArray of NSString objects that were parsed out of the XML document.

Time for action – implementing the program code for the pop-up menu

Now, we need to handle the user interaction with the pop-up menu so that the Global Currency App updates the table view when the user selects a currency code from the menu.

1. In Xcode, click on the file named BTSAppDelegate.h in the project navigator and add the following interface method definition:

```
// Handle the Pop Up Menu selection
- (IBAction)selectToCurrency:(id)a_sender;
```

2. Click on the file named BTSAppDelegate.m in the project navigator and add the following method implementation stub:

```
// This method will be invoked whenever a currency
// code is selected from the Pop Up Menu
- (IBAction)selectToCurrency:(id)a_sender
{

        NSBeep();
}
```

3. Click on the file named MainMenu.xib in the project navigator.
4. Right-click on the pop-up menu and drag to the **App Delegate** object and release the mouse button.
5. When the **Received Actions** item is displayed, select **selectToCurrency:**.
6. Click the **Run** button to run the project.

7. Select any currency from the pop-up menu and the App will beep.

 We do this stub implementation so that we can easily verify that everything is connected properly between the interface and the program implementation. Once we are sure the connections are established correctly, we can proceed with the implementation without worrying about or forgetting about connecting the two parts.

8. Quit the Global Currency App.

9. Click on the file named BTSAppDelegate.m in the project navigator and change the implementation of **selectToCurrency:** as follows:

```
- (IBAction)selectToCurrency:(id)a_sender
{

//       NSBeep();

    // Send a message to the table view telling it that
    // it needs to reload its data
    [mConvertedCurrencyTableView reloadData];
}
```

What just happened?

We changed the implementation so that it does not beep. Instead it will send a message to the table view that tells it to reload its data. Of course, we haven't yet implemented the code that is required to reload the table view so if we run our App now, it will look as though selecting a currency from the pop-up menu isn't doing anything.

Creating the Table View Interface

The final GUI element that needs to be managed is the NSTableView. When the user selects a currency to convert from, we want our App to display a table that shows the value in all the other currencies.

Time for action – configuring the table view in Interface Builder

The first thing that we need to do is update the table view in Interface Builder so that we can access the components that we need in our program code.

1. Open the Global Currency project in Xcode.

2. In the project navigator, click on the folder named **Global Currency**.

3. From the **File** menu, select **New**, and then select **File...**.

4. Under Mac OS X, select **Cocoa**.

5. For the template, select **Objective-C class**.

6. Then click on the **Next** button as shown in the following screenshot:

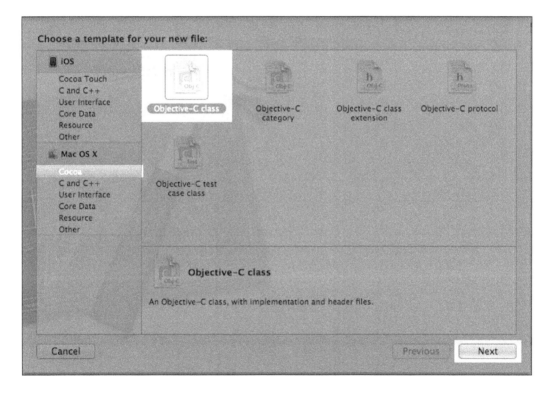

7. For the new file options, select a **Class** of `BTS_GCTableViewDelegate` and a Subclass of `NSObject` and then click on the **Next** button.

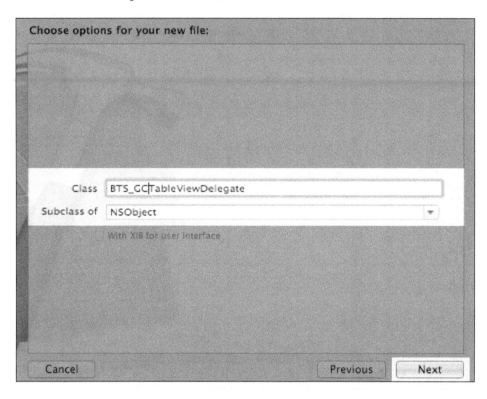

8. When the create file sheet is displayed, click on the **Create** button to create the new files in the default location. The new files will appear in the project navigator pane as shown in the following screenshot:

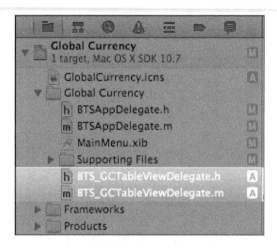

9. In the project navigator, click on the file named **MainMenu.xib**.

10. In the **Object Library**, locate the generic **Object** object as shown in the following screenshot:

11. Drag an **Object** from the **Object Library** to the **Objects** pane of the editor to create a new instance of the **Object**.

12. Rename the **Object** as **BTS_GCTableViewDelegate**.

13. In the **Identity Inspector**, change the **Class** of the **Custom Class** to **BTS_GCTableViewDelegate** as shown in the following screenshot:

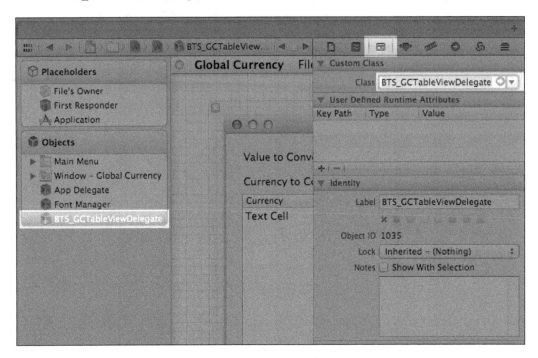

14. In the editor, click on the table view two times, the first click to select the NSScrollView and the second click to select the NSTableView. Make sure the NSTableView is selected.

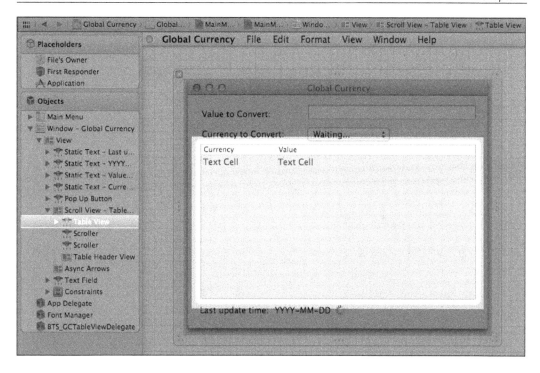

15. Right-click on the table view and drag to the new **BTS_GCTableViewDelegate** object and release the mouse button.

16. From the **Outlets** pop-up dialog, select **dataSource**.

17. Right-click on the table view a second time and drag to the new **BTS_GCTableViewDelegate** object and release the mouse button.

18. From the outlets pop-up dialog, select **delegate**.

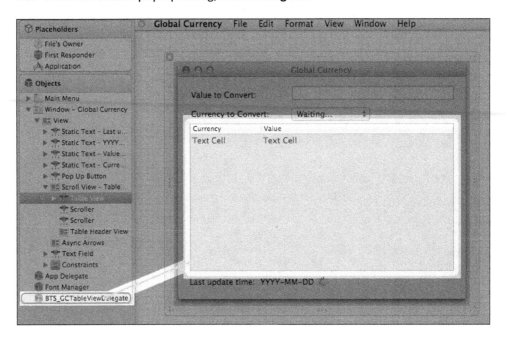

19. Click on the left-hand side of the table view three times to select the **Currency** table column.

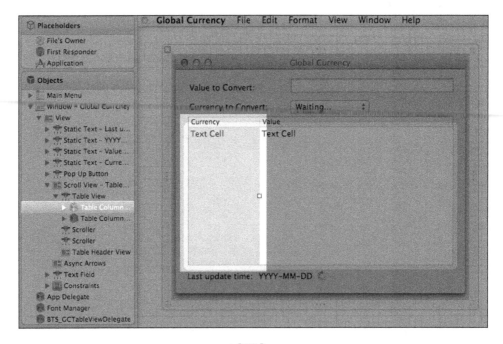

20. In the **Identity Inspector**, locate the **Identifier** and set it to **currency** as shown in the following:

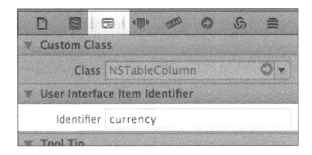

21. Click on the right-hand side of the table view one time to select the **Value** table column.

22. In the **Identity Inspector**, locate the identifier and set it to **value**.

What just happened?

We created a new custom class and created an instance of that class in Interface Builder. We then assigned that instance object as both the delegate and dataSource for the NSTableView.

The delegate object is an object that implements the NSTableViewDelegate protocol methods that will be invoked when the table view needs to perform actions such as informing the delegate the selection has changed or asking the delegate if a column should be selected.

The dataSource object is an object that implements the NSTableViewDataSource protocol methods that will be automatically invoked when the table view needs to display data.

Sometimes we may want to know more about a specific object or protocol. We can use Xcode's built-in documentation to learn more. First, we highlight the keyword we are interested in by double-clicking it, for example, we could double-click the keyword NSTableView. Then we select the **Show Quick Help Inspector** icon above the inspector pane to see a summary of the object and links to further reading and resources for that object and its protocols.

Creating the table view implementation

Once the GUI for the `NSTableView` has been connected to its `delegate` and `dataSource` object in Interface Builder, we need to implement the required methods to support those protocols.

There are two methods that the `delegate` and `dataSource` object need to implement in order for our table view to be populated. They are as follows:

◆ `numberOfRowsInTableView:`

◆ `tableView objectValueForTableColumn:row:`

There is also one other method, `awakeFromNib:` that is called automatically when an object is created from the `.xib` file. We will use this method to perform initialization that is required when the object is created.

Time for action – implementing the dataSource and delegate

We are now ready to write the program code to implement the required dataSource and delegate methods.

1. Open the Global Currency project in Xcode.

2. Click on the file named `BTS_GCTableViewDelegate.h` and add the following `#defines` to create literal values that can be used to identify each column of the table view:

```
// Create defines that will be used
// to identify the column in the
// table view

#define kBTSGCCurrency @"currency"
#define kBTSGCValue @"value"
```

3. Click on the file named `BTS_GCTableViewDelegate.h` and add the following code to create a reference to a single member variable that we will use to cache a reference to the `AppDelegate` object:

```
#import "BTSAppDelegate.h"
#import <Foundation/Foundation.h>

// Create defines that will be used
// to identify the column in the
// table view
```

```
#define kBTSGCCurrency @"currency"
#define kBTSGCValue @"value"

@interface BTS_GCTableViewDelegate : NSObject
{
    // Create a reference to the AppDelegate so
    // that we only need to look it up one time
    BTSAppDelegate *mAppDelegate;
}
```

Cache frequently used objects

We can look up the AppDelegate each time we need to use it, but instead we will look it up one time, when the object is created, and save that reference. Later, when we need to refer to the object, we use this cached reference. It is common practice in programming to cache values that are used frequently.

4. Click on the file named BTS_GCTableViewDelegate.m and enter the following code to obtain and cache the reference to the AppDelegate object:

```
/*
    This method is invoked automatically
    when the object instance is revived
    from the .xib file

    This is where we do any initialization
    needed by the .xib object
 */


-(void) awakeFromNib
{
    // Get a reference to our AppDelegate
    // object and save it for later use
    mAppDelegate = [NSApp delegate];
}
```

Note that the method name is awakeFromNib and not awakeFromXib. Apple is in the process of renaming Nib files to Xib files but the transition is not yet complete so we are seeing a mix of Xib and Nib. When the transition is complete, Nib references will go away. Until that time, it's very important to use Nib in the correct places or the App will not work.

5. NSTableView objects need to know how many rows of data they have to display. The way they do this is by invoking the numberOfRowsInTableView; method on the dataSource object. Every dataSource object must implement this method. Enter the following code to return the number of rows in the table view:

```
/*
This method is invoked automatically
when the table view GUI element needs
to know how many rows it has to
display

All dataSource objects must implement
this method.
*/

- (NSInteger)numberOfRowsInTableView:(NSTableView *)aTableView
{
    // Ask the AppDelegate to lookup the mCurrencyRates
    // member variable and then ask it for the number
    // of objects it contains.  That is the number of
    // rows in the table view
    return mAppDelegate.mCurrencyRates.count;

}
```

6. The NSTableView objects need to know the values to display for each row and column. The way they do this is by invoking the tableView objectValueForTableColumn: row; method on the dataSource object. Every dataSource object must implement this method. Enter the following code to return the values for each row and column of the table view:

```
- (id)tableView:(NSTableView *)a_tableView objectValueForTableColu
mn:(NSTableColumn *)a_tableColumn row:(NSInteger)a_rowIndex
{
    // Retrive the identifier for the row.  These are
    // set in the .xib file

    NSString *l_identifier = [a_tableColumn identifier];

    // If the desired column is the currency, then
    // return the value for the currency code
    if ([kBTSGCCurrency isEqual: l_identifier])
    {
        return [mAppDelegate.mCurrencyRates.allKeys
                objectAtIndex:a_rowIndex];
```

```objc
    }

    // If the desired column is the value, then
    // return the value for the value for that currency code
    if ([kBTSGCValue isEqual: l_identifier])
    {
        // Get the value to convert from
        // the AppDelegate
        double l_valueToConvert =
          [mAppDelegate.mValueToConvertTextField doubleValue];

        // Get the currency code of the value
        // to convert from the AppDelegate
        NSString * l_selectedCurrency =
          [mAppDelegate.mCurrencyToConvertPopUp
titleOfSelectedItem];

        // Get the exchange rate to Euros for
        // the value to convert from the AppDelegate
        double l_rateFrom =
          [[mAppDelegate.mCurrencyRates
            objectForKey:l_selectedCurrency] doubleValue];

        // Get the currency codes from the AppDelegate
        // and look up the currency code for the
        // requested table row
        NSString *l_toCurrency =
          [mAppDelegate.mCurrencyRates.allKeys
            objectAtIndex:a_rowIndex];

        // Get the exchange rate to Euros for
        // the row from the AppDelegate
        double l_rateTo =
          [[mAppDelegate.mCurrencyRates objectForKey:l_toCurrency]
            doubleValue];

        // Calculate the converted value.
        // First by converting the from currency to
        // Euros, then by converting the result
        // from Euors to the desired currency
        double l_euroValue = l_valueToConvert / l_rateFrom;
        double l_finalValue = l_euroValue * l_rateTo;

        // Return the result as an NSString
        return [NSString stringWithFormat:@"%f",l_finalValue];
    }
```

What just happened?

We completed the implementation of the NSTableView. Now, when we enter a value and pick its currency from the pop-up menu, we get a list of the converted amount for all of the other currencies, as shown in the following screenshot:

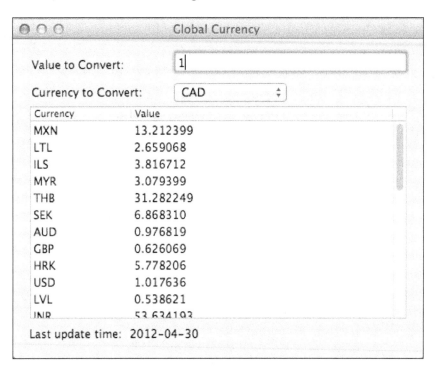

Have a go hero – adding a rate column

Our program shows the currency and the exchanged value but it does not show the exchange rate. In Interface Builder, add a third column (that will display the exchange rate) to the table view and set its identifier to be rate. Then modify the dataSource to return the exchange rate value for that column.

Summary

In this chapter, we have implemented a business application that accesses the Internet to get its list of exchange rates and displays the exchanged values in a table.

Specifically, we covered the basics of XML and how to use `NSURL` and `NSXMLDocument` to download an XML file from the Internet. We continued by covering how to access, using paths, the XML Elements that we want in the XML document and how to use a background `NSThread` so that our main user interface thread is not tied up by another task. Then we looked at how to populate and act on `NSPopUpButton` objects and how to populate `NSTableView` objects. Finally, we covered how to access the `AppDelegate` from another object to retrieve values and then perform arithmetic operations on them.

Now that we've learned how to access XML files from the Internet, we are going to look at the Internet using its new marketing name of, the Cloud. We will look at how so-called "Cloud services", specifically iCloud, can be used to not only retrieve information but also store information. Numbers in the cloud will be the topic of our next chapter.

5

Personal Information – Numbers in the iCloud

This chapter will walk us through the steps needed to create a personal information App that allows us to store our important numbers in iCloud so that we can access them from anywhere in the world.

In this chapter, we shall learn the following:

- What is iCloud?
- Creating an iCloud enabled development provisioning profile
- Implementing two tables in one window
- Implementing a toolbar
- Storing and retrieving our important numbers in iCloud

What is iCloud?

When software designers, network architects, system designers, and other assorted technical geeks draw pictures of networks they use the cloud symbol to represent wide area networks. More specifically, in many network diagrams, they use the cloud symbol to represent the most famous wide area network of them all, the Internet. Companies have been trying, with varying degrees of success, to provide wide area network (AOL and CompuServe) and Internet based (MobileMe, Yahoo, and MSN) services for decades.

With the introduction of mobile computing platforms (phones and tablets), a real need for Internet based services has finally arrived, and since the marketing folks want consumers to distinguish these needed services from the previous efforts to provide unneeded services, they have decided to call them cloud-based services.

So in answer to the question, iCloud is nothing more than Apple's marketing, or brand name, for its Internet based services. Specifically, iCloud provides:

- Authentication (login)
- Security (trusted developers)
- Automatic backup
- A set of standard application programming interfaces (APIs) for developers to access files and preferences
- Automatic services to synchronize files and preferences across multiple devices that are connected to the Internet

Be aware that iCloud services do not behave the same on Mac OS X as on iOS. When an iOS user enabled iCloud backups data is sometimes moved to iCloud and removed from the device. In this case, if the device is not connected to the Internet, critical data may not be available to the App. It is not safe to assume that what works on Mac OS X will also work on iOS. Rather iOS Apps need to consider things that are not, yet, issues for Mac OS X Apps.

To develop applications that use iCloud, developers must register with Apple and digitally sign their applications so that they are trusted.

To use applications that access iCloud, users must register with Apple and login using the iCloud system preference.

Installing an iCloud enabled development profile

In a later chapter, we are going to discuss the Mac OS X App store and the details of how to sign up as a registered Mac developer to distribute our App in the App store. This section assumes we are already a registered Mac developer and discusses just the steps needed to create a development profile for an iCloud enabled Mac App.

If you are not currently a registered Mac App developer skip this section. The sample App can be built but access to iCloud will not be enabled. The App can be rebuilt later with iCloud access enabled, by following these steps. If you decide to join the Mac App developer program.

Time for action – creating and installing an iCloud enabled development profile

We are going to start by creating a new App ID and making sure it is enabled for iCloud access. Using the new App ID we can create, download, and install the development provisioning profile that will enable iCloud access. Let's get started!

1. Go to `http://developer.apple.com` and select the **Mac Dev Center** option.

2. Login to the **Mac Dev Center** and select **Developer Certificate Utility**.

3. Create a new App ID making sure to **Enable for iCloud**.

4. Create a new **Development Provisioning Profile** for the iCloud enabled App ID by selecting **Provisioning Profiles** and clicking on the **Create Profile** button.

5. On the **Create Mac Provisioning Profile** detail screen, select **Development Provisioning Profile** for the **Kind** field, give it whatever name you like, and select **Numbers In The Cloud** for the Mac App ID.

6. Finally, click on the **Generate** button.

7. Next, download the **Profile**.

8. Double-click on the downloaded `.provisionprofile` file to install the profile in the System Preferences.

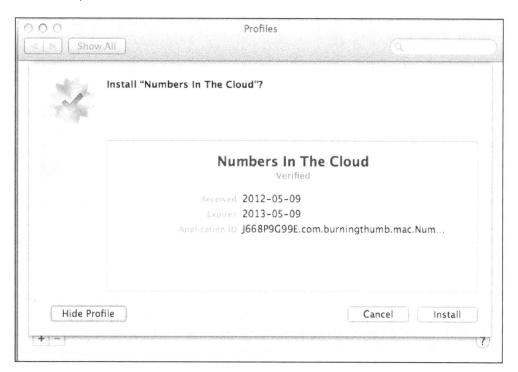

9. Drag the downloaded `.provisionprofile` file into the Xcode **Organizer** to install the profile in Xcode.

What just happened?

We created a new iCloud enabled Mac App ID, we created a new development profile for the iCloud enabled Mac App ID, and we downloaded and installed the profile.

Designing the GUI for numbers in the cloud

Our App will be used to store values for our important, personal numbers in iCloud. Because we want our numbers to be organized, we are going to store the numbers by category, such as, phone numbers, credit card numbers, and PIN numbers. We are going to use a toolbar with toolbar items that allow us to add and delete both categories and numbers within those categories as shown in the following figure:

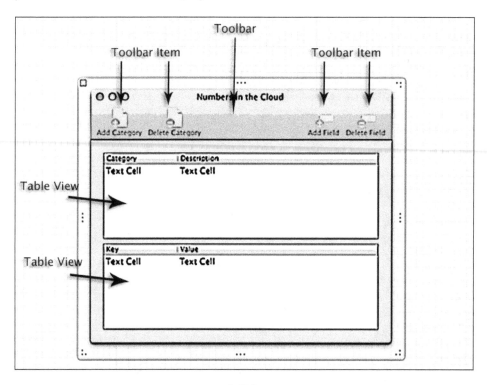

Time for action – creating our project and GUI

We are going to start by creating a new project and designing the `.xib` file to match our GUI design. Once we have the interface laid out, we will continue to implement the App.

1. To create a new Xcode project, launch the Xcode App. If you have any projects open from a previous chapter, close them.

2. If you don't see the **Welcome to Xcode** window, then select **Welcome to Xcode** from the **Window** menu.

3. Click on the **Create a new Xcode project** button in the **Welcome to Xcode** window.

4. When Xcode asks us to select a template, select **Application** under **Mac OS X** and **Cocoa Application** as the template. Then, click on the **Next** button.

5. When we click the **Next** button, Xcode will ask us to select options for our new project. The options that we need to select are as follows:

Option	Value
Product Name	`Numbers in the Cloud`
Company Identifier	`com.yourdomain`
Class Prefix	Your initials (we have used `BTS` throughout this book)

6. Enable the **Use Automatic Reference Counting** option.

7. Click on the **Next** button, locate our projects folder, and then click on the **Create** button.

8. After Xcode creates the new project, design an icon, and drag it in to the **App Icon** field on **TARGET Summary**.

9. Click on the filename `MainMenu.xib` in the project navigator.

10. Using our GUI design, drag the following items from the **Objects** library into the **Numbers In The Cloud** window, then rename and position them to match the design. The Object Kind is the thing that you want to drag, and the value is the name you want to give it. All you need to do here is create these GUI objects so that the GUI looks like the design shown in the previous screenshot.

Object Kind	Value
Toolbar	
Toolbar item	**Add Category**
Toolbar item	**Delete Category**
Toolbar item	**Add Key**
Toolbar item	**Delete Key**
Table view	Two columns titled **Category** and **Description**
Table view	Two columns titled **Key** and **Value**

11. Select each table column and in the **Identity Inspector** tool set the identifier to match the column titles so that the identifier for the **Category** column is `category`, the identifier for the **Description** column is `description`, the identifier for the **Key** column is `key`, and the identifier for the **Value** column is `value`. Our program code will use these identifiers in its `dataSource` implementation to determine for which column it must return a value.

12. Create images for the four different toolbar item objects. The images can be anything we want them to be and should be designed in the same way as we would design any icon on Mac OS X.

13. Drag these image files into the **Supporting Files** group in Xcode as shown in the following screenshot:

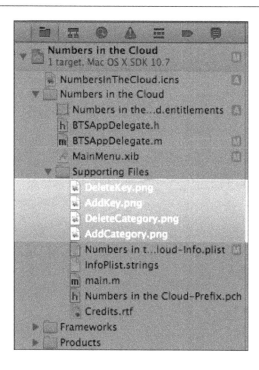

14. For each **Toolbar Item**, in the Xcode **Attributes Inspector**, set the values for the **Image Name**, **Label**, **Palette Label**, and **Identifier** so that we have the four toolbar items.

Name	Label	Palette Label	Identifier
Add category	**Add Category**	**Add Category**	addcategory
Delete category	**Delete Category**	**Delete Category**	deletecategory
Add key	**Add Key**	**Add Key**	addkey
Delete key	**Delete Key**	**Delete Key**	deletekey

In the following screenshot, each **Toolbar Item** has an icon and a label. We also need to drag the **Toolbar Item** objects into the **Toolbar** as shown in the following screenshot:

What just happened?

We created our Xcode project and designed our user interface using Interface Builder. Now when we click on the **Run** button, our project displays our interface.

Note that the **Toolbar Item** objects are grayed out. This is because we have not assigned them a target action so they are disabled automatically. As soon as we assign a target action to the **Toolbar Item** objects, they will automatically enable.

The following screenshot shows the final interface after we have designed it in Xcode:

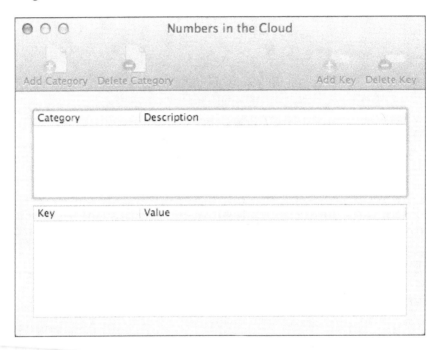

Connecting the GUI to program elements

Now that we have created the GUI in Interface Builder we need to connect the elements to variables defined in our App Delegate so that we can update the GUI from inside our program code. We will always need these references to GUI elements in our programs.

Time for action – connecting the App Delegate to the GUI

Since we have already created the `.xib` file we just need to add the reference to the GUI objects in to our App Delegate and then connect them to our GUI. Let's get started!

1. In Xcode, click on the file name `BTSAppDelegate.h` in the project navigator and add the following properties:

```
//
// Define the GUI object references
//

@property (strong) IBOutlet NSToolbar *m_toolbar;
@property (strong) IBOutlet NSToolbarItem *m_
addCategoryToolbarItem;
@property (strong) IBOutlet NSToolbarItem *m_
deleteCategoryToolbarItem;
@property (strong) IBOutlet NSToolbarItem *m_addKeyToolbarItem;
@property (strong) IBOutlet NSToolbarItem *m_deleteKeyToolbarItem;
@property (strong) IBOutlet NSTableView *m_categoryTableView;
@property (strong) IBOutlet NSTableView *m_keyTableView;
```

2. Click on the filename `BTSAppDelegate.m` in the project navigator and add the following lines of code to synthesize the properties:

```
//
// Define the GUI object references
//

@synthesize m_toolbar;
@synthesize m_addCategoryToolbarItem;
@synthesize m_deleteCategoryToolbarItem;
@synthesize m_addKeyToolbarItem;
@synthesize m_deleteKeyToolbarItem;
@synthesize m_categoryTableView;
@synthesize m_keyTableView;
```

3. Click on the file named **MainMenu.xib**.

4. In the **Editor** toolbar, click on the **Show the Assistant editor** icon to display the assistant editor. The assistant editor allows us to connect interface elements in the `.xib` file directly to program code.

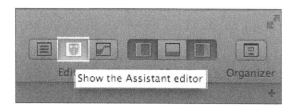

5. After clicking on the **Show the Assistant editor** icon, the **Editor** pane will split to display program code that is related to the selected user interface object. It will look like the following screenshot:

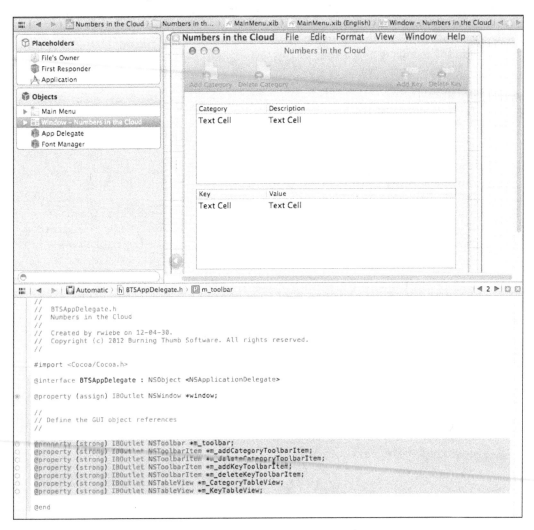

6. In the bottom pane of the **Editor** window, there is an assistant denoted by the tuxedo shaped icon. You can choose various kinds of assistance based on the assistant that you choose from the pop-up menu. Make sure the selected pop-up assistant is set to **Automatic** and click on the arrows until the BTSAppDelegate.h file is displayed as shown in the following screenshot:

7. By left-clicking in the circle beside an `@property` declaration, we can drag to either the `.xib` document or the document outline to connect the code directly to the user interface objects as shown in the following screenshot:

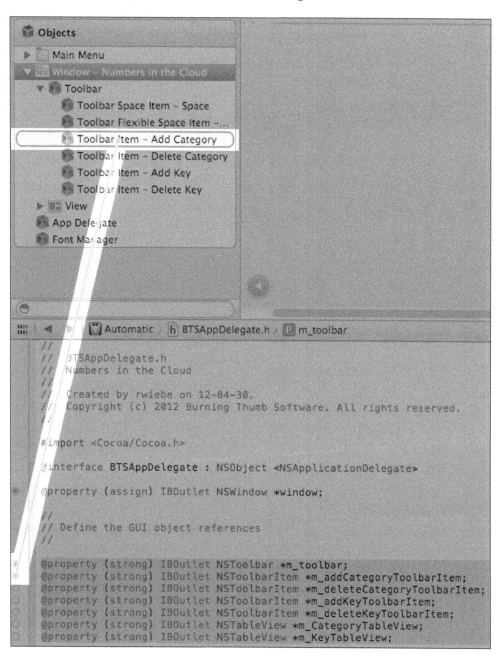

8. Using the assistant editor, connect the user interface objects as shown in the following screenshot:

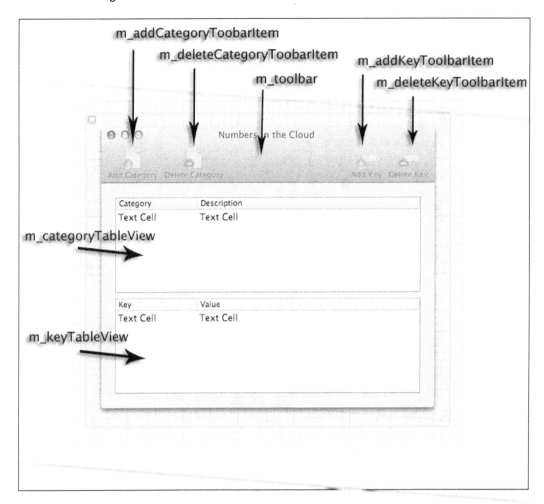

What just happened?

We created and synthesized the properties for the **Numbers in the Cloud** GUI objects and connected them directly to our program code using the assistant editor. Now we know a second way that we can use Xcode to connect program code and GUI objects. With the user interface objects connected, we are ready to start implementing our program behavior.

Using two tables in one window

Whenever we want to display a table of rows and columns in a Mac OS X App, we can use a GUI object called a table view, or in programming terms an NSTableView object. We can have any number of rows, any number of columns, and even multiple NSTableView objects in our GUI.

Since we have an NSTableView object for both our number categories and our number key-value pairs, we need to think of a way to store the information inside our program code. Since NSTableViews lend themselves naturally to NSArrays, we may choose to represent the rows of each table with the row of an array. In turn, the array rows can contain an NSDictionary object, where the dictionary key corresponds to a table column identifier. We end up with something like the following screenshot:

Item 0	⊙ ⊖	Diction... ↕	(3 items)
category	⊙ ⊖	String	Credit Cards
description		String	My Credit Cards
▼ keys		Array	(2 items)
▼ Item 0		Diction...	(2 items)
key		String	Mastercard
value		String	9999 9999 9999 9999
▼ Item 1		Diction...	(2 items)
key		String	Visa
value		String	8888 8888 8888 8888
▼ Item 1		Diction...	(3 items)
category		String	PINS
description		String	My PIN Numbers
▼ keys		Array	(2 items)
▼ Item 0		Diction...	(2 items)
key		String	Wells Fargo
value		String	9999
▼ Item 1		Diction...	(2 items)
key		String	Bank of America
value		String	8888

This "array of dictionaries" seems like a good choice for storing the information in our program.

Time for action – implementing the TableView delegate

In order for our table view to display values, we need to implement something called a **delegate**. As its name implies, a delegate performs a task on behalf of another object. In this case our table view delegate will handle any clicks on our table and will implement the methods that return the information that will be displayed in the table's rows and columns.

1. Add the member variable to BTSAppDelegate.h as follows:

```
//
// Define the Member elements
//

@property (strong)  NSMutableArray *m_numbersArray;
```

2. Add the member variable to BTSAppDelegate.m as follows:

```
//
// Define the Member elements
//

@synthesize m_numbersArray;
```

3. From the **File** menu, select **New**, then select **New File...** and create a new class named **BTS_NCTableViewDelegate** that will be used to manage the table views.

4. Select the MainMenu.xib file and create a new object from the **Object Library**.

5. Change the name of the new object to **BTS_NCTableViewDelegate**.

6. Change the class of the new object to **BTS_NCTableViewDelegate**.

7. Connect the **dataSource** object and **delegate** outlets of both the table views to the new **BTS_NCTableViewDelegate** object.

8. In the BTS_NCTableViewDelegate.h file, add a #define for the key that we will use to access the numbers in the categories dictionary. Also create an object reference for the AppDelegate object so that we can cache the reference when our new object awakes.

```
#import <Foundation/Foundation.h>
#import "BTSAppDelegate.h"

// Define the key that will be used
// to access the keys array in the categories dictionary
#define kBTSNCKeysKey @"keys"

@interface BTS_NCTableViewDelegate : NSObject
{
    // Create a reference to the AppDelegate so
    // that we only need to look it up one time
    BTSAppDelegate *m_appDelegate;
}
```

9. In the `BTS_NCTableViewDelegate.m` file, implement the code in the `awakeFromNib:` method that caches a reference to the `AppDelegate` object so that we can use the reference in our other methods as follows:

```
/*

 This method is invoked automatically
 when the object instance is revived
 from the .xib file

 This is where we do any initialization
 needed by the .xib object

 */

-(void) awakeFromNib
{
    // Get a reference to our AppDelegate
    // object and save it for later use
m_appDelegate = [NSApp delegate];
}
```

10. Our table view delegate needs to return the number of rows for both of the tables and does so by determining which table view has asked for the information and then returning the number of rows in the array for that table to the table view that asked. Add the following code to the `BTS_NCTableViewDelegate.m` file to implement the method:

```
/*

 This method is invoked automatically
 when the table view GUI element needs
 to know how many rows it has to
 display

 All dataSource objects must implement
 this method.

 */

- (NSInteger)numberOfRowsInTableView:(NSTableView *)a_tableView
{
    // Create the reference that will be returned
    NSInteger l_numberOfRows = 0;

    // Create a reference to the row of the
    // categories table that is selected
    NSInteger l_selectedCategory = -1;
```

```
            // We need to behave differently based on
            // which table view wants to know how many
            // rows it must display

            // We can inspect the value of a_tableView to
            // determine which table view is asking for
            // information

            // Is it the category table view ?
            if (a_tableView == m_appDelegate.m_categoryTableView)
            {
                // Set the return value to the number of rows
                // in the array
                l_numberOfRows = m_appDelegate.m_numbersArray.count;
            }
            // Is it the keys table view ?
            else if (a_tableView == m_appDelegate.m_keyTableView )
            {
                // Determine which category row is selected
                l_selectedCategory =
m_appDelegate.m_categoryTableView.selectedRow;

                // If a row was selected
                if (l_selectedCategory >= 0)
                {
                    // Find the category row in the m_numbersArray.
                    // Locate the second array using the kBTSNCKeysKey.
                    // Set the return value to the number of rows
                    // in the array.
                    l_numberOfRows = [[[m_appDelegate.m_numbersArray
                                     objectAtIndex:l_selectedCategory]
                                     objectForKey:kBTSNCKeysKey]
count];
                }
            }

            // Return the number of rows
            return l_numberOfRows;

        }
```

11. Our table view delegate needs to return the value for a cell in a specific column and a specific row for a table. It does so by determining which table view has asked and then returning the value for that cell in the table to the table view that asked for it. Add the following code to the BTS_NCTableViewDelegate.m file to implement the method:

```
/*

    This method is invoked automatically
    when the table view GUI element needs
```

```
to display a column value for any
column row

All dataSource objects must implement
this method.

*/

- (id)tableView:(NSTableView *)a_tableView objectValueForTableColu
mn:(NSTableColumn *)a_tableColumn row:(NSInteger)a_rowIndex
{
```

12. First we set up some initial references for the value that will be returned and the value that has been selected in the table:

```
// Create a reference to the value that
// will be returned
id l_columnValue;

// Create a reference to the row of the
// categories table that is selected
NSInteger l_selectedCategory = -1;

// Determine which table column the value is
// for by looking up the identifier.  Remember to
// set the identifier in the .xib file for each
// table column or this method will not work
NSString *l_identifier = [a_tableColumn identifier];

// We need to behave differently based on
// which table view wants to know how many
// rows it must display
```

13. Then we examine the value of the passed in `NSTableView` object and create a reference to the object that should be returned for that table view. This is needed because the delegate method for both table views is the same object. If instead we had created a second object and made it the delegate for the second table view then we would not need to make this determination.

```
// We can inspect the value of a_tableView to
// determine which table view is asking for
// information

// Is it the category table view ?
if (a_tableView == m_appDelegate.m_categoryTableView)
{
    // Set the return value from dictionary item in
    // the array for the row.  Use the table identifer
    // set in the .xib file as the key to access the
```

```
            // dictionary
            l_columnValue =
            [[m_appDelegate.m_numbersArray objectAtIndex:a_rowIndex]
                objectForKey:l_identifier];
        }


        // Is it the keys table view ?
        else if (a_tableView == m_appDelegate.m_keyTableView)
        {
            // Determine which category row is selected
            l_selectedCategory =
    m_appDelegate.m_categoryTableView.selectedRow;


            // If a row was selected
            if (l_selectedCategory >= 0)
            {
                // Set the return value from dictionary item in
                // the array for the selected row.  Use the table
                // identifer set in the .xib file as the key to access
                // thedictionary
                l_columnValue =
                  [[[[m_appDelegate.m_numbersArray
                        objectAtIndex:l_selectedCategory]
                       objectForKey:kBTSNCKeysKey]
                      objectAtIndex:a_rowIndex]
                       objectForKey:l_identifier];
            }
        }


    return l_columnValue;
    }
```

14. Because we want to be able to double-click on any cell in either of the table views in our GUI, we need to implement the optional NSTableView delegate method that is called when a GUI value changes. We use the changed value passed in to this method to update the NSDictionary storage in our App. Add the following code to the BTS_NCTableViewDelegate.m file to implement the method:

```
/*

This method is invoked automatically
when any cell in the table view GUI element
changes.

It is optional to implement this method but
it must be implemented if cells are editable
```

```
    */

- (void)tableView:(NSTableView *)a_tableView
    setObjectValue:(id)a_object
    forTableColumn:(NSTableColumn *)a_tableColumn
               row:(int)a_rowIndex
{
```

15. We set up some initial references that we will use to examine the value that has been selected in the table as follows:

```
// Create a reference to the row of the
// categories table that is selected
NSInteger l_selectedCategory = -1;

// Create a reference to the mutable
// dictionary that stores the data
// for a row
NSMutableDictionary *l_row;
```

16. Again we examine the table view object that was passed in and use its value to decide which object needs to be modified:

```
// Is it the category table view ?
if (a_tableView == m_appDelegate.m_categoryTableView)
{
    // Assign the row reference to the
    // selected category dictionary
    l_row = [m_appDelegate.m_numbersArray
            objectAtIndex:a_rowIndex];

    // Update the dictionary with the
    // new value
    [l_row setObject:a_object
            forKey:[a_tableColumn identifier]];
}

// Is it the keys table view ?
else if (a_tableView == m_appDelegate.m_keyTableView)
{
    // Determine which category row is selected
    l_selectedCategory =
m_appDelegate.m_categoryTableView.selectedRow;

    if (l_selectedCategory >= 0)
    {
        // Assign the row reference to the
        // selected key dictionary
```

```
            l_row =
            [[[m_appDelegate.m_numbersArray
                objectAtIndex:l_selectedCategory]
              objectForKey:kBTSNCKeysKey]
             objectAtIndex:a_rowIndex];

            // Update the dictionary with the
            // new value
            [l_row setObject:a_object
                    forKey:[a_tableColumn identifier]];

        }

    }
}
```

17. If the user clicks on a new category in the table view, we need to load the key table with the values associated with that category. We can do this by using the optional `tableViewSelectionDidChange:` notification method. This method is invoked whenever a new row is selected in a table view. Add the following code to the `BTS_NCTableViewDelegate.m` file to implement the method:

```
/*

This method is invoked automatically
when the table view GUI element selection
changes.

It is optional to implement this method

*/

- (void) tableViewSelectionDidChange: (NSNotification *) a_
notification
{
    // The notification object is
    // the table view that has a new
    // selection.  We need a reference
    // to that object
    NSTableView *l_tableView = [a_notification object];

    // Is it the category table view ?
    if (l_tableView == m_appDelegate.m_categoryTableView)
    {
        // Tell the key table view to reload its
        // data
        [m_appDelegate.m_keyTableView reloadData];
    }

}
```

What just happened?

We implemented the program code that will provide data to two tables in a single window. We did this by using a single `dataSource` and `delegate` object that examined the table view that was requesting the data and returning different values depending on which table view required the information.

Have a go hero – using two dataSource and delegate objects

Another way to implement this would be to have two distinct delegate objects. We could have connected the category table view to one of the objects and the key table view to the other object. If it was done that way the program code could be split and the if conditions removed because each object would only be handling a single table view.

Go ahead and make those changes now, by following these steps:

1. Add a new `dataSource` and delegate object by adding a new file and creating an instance of the object in the `.xib` file.
2. Connect one of the two table views to the new object in the `.xib` file.
3. Duplicate the program code across the two `dataSource` and delegate objects.
4. Remove the `if` conditions from the program code so that each object handles one table view or the other.

Implementing the toolbar

Similar to a table view, a toolbar uses a delegate object to implement much of its behavior. We can create the delegate object for the toolbar in the same way as we have done for table views with the difference being that the implementation methods will be toolbar rather than the table view methods.

Time for action – implementing the Toolbar delegate

Similar to a table view, we need to implement a delegate for our toolbar. Again, as its name implies, the toolbar delegate will implement behaviors on behalf of the GUI object.

1. From the **File** menu, select **New**, then select **New File...** and create a new class named `BTS_NCToolbarDelegate` that will be used to manage the table views.
2. Select the **MainMenu.xib** file and create a new object from the **Object Library**.
3. Change the name of the new object to **BTS_NCToolbarDelegate**.
4. Change the class of the new object to **BTS_NCToolbarDelegate**.

5. In the .xib file, connect the **Toolbar** object to the **BTS_NCToolbarDelegate** object and select **delegate** from the **Outlets** menu as shown in the following screenshot:

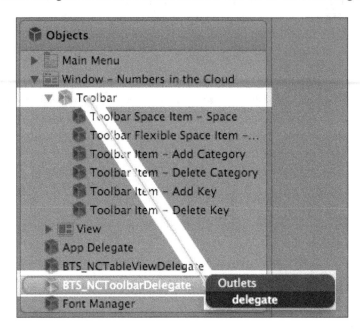

6. In BTS_NCToolbarDelegate.h, add the following code to define the interface. It defines a single method that will be used to handle all the **Toolbar Item** objects.

```
// Handle the Toolbar Item selection
- (IBAction)selectToolbarItem:(id)a_sender;
```

7. Connect the **dataSource** and **delegate** outlets of both the table views to the new **BTS_NCToolbarDelegate** object.

8. Add the member variable to BTSAppDelegate.h that will be used to cache a reference to the AppDelegate object as follows:

```
#import <Foundation/Foundation.h>
#import "BTSAppDelegate.h"

@interface BTS_NCToolbarDelegate : NSObject
{
// Create a reference to the AppDelegate so
// that we only need to look it up one time
BTSAppDelegate *m_appDelegate;
}
```

9. Because we are going to reference kBTSNCKeysKey in the file named BTS_
NCToolbarDelegate.m, we will #import the BTS_NCTableViewDelegate.h
file so that we don't need to #define the value twice. Using multiple defines for
a constant value can be error prone so we never want to define them more than
one time:

```
#import "BTS_NCToolbarDelegate.h"
#import "BTS_NCTableViewDelegate.h"
```

10. In the BTS_NCToolbarDelegate.m file, implement the code in the
awakeFromNib: method that caches a reference to the AppDelegate object
so that we can use the reference in our other methods:

```
/*

 This method is invoked automatically
 when the object instance is revived
 from the .xib file

 This is where we do any initialization
 needed by the .xib object

 */

-(void) awakeFromNib
{
    // Get a reference to our AppDelegate
    // object and save it for later use
m_appDelegate = [NSApp delegate];
}
```

11. In the BTS_NCToolbarDelegate.m file, implement the code in the
selectToolbarItem: method that handles toolbar item clicks. This method
adds a new row to the selected table and populates the column values with the
identifiers that were assigned in the .xib file:

```
/*

 This method is assigned in the .xib
 file as the target action for
 the toolbar items.  As a result, it
 is invoked whenever a toolbar item
 is clicked.

 Input: a_sender - the object that was
                   clicked
```

```
    Output: None


    */
-   (IBAction)selectToolbarItem:(id)a_sender
{
```

12. The first thing that we need to do is create some variables for the items that we want to reference in our method:

```
// Create a reference to the row of the -
// categories table that is selected -
    NSInteger l_selectedCategory = -1;

// Create a reference to the row of the -
// key table that is selected -
    NSInteger l_selectedKey = -1;

// Create a reference to an array that
// will hold a list of all the columns
// in the selected table view
    NSArray *l_columns;

// Create a reference to an array that
// will hold a list of all the rows
// in the dataSource for the table view
    NSMutableArray *l_rows;

// Get the number of the selected
// row in the Category table view
    l_selectedCategory =
m_appDelegate.m_categoryTableView.selectedRow;

// Get the number of the selected
// row in the Key table view
    l_selectedKey = m_appDelegate.m_keyTableView.selectedRow;
```

13. Next we need to compare the value of the sender to determine which item invoked the method. If it was the **Delete Key** toolbar item then we will remove a row and redisplay the table as follows:

```
        // Was the Delete Key toolbar item clicked
        if (a_sender == m_appDelegate.m_deleteKeyToolbarItem)
        {
            // Was a row in the Key table view selected
            if (l_selectedKey >= 0)
{
                // Get all the rows
                l_rows = [[m_appDelegate.m_numbersArray
objectAtIndex:l_selectedCategory]
objectForKey:kBTSNCKeysKey];
```

```
            // Remove the selected row
            [l_rows removeObjectAtIndex: l_selectedKey];

            // Re-display the table
            [m_appDelegate.m_keyTableViewreloadData];

        }
    }
```

14. If it was the **Delete Category** toolbar item, then we will remove a row and redisplay the table as follows:

```
    // Was the Delete Category toolbar item clicked
    else
if (a_sender == m_appDelegate.m_deleteCategoryToolbarItem)
    {
        // Was a row in the Category table view selected
        if (l_selectedCategory >= 0)
        {
            // Remove the selected row
            [m_appDelegate.m_numbersArray
removeObjectAtIndex: l_selectedCategory];

            // Re-display both tables
            [m_appDelegate.m_categoryTableViewreloadData];
            [m_appDelegate.m_keyTableViewreloadData];

        }
    }
```

15. If it was the **Add Key** toolbar item, then we will add a row, set the default values based on the column identifiers, and redisplay the table as follows:

```
    // Was the Add Key toolbar item clicked
    else
if (a_sender == m_appDelegate.m_addKeyToolbarItem)
    {
        // Was a row in the Category table view selected
        if (l_selectedCategory >= 0)
        {
            // Create a new empty dictionary
NSMutableDictionary *l_newRow =
            [[NSMutableDictionaryalloc] init];

            // Get a list of table columns
            l_columns = m_appDelegate.m_keyTableView.tableColumns;

            // For each column, add an entry
            // to the dictioary that matches
            // the column identifier
            for (id l_column in l_columns)
```

```
          {
                [l_newRow setObject:[l_column identifier]
     forKey:[l_column identifier]];
          }

          // Get the key array for the selected
          // category
          l_rows = [[m_appDelegate.m_numbersArray
     objectAtIndex:l_selectedCategory]
     objectForKey:kBTSNCKeysKey];

          // Add the newly create row
          [l_rows insertObject:l_newRow
     atIndex: l_selectedKey + 1];

          // Re-display the table
          [m_appDelegate.m_keyTableViewreloadData];
     }
}
```

16. Finally, if it was the **Add Category** toolbar item, then we will add a row, set the default values based on the column identifiers, and redisplay the table as follows:

```
     // Was the Add Category toolbar item clicked
     else
     if (a_sender == m_appDelegate.m_addCategoryToolbarItem)
     {

          // Create a new empty dictionary
          NSMutableDictionary *l_newRow =
            [[NSMutableDictionary alloc] init];

          // Get a list of table columns
          l_columns = m_appDelegate.m_categoryTableView.
     tableColumns;


          // For each column, add an entry
          // to the dictioary that matches
          // the column identifier
          for (id l_column in l_columns)
          {
               [l_newRow setObject:[l_column identifier]
                         forKey:[l_column identifier]];
          }

          // Add an empty set of Keys to
          // the dictionary
          [l_newRow setObject:[[NSMutableArray alloc] init]
                    forKey:kBTSNCKeysKey];
```

```
        // Add the newly create row
        [m_appDelegate.m_numbersArray insertObject: l_newRow
                        atIndex:l_selectedCategory + 1];


        // Re-display both tables
        [m_appDelegate.m_categoryTableView reloadData];
        [m_appDelegate.m_keyTableView reloadData];
    }


}
```

What just happened?

We implemented the delegate for the toolbar items which also included the target action method that is invoked when a toolbar item is clicked. The following screenshot shows an example of the rows inserted by clicking on the add buttons. To change the values to something more meaningful, the App user would double-click on each value and type a new value.

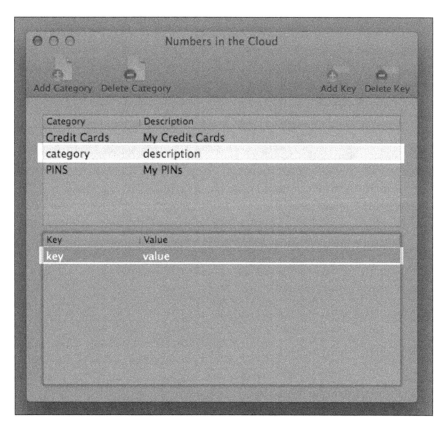

Have a go hero – using four different target actions

Another way to implement this would be to create a distinct target action method for each toolbar item object. We could have connected the toolbar to its own action method. If it was done that way the program code could be split and the `if` conditions removed because each target action method would only be handling a single toolbar item.

Go ahead and make those changes now, by following these steps:

1. Add a new target action in the `BTS_NCToolbarDelegate.h` file.

2. Connect each of the toolbar items to the individual action in the `.xib` file.

3. Remove the `if` conditions from the program code and moving the corresponding program code to the appropriate target action method.

Accessing iCloud

Now that we can create and manage our numbers using our App, we need to store them and retrieve them from iCloud. We are going to approach writing the program code in what may seem like a backwards approach. It is, however, quite common in programming to "assume" something is true even when we know that the first time the program runs it will be false. We do this because we expect it will be true every time, except the first time. In this case, we are going to assume the numbers have already been saved in iCloud, and read them into our App when it starts, even though we know the very first time we run our App that this won't be true but our program code will handle that condition.

Time for action – accessing iCloud for key-value storage

Because we are going to store our numbers in iCloud using a key-value pairing, we need to use a key to access the value. Since iCloud will automatically associated the key with our App's bundle identifier, it can be any arbitrary value. We will choose to use @`"numbers"`.

1. Add the following define to **BTSAppDelegate.h** to create the key:

```
// Define the key that we will use
// to access our numbers in the
// iCloud key / value data store
#define kBTSNCNumbersKey @"numbers"
```

2. Add the code to `BTSAppDelegate.m` that creates the mutable array we will use to store our numbers. This code will first try to load the numbers from iCloud and if they are not found in iCloud then it will create a new empty NSMutableArray object as shown in the following code snippet:

```
// This method is invoked automatically
// when our App finishes launching
```

```objc
- (void)applicationDidFinishLaunching:
        (NSNotification *)aNotification
{
    // Insert code here to initialize your application

    // Create a variable to hold the error code
    BOOL l_result;

    // The NSUbiquitousKeyValueStore class provides a
    // programmatic interface for storing small amounts of
    // configuration data in iCloud.

    // An application must always use the default store
    // object to get and set values. This store is tied to
    // the unique identifier string your application provides
    // in its entitlements.
    NSUbiquitousKeyValueStore *l_store =
    [NSUbiquitousKeyValueStore defaultStore];

    // When the value of a key changes externally, the shared
    // key-value store object posts a
    // NSUbiquitousKeyValueStoreDidChangeExternallyNotification
    // notification to your application. This notification is sent
    // only when a  key changes externally or when there was a
    // problem writing a local change to iCloud. It is not sent
when
    // your application succeeds in setting a value.

    // Register for notifications so that we can detect errors
    [[NSNotificationCenter defaultCenter]
     addObserver:self
     selector:@selector(updateKVStoreItems:)
     name:NSUbiquitousKeyValueStoreDidChangeExternallyNotification
     object:l_store];

    // Synchronize the store so that any changes that were made
    // are known to our App
    l_result = [l_store synchronize];

    // Retrieve the numbers from iCloud, if they are
    // not found the object will not be created

    // This code uses CFPropertyListCreateDeepCopy to
    // make a mutable copy of the retrieved item
    // which would otherwise have some immutable
    // items
    m_numbersArray =
```

```
  (__bridge_transfer  NSMutableArray*)
   CFPropertyListCreateDeepCopy(
     kCFAllocatorDefault,
     (__bridge_retained  CFPropertyListRef)
      [l_store arrayForKey:kBTSNCNumbersKey],
     kCFPropertyListMutableContainers);

 // If the numbers were not found in iCloud then
 // create a new, empty numbers object
 if (m_numbersArray == NULL)
 {
     m_numbersArray = [[NSMutableArray alloc] init];
 }

 // Update the GUI
 [m_categoryTableView reloadData];
}
```

The NSUbiqitousKeyValueStore is an object that uses the iCloud key-value store to make preference, configuration, and app-state data available to every instance of our app on every device connected to a user's iCloud account.

Changes our app writes to the key-value store object are initially held in memory, then written to disk by the system at appropriate times. The system automatically reconciles our local, on-disk keys and values with those in iCloud.

3. Finally we need to implement the notification method that will be received whenever a key-value is pushed from iCloud to our App. Since we only use the single key @"numbers" the implementation could simply re-read the numbers from the iCloud store but we have added a little extra code that would work if there were multiple keys returned in the notification. Enter the following program code in the file:

```
/*
    This notification is posted when the Key-Value
    Store changes.  We register to receive this
    notification in the applicationDidFinishLaunching
    method

    Input: A notification whose userInfo contains
           the changed item reason or error and
           keys.

    Output: none
*/
```

```objc
- (void)updateKVStoreItems:(NSNotification*)a_notification
{

    // Get the userInfo dictionary from
    // the notification object
    NSDictionary* l_userInfo = [a_notification userInfo];

    // Get the reason for the change
    // from the userInfo dictionary
    NSNumber* reasonForChange =
     [l_userInfo
      objectForKey:NSUbiquitousKeyValueStoreChangeReasonKey];

    NSInteger l_reason = -1;

    // If a reason could not be determined, do not update
anything.
    if (!reasonForChange)

        return;

    // Convert the NSNumber object to an
    // integer
    l_reason = [reasonForChange integerValue];

    // Update only for changes from the server.
    if ((l_reason == NSUbiquitousKeyValueStoreServerChange) ||
        (l_reason == NSUbiquitousKeyValueStoreInitialSyncChange))
    {

        // Get the array of keys that changed
        // This should only ever include one string
        // with the value kBTSNCNumbersKey
        NSArray* l_changedKeys =
            [l_userInfo
             objectForKey:NSUbiquitousKeyValueStoreChangedKeysKey];

        // An application must always use the default store
        // object to get and set values. This store is tied to
        // the unique identifier string your application provides
        // in its entitlements.
        NSUbiquitousKeyValueStore *l_store =
        [NSUbiquitousKeyValueStore defaultStore];

        // Loop over the keys
        for (NSString* key in l_changedKeys)
        {
```

```
                        // This should be the only key
                        if ([key isEqual:kBTSNCNumbersKey ])
                        {
                            // This code uses CFPropertyListCreateDeepCopy to
                            // make a mutable copy of the retrieved item
                            // which would otherwise have some immutable
                            // items
                            m_numbersArray =
                              (__bridge_transfer  NSMutableArray*)
                               CFPropertyListCreateDeepCopy(
                                 kCFAllocatorDefault,
                                  (__bridge_retained  CFPropertyListRef)
                                   [l_store arrayForKey:kBTSNCNumbersKey] ,
                                 kCFPropertyListMutableContainers) ;


                            // Update the GUI
                            [m_categoryTableView reloadData] ;


                        }
                    }
                }
            }
```

4. Our `AppDelegate` is also going to be responsible for saving our numbers array to iCloud. Modify the `BTS_AppDelegate.h` file to include the interface definition for the method that will perform that work as shown in the following code snippet:

```
// This method will be invoked to
// save our numbers to iCloud
- (void)saveNumbersToCloud;
```

5. Once we define the interface, we need to implement the method. Enter the following code into `BTS_AppDelegate.m` to implement the `saveNumbersToCloud` method:

```
// This method will be invoked by the toolbar
// and tableview delegate methods whenever they
// need to update iCloud
//
// Input: none
//
// Output: none

- (void)saveNumbersToCloud
{
    // Create a variable to hold the error code
    BOOL l_result;
```

```
// The NSUbiquitousKeyValueStore class provides a
// programmatic interface for storing small amounts of
// configuration data in iCloud.

// An application must always use the default store
// object to get and set values. This store is tied to
// the unique identifier string your application provides
// in its entitlements.
NSUbiquitousKeyValueStore *l_store =
[NSUbiquitousKeyValueStore defaultStore];

// Write the Array to local memory
// in such a way that it will automatically
// be written to disk and then automatically
// be transferred to iCloud
[l_store setArray:m_numbersArray forKey:kBTSNCNumbersKey];

// Synchronize the store so that any changes that were made
// are known to our App
l_result = [l_store synchronize];
}
```

6. In `BTS_NCToolbarDelegate.m`, add the following code to the end of the `selectToolbarItem:` method to update iCloud whenever a row is added to or deleted from a table:

```
// Save the changed array to iCloud
[m_appDelegate saveNumbersToCloud];
}
```

7. Similarly, in `BTS_NCTableViewDelegate.m`, add the following code to the end of the method to update iCloud whenever a cell value is modified:

```
// Save the changed array to iCloud
[m_appDelegate saveNumbersToCloud];

return l_columnValue;
}
```

8. Apps that access iCloud must be signed using an iCloud enabled provisioning profile and must include the iCloud entitlement. To enable our App Target, we must select it in the Xcode **Editor** and do the following:

   ❏ Enable **Code Sign Application**
   ❏ Enable **Entitlements**

- ☐ Enable iCloud key-value store (`com.domain.Numbers-In-The-Clouds` will be automatically added by Xcode as the default value)

- ☐ Add an item to iCloud Containers (`com.domain.Numbers-in-the-Clouds` will be automatically added by Xcode as the default value)

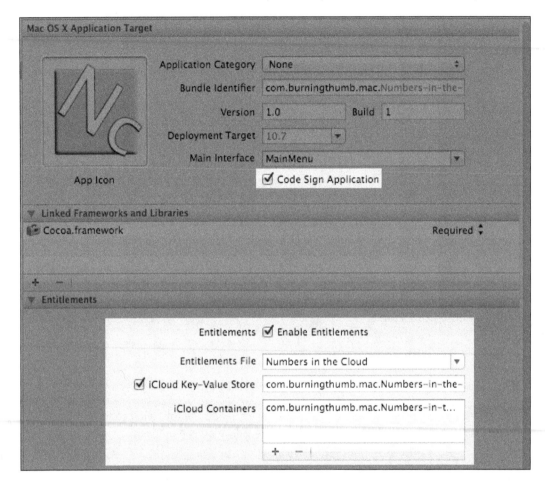

9. Finally, we must enable code signing in the build settings using the provisioning profile with iCloud enabled that we created earlier, as shown in the following screenshot:

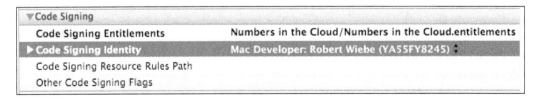

What just happened?

We implemented the methods required to update the iCloud key-value data store and configured the App Target to allow the built App to access iCloud. Now when we run our App, we can add entries and they will be stored in iCloud. When we quit the App and relaunch it, we will see the saved values as shown in the following screenshot:

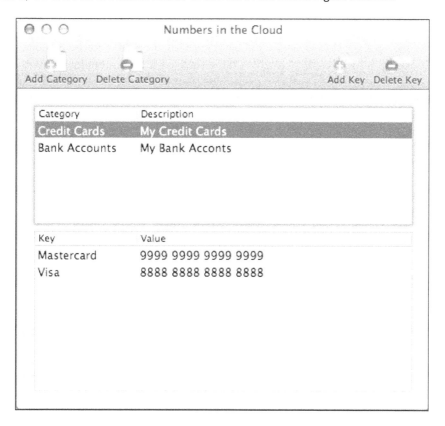

Summary

In this chapter, we have implemented an application that uses a toolbar and two table views backed by a mutable array that contains mutable dictionaries and arrays. The backing data was stored in iCloud rather than on the local computer so that multiple copies of the App running on different computers can access the data on iCloud and iCloud will push changes that occurred on one computer to the other.

Specifically, we covered what is iCloud and what entitlements are required to use iCloud. Then we looked at how to manage multiple table views and how to implement a toolbar. Next, we covered how to read and write key-value pairs to iCloud. We finished by looking at how to register for notifications of changes from iCloud and how to use those notifications to update our program data.

Now that we have spent some time looking at business applications and data synchronization we are going to move on to something a bit more fun and look at some of the multi-touch features of Mac OS X. Every Macbook comes with a multi-touch trackpad and Apple sells the magic trackpad for use with desktop computers. We are going to explore, in the next chapter, how to use multi-touch events in a finger painting App.

6
Painting – Multi-finger Paint

This chapter will walk us through the steps needed to create a bitmapped painting App that uses the multi-touch track pad to allow the App user to paint with multiple fingers.

In this chapter, we shall learn the following:

- ◆ What is multi-touch?
- ◆ Implementing a custom view
- ◆ Receiving multi-touch events
- ◆ Managing the mouse cursor
- ◆ Drawing using the 2D drawing APIs
- ◆ Receiving keyboard events
- ◆ Receiving gesture events

What is multi-touch?

The genesis of **multi-touch** on Mac OS X was the ability to perform two finger scrolling on a trackpad. The technology was further refined on mobile touch screen devices such as the iPod Touch, iPhone, and iPad. And it has also matured on the Mac OS X platform to allow the use of multi-touch or magic trackpad combined with one or more fingers and a motion to interact with the computer. **Gestures** are intuitive and allow us to control what is on the screen with fluid motions. Some of the things that we can do using multi-touch are as follows:

- **Two finger scrolling**: This is done by placing two fingers on the trackpad and dragging in a line
- **Tap or pinch to zoom**: This is done by tapping once with a single finger, or by placing two fingers on the trackpad and dragging them closer to each other
- **Swipe to navigate**: This is done by placing one or more fingers on the trackpad and quickly dragging in any direction followed by lifting all the fingers
- **Rotate**: This is done by placing two fingers on the trackpad and turning them in a circular motion while keeping them on the trackpad

But these gestures just touch the surface of what is possible with multi-touch hardware. The magic trackpad can detect and track all 10 of our fingers with ease. There are plenty of new things that can be done with multi-touch – we are just waiting for someone to invent them.

Implementing a custom view

Multi-touch events are sent to the NSView objects. So before we can invent that great new multi-touch thing, we first need to understand how to implement a custom view.

Essentially, a custom view is a subclass of NSView that overrides some of the behavior of the NSView object. Primarily, it will override the drawRect: method and some of the event handling methods.

Time for action – creating a GUI with a custom view

By now we should be familiar with creating new Xcode projects so some of the steps here are very high level. We can look back at the earlier chapters for help if we cannot remember some of the details of each high-level step. Let's get started!

1. Create a new Xcode project with **Automatic Reference Counting** enabled and these options enabled as follows:

Option	Value
Product Name	Multi-Finger Paint
Company Identifier	com.yourdomain
Class Prefix	Your initials (For consistency throughout this book, we used BTS)

2. After Xcode creates the new project, design an icon and drag it in to the **App Icon** field on the **TARGET Summary**.

3. Remember to set the **Organization** in the **Project Document** section of the **File inspector**.

4. Click on the filename **MainMenu.xib** in the project navigator.

5. Select the **Multi-Finger Paint** window and in the **Size** inspector change its **Width** and **Height** to **700** and **600** respectively.

6. Enable both the **Minimum Size** and **Maximum Size Constraints** values.

7. From the **Object Library**, drag a custom view into the window.

8. In the **Size inspector**, change the **Width** and **Height** of the custom view to **400** and **300** respectively.

9. Center the window using the guides that appear.

10. From the **File** menu, select **New>**, then select the **File...**option.

11. Select **the Mac OS X Cocoa Objective-C class** template and click on the **Next** button.

12. Name the class BTSFingerView and select subclass of **NSView**.

 It is very important that the subclass is NSView. If we make a mistake and select the wrong subclass, our App won't work.

13. Click on the button titled **Create** to create the .h and .m files.

14. Click on the filename BTSFingerView.m and look at it carefully. It should look similar to the following code:

```
//
//  BTSFingerView.m
//  Multi-Finger Paint
//
//  Created by rwiebe on 12-05-23.
//  Copyright (c) 2012 BurningThumb Software. All rights reserved.
//

#import "BTSFingerView.h"

@implementation BTSFingerView

- (id)initWithFrame:(NSRect)frame
{
    self = [super initWithFrame:frame];
    if (self) {
        // Initialization code here.
    }

    return self;
}

- (void)drawRect:(NSRect)dirtyRect
{
    // Drawing code here.
}

@end
```

15. By default, custom views do not receive events (keyboard, mouse, trackpad, and so on) but we need our custom view to receive events. To ensure our custom view will receive events, add the following code to the BTSFingerView.m file to accept the first responder:

```
/*
 ** - (BOOL) acceptsFirstResponder
 **
 ** Make sure the view will receive
 ** events.
 **
 ** Input: none
```

```
**
** Output: YES to accept, NO to reject
*/

- (BOOL) acceptsFirstResponder
{
    return YES;
}
```

16. And, still in the `BTSFingerView.m` file, modify the `initWithFrame` method to allow the view to accept touch events from the trackpad as follows:

```
- (id) initWithFrame: (NSRect) frame
{
    self = [super initWithFrame:frame];
    if (self) {
        // Initialization code here.

        // Accept trackpad events
        [self setAcceptsTouchEvents: YES];

    }

    return self;
}
```

17. Once we are sure our custom view will receive events, we can start the process of drawing its content. This is done in the `drawRect:` method. Add the following code to the `drawRect:` method to clear it with a transparent color and draw a focus ring if the view is first responder:

```
/*
 ** - (void) drawRect: (NSRect) dirtyRect
 **
 ** Draw the view content
 **
 ** Input: dirtyRect - the rectangle to draw
 **
 ** Output: none
 */

- (void) drawRect: (NSRect) dirtyRect
{
    // Drawing code here.

    // Preserve the graphics content
```

```
    // so that other things we draw
    // don't get focus rings
    [NSGraphicsContext saveGraphicsState];

    // color the background transparent
    [[NSColor clearColor] set];

    // If this view has accepted first responder
    // it should draw the focus ring
    if ([[self window] firstResponder] == self)
    {
        NSSetFocusRingStyle(NSFocusRingAbove);
    }

    // Fill the view with fully transparent
    // color so that we can see through it
    // to whatever is below
    [[NSBezierPath bezierPathWithRect:[self bounds]] fill];

    // Restore the graphics content
    // so that other things we draw
    // don't get focus rings
    [NSGraphicsContext restoreGraphicsState];

}
```

18. Next, we need to go back into the `.xib` file, and select our custom view, and then select the **Identity Inspector** where we will see that in the section titled **Custom Class**, the **Class** field contains **NSView** as the class.

19. Finally, to connect this object to our new custom view program code, we need to change the **Class** to BTSFingerView as shown in the following screenshot:

What just happened?

We created our Xcode project and implemented a custom NSView object that will receive events. When we run the project we notice that the focus ring is drawn so that we can be confident the view has accepted the firstResponder status.

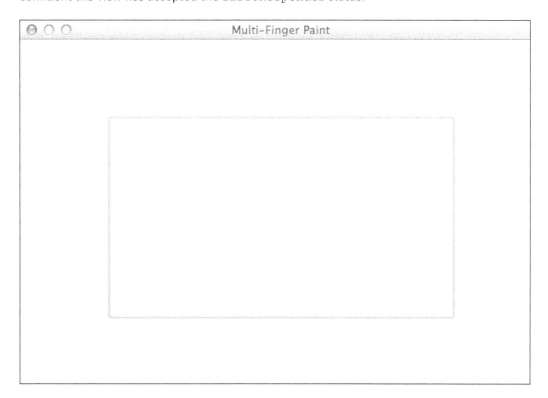

How to receive multi-touch events

Because our custom view accepts first responder, the Mac OS will automatically send events to it. We can override the methods that process the events that we want to handle in our view. Specifically, we can override the following events and process them to handle multi-touch events in our custom view:

- ◆ - (void)touchesBeganWithEvent:(NSEvent *)event
- ◆ - (void)touchesMovedWithEvent:(NSEvent *)event
- ◆ - (void)touchesEndedWithEvent:(NSEvent *)event
- ◆ - (void)touchesCancelledWithEvent:(NSEvent *)event

Time for action – drawing our fingers

When the multi-touch or magic trackpad is touched, our custom view methods will be invoked and we will be able to draw the placement of our fingers on the trackpad in our custom view.

1. In Xcode, click on the filename `BTSFingerView.h` in the project navigator and add the following highlighted property:

```
//
//  BTSFingerView.h
//  Multi-Finger Paint
//
//  Created by rwiebe on 12-05-23.
//  Copyright (c) 2012 BurningThumb Software. All rights reserved.
//

#import <Cocoa/Cocoa.h>

@interface BTSFingerView : NSView

// A reference to the object that will
// store the currently active touches
@property (strong) NSMutableDictionary *m_activeTouches;

@end
```

2. In Xcode, click on the file `BTSFingerView.m` in the project navigator and add the following program code to synthesize the property:

```
//
//  BTSFingerView.m
//  Multi-Finger Paint
//
//  Created by rwiebe on 12-05-23.
//  Copyright (c) 2012 BurningThumb Software. All rights reserved.
//

#import "BTSFingerView.h"

@implementation BTSFingerView

// Synthesize the object that will
// store the currently active touches
@synthesize m_activeTouches;
```

3. Add the following code to the `initWithFrame:` method in the
`BTSFingerView.m` file to create the dictionary object that will be
used to store the active touch objects:

```
- (id)initWithFrame:(NSRect)frame
{
    self = [super initWithFrame:frame];
    if (self) {
        // Initialization code here.

        // Create the mutable dictionary that
        // will hold the list of currently active
        // touch events
        m_activeTouches = [[NSMutableDictionary alloc] init];

    }

    return self;
}
```

4. Add the following code to the `BTSFingerView.m` file to add `BeganWith` touch
events to the dictionary of active touches:

```
/**
 ** - (void)touchesBeganWithEvent:(NSEvent *)event
 **
 ** Invoked when a finger touches the trackpad
 **
 ** Input: event - the touch event
 **
 ** Output: none
 */

- (void)touchesBeganWithEvent:(NSEvent *)event
{
    // Get the set of began touches
    NSSet *l_touches =
      [event touchesMatchingPhase:NSTouchPhaseBegan
                          inView:self];

    // For each began touch, add the touch
    // to the active touches dictionary
    // using its identity as the key
    for (NSTouch *l_touch in l_touches)
    {
```

```
            [m_activeTouches setObject:l_touch forKey:l_touch.
    identity];
        }

        // Redisplay the view
      [self setNeedsDisplay:YES];
    }
```

5. Add the following code to the `BTSFingerView.m` file to add moved touch events to the dictionary of active touches:

```
/**
 ** - (void)touchesMovedWithEvent:(NSEvent *)event
 **
 ** Invoked when a finger moves on the trackpad
 **
 ** Input: event - the touch event
 **
 ** Output: none
 */

- (void)touchesMovedWithEvent:(NSEvent *)event
{
    // Get the set of move touches
    NSSet *l_touches =
      [event touchesMatchingPhase:NSTouchPhaseMoved
                            inView:self];


    // For each move touch, update the touch
    // in the active touches dictionary
    // using its identity as the key
    for (NSTouch *l_touch in l_touches)
    {
        // Update the touch only if it is found
        // in the active touches dictionary
        if ([m_activeTouches objectForKey:l_touch.identity])
        {
            [m_activeTouches setObject:l_touch
                                forKey:l_touch.identity];
        }
    }

    // Redisplay the view
    [self setNeedsDisplay:YES];
}
```

6. Add the following code to the `BTSFingerView.m` file to remove the touch from the dictionary of active touches when the touch ends:

```
/**
 ** - (void)touchesEndedWithEvent:(NSEvent *)event
 **
 ** Invoked when a finger lifts off the trackpad
 **
 ** Input: event - the touch event
 **
 ** Output: none
 */


- (void)touchesEndedWithEvent:(NSEvent *)event
{

    // Get the set of ended touches
    NSSet *l_touches =
      [event touchesMatchingPhase:NSTouchPhaseEnded
                          inView:self];


    // For each ended touch, remove the touch
    // from the active touches dictionary
    // using its identity as the key
    for (NSTouch *l_touch in l_touches)
    {
        [m_activeTouches removeObjectForKey:l_touch.identity];
    }

    // Redisplay the view
    [self setNeedsDisplay:YES];
}
```

7. Add the following code to the `BTSFingerView.m` file to remove the touch from the dictionary of active touches when the touch is cancelled:

```
/**
 ** - (void)touchesCancelledWithEvent:(NSEvent *)event
 **
 ** Invoked when a touch is cancelled
 **
 ** Input: event - the touch event
 **
 ** Output: none
 */
```

```
- (void)touchesCancelledWithEvent:(NSEvent *)event
{
    // Get the set of cancelled touches
    NSSet *l_touches =
      [event touchesMatchingPhase:NSTouchPhaseCancelled
                           inView:self];

    // For each cancelled touch, remove the touch
    // from the active touches dictionary
    // using its identity as the key
    for (NSTouch *l_touch in l_touches)
    {
        [m_activeTouches removeObjectForKey:l_touch.identity];
    }

    // Redisplay the view
    [self setNeedsDisplay:YES];
}
```

8. When we touch the trackpad we are going to draw a "finger cursor" in our custom view. We need to decide how big we want that cursor to be and the color that we want the cursor to be. Then we can add a series of #define to the file named BTSFingerView.h to define that value:

```
// Define the size of the cursor that
// will be drawn in the view for each
// finger on the trackpad
#define D_FINGER_CURSOR_SIZE 20

// Define the color values that will
// be used for the finger cursor
#define D_FINGER_CURSOR_RED 1.0
#define D_FINGER_CURSOR_GREEN 0.0
#define D_FINGER_CURSOR_BLUE 0.0
#define D_FINGER_CURSOR_ALPHA 0.5
```

9. Now we can add the program code to our drawRect: implementation that will draw the finger cursors in the custom view.

```
// For each active touch
for (NSTouch *l_touch in m_activeTouches.allValues)
{
    // Create a rectangle reference to hold the
    // location of the cursor
    NSRect l_cursor;

    // Determine where the touch point
    NSPoint l_touchNP = [l_touch normalizedPosition];
```

```
            // Calculate the pixel position of the touch point
            l_touchNP.x = l_touchNP.x * [self bounds].size.width;
            l_touchNP.y = l_touchNP.y * [self bounds].size.height;

            // Calculate the rectangle around the cursor
            l_cursor.origin.x = l_touchNP.x - (D_FINGER_CURSOR_SIZE /
    2);

            l_cursor.origin.y = l_touchNP.y - (D_FINGER_CURSOR_SIZE /
    2);

            l_cursor.size.width = D_FINGER_CURSOR_SIZE;
            l_cursor.size.height = D_FINGER_CURSOR_SIZE;

            // Set the color of the cursor
            [[NSColor colorWithDeviceRed: D_FINGER_CURSOR_RED
                                   green: D_FINGER_CURSOR_GREEN
                                    blue: D_FINGER_CURSOR_BLUE
                                   alpha: D_FINGER_CURSOR_ALPHA] set];

            // Draw the cursor as a circle
            [[NSBezierPath bezierPathWithOvalInRect: l_cursor] fill];
    }
```

What just happened?

We implemented the methods required to keep track of the touches and to draw the location of the touches in our custom view. If we run the App now, and move the mouse pointer over the view area, and then touch the trackpad, we will see red circles that track our fingers being drawn in the view as shown in the following screenshot:

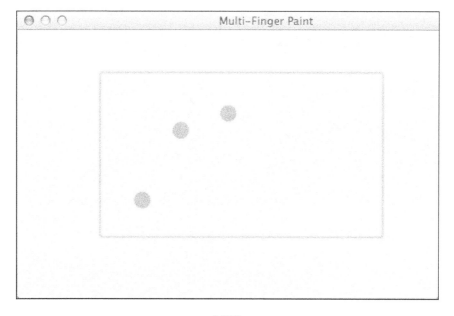

What is an NSBezierPath?

A **Bezier Path** consists of straight and curved line segments that can be used to draw recognizable shapes. In our program code, we use Bezier Paths to draw a rectangle and a circle but a Bezier Path can be used to draw many other shapes.

How to manage the mouse cursor

One of the interesting things about the trackpad and the mouse is the association between a single finger touch and the movement of the mouse cursor. Essentially, Mac OS X treats a single finger movement as if it was a mouse movement. The problem with this is that when we move just a single finger on the trackpad, the mouse cursor will move away from our NSView causing it to lose focus so that when we lift our finger we need to move the mouse cursor back to our NSView to receive touch events.

Time for action – detaching the mouse cursor from the mouse hardware

The solution to this problem is to detach the mouse cursor from the mouse hardware (typically called capturing the mouse) whenever a touch event is active so that the cursor is not moved by touch events. In addition, since a "stuck" mouse cursor may be cause for concern to our App user, we can hide the mouse cursor when touches are active.

1. In Xcode, click on the file named BTSFingerView.h in the project navigator and add the following flag to the interface:

```
@interface BTSFingerView : NSView
{

// Define a flag so that touch methods can behave
    // differently depending on the visibility of
    // the mouse cursor
    BOOL m_cursorIsHidden;

}
```

2. In Xcode, click on the file named BTSFingerView.m in the project navigator.

3. Add the following code to the beginning of the `touchesBeganWithEvent:` method to detach and hide the mouse cursor when a touch begins. We only want to do this one time so it is guarded by a BOOL flag and an *if* statement to make sure we don't do it for every touch that begins.

```
- (void)touchesBeganWithEvent:(NSEvent *)event
{

    // If the mouse cursor is not already hidden,
    if (NO == m_cursorIsHidden)
    {
        // Detach the mouse cursor from the mouse
        // hardware so that moving the mouse (or a
        // single finger) will not move the cursor
        CGAssociateMouseAndMouseCursorPosition(false);

        // Hide the mouse cursor
        [NSCursor hide];

        // Remember that we detached and hid the
        // mouse cursor
        m_cursorIsHidden = YES;
    }
```

4. Add the following code to the end of the `touchesEndedWithEvent:` method to attach and unhide the mouse cursor when all touches end. We use a BOOL flag to remember the state of the cursor so that the `touchesBeganWithEvent:` method will re-hide it when the next touch begins.

```
    // If there are no remaining active touches
    if (0 == [m_activeTouches count])
    {
        // Attach the mouse cursor to the mouse
        // hardware so that moving the mouse (or a
        // single finger) will  move the cursor
        CGAssociateMouseAndMouseCursorPosition(true);

        // Show the mouse cursor
        [NSCursor unhide];

        // Remember that we attached and unhid the
        // mouse cursor so that the next touch that
        // begins will detach and hide it
        m_cursorIsHidden = NO;
    }

    // Redisplay the view
    [self setNeedsDisplay:YES];
}
```

5. Add the following code to the end of the `touchesCancelledWithEvent:` method to attach and unhide the mouse cursor when all touches end. We use a BOOL flag to remember the state of the cursor so that the `touchesBeganWithEvent:` method will re-hide it when the next touch begins.

```
// If there are no remaining active touches
if (0 == [m_activeTouches count])
{
    // Attach the mouse cursor to the mouse
    // hardware so that moving the mouse (or a
    // single finger) will  move the cursor
    CGAssociateMouseAndMouseCursorPosition(true);

    // Show the mouse cursor
    [NSCursor unhide];

    // Remember that we attached and unhid the
    // mouse cursor so that the next touch that
    // begins will detach and hide it
    m_cursorIsHidden = NO;
}

// Redisplay the view
[self setNeedsDisplay:YES];
}
```

6. While we are looking at the movement of the mouse, we also notice that the focus ring for our custom view is being drawn regardless of whether or not the mouse cursor is over our view. Since touch events will only be sent to our view if the mouse cursor is over it, we want to change the program code so that the focus ring only appears when the mouse cursor is over the custom view. This is something we can do with another BOOL flag. Add the following code to the file to define a BOOL flag that will allow us to determine if the mouse cursor is over our custom view:

```
// Define a flag so that view methods can behave
// differently depending on the position of the
// mouse cursor
BOOL m_mouseIsInFingerView;
```

7. In the file named `BTSFingerView.m`, add the following code to create a tracking rectangle that matches the bounds of our custom view. Once the tracking rectangle is active, the methods `mouseEntered:` and `mouseExited:` will be automatically invoked as the mouse cursor enters and exits our custom view.

```
/**
 ** - (void)viewDidMoveToWindow
 **
 ** Informs the receiver that it has been added to
 ** a new view hierarchy.
```

```
**
** We need to make sure the view window is valid
** and when it is, we can add the tracking rect
**
** Once the tracking rect is added the mouseEntered:
** and mouseExited: events will be sent to our view
**
*/

- (void)viewDidMoveToWindow
{
    // Is the views window valid
    if ([self window] != nil)
    {
        // Add a tracking rect such that the
        // mouseEntered; and mouseExited: methods
        // will be automatically invoked
        [self addTrackingRect:[self bounds]
                        owner:self
                     userData:NULL
                  assumeInside:NO];
    }
}
```

8. In the file named `BTSFingerView.m,` add the following code to implement the `mouseEntered:` and `mouseExited:` methods. In those methods, we set the BOOL flag so that the `drawRect:` method knows whether or not to draw the focus ring.

```
/**
 ** - (void)mouseEntered:
 **
 ** Informs the receiver that the mouse cursor
 ** entered a tracking rectangle
 **
 ** Since we only have a single tracking rect
 ** we know the mouse is over our custom view
 **
 */

- (void)mouseEntered:(NSEvent *)theEvent
{
    // Set the flag so that other methods know
    // the mouse cursor is over our view
    m_mouseIsInFingerView = YES;
```

```
        // Redraw the view so that the focus ring
        // will appear
        [self setNeedsDisplay:YES];
    }


    /**
     ** - (void)mouseExited:
     **
     ** Informs the receiver that the mouse cursor
     ** exited a tracking rectangle
     **
     ** Since we only have a single tracking rect
     ** we know the mouse is not over our custom view
     **
     */

    - (void)mouseExited:(NSEvent *)theEvent
    {
        // Set the flag so that other methods know
        // the mouse cursor is not over our view
        m_mouseIsInFingerView = NO;

        // Redraw the view so that the focus ring
        // will not appear
        [self setNeedsDisplay:YES];
    }
```

9. Finally, in the `drawRect:` method, change the program code that draws the focus ring to only do so if the mouse cursor is in the tracking rectangle:

```
        // If this view has accepted first responder
        // it should draw the focus ring but only if
        // the mouse cursor is over this view
        if (
                ([[self window] firstResponder] == self) &&
                (YES == m_mouseIsInFingerView)
                )
        {
            NSSetFocusRingStyle(NSFocusRingAbove);
        }
```

What just happened?

We implemented the program code that will prevent the mouse cursor from moving out of our custom view when touch events are active. In doing so we noticed that our focus ring behavior could be improved. Therefore we added additional program code to ensure the focus ring is visible only when the mouse pointer is over our view.

Performing 2D drawing in a custom view

Mac OS X provides a number of ways to perform drawing. The methods provided range from very simple methods to very complex methods. For our multi-finger painting program we are going to use the core graphics APIs designed to draw a path. We are going to collect each stroke as a series of points and construct a path from those points so that we can draw the stroke.

Each active touch event will have a corresponding active stroke object that needs to be drawn in our custom view. When a stroke is finished, and the App user lifts the finger, we are going to send the finished stroke to another custom view so that it is drawn only one time and not each time fingers move. The optimization of using the second view will ensure our finger tracking is not slowed down too much by drawing.

Before we can begin drawing, we need to create two new objects that will be used to store individual points and strokes. The program code for these two objects is not shown but the objects are included in the Multi-Finger Paint Xcode project. The two objects are as follows:

◆ `BTSPoint`

◆ `BTSStroke`

The `BTSPoint` object is a wrapper for an `NSPoint` structure. The `NSPoint` structure needs to be wrapped in an object so that it can be stored in an `NSArray` object. It has a single instance variable:

```
NSPoint m_point;
```

It implements the following methods which allows it to be initialized: return the point (x and y), return just the x value, or return just the y value. For more information on the object, we can read the source code file in the project:

```
- (id) initWithNSPoint:(NSPoint)a_point;
- (NSPoint) point;
- (CGFloat)x;
- (CGFloat)y;
```

The `BTSStroke` object is a wrapper for an array of `BTSPoint` objects, a color, and a stroke width. It is used to store strokes that are drawn in our custom `NSView`. It has the following instance variables and properties:

```
float m_red;
float m_green;
float m_blue;
float m_alpha;
float m_width;

@property (strong) NSMutableArray *m_points;
```

It implements the following methods which allows it to be initialized: a new point to be added, return the array of points, return any of the color components, and return the stroke width. For more information on the object, we can read the source code file in the project:

```
- (id) initWithWidth:(float)a_width
                red:(float)a_red
              green:(float)a_green
               blue:(float)a_blue
              alpha:(float)a_alpha;
- (void) addPoint:(BTSPoint *)a_point;
- (NSMutableArray *) points;
- (float) red;
- (float) green;
- (float) blue;
- (float) alpha;
- (float) width;
```

Time for action – drawing the active strokes

We can now look back at our project and implement the program code needed to draw the strokes that are active. There are two classes that are included in the sample code project but that are not discussed in detail here. While they are not essential to understanding multi-touch it is recommended that we examine the code, for completeness. We will need the files that implement these classes included in our project so that our multi-touch paint program can run.

1. In Xcode, examine the program code in the files named BTSPoint.h, BTSPoint.m, BTSStroke.h, and BTSStroke.m so that we are familiar with these two objects that will be used during the painting process to create colored strokes in our custom NSView object.

2. Create new files that match these files so that the project we are working on has these objects implemented.

3. We are going to need to allow the App user to select the color for each finger to paint. To do this, we need to add a new custom view to our .xib file and add the NSColorWell objects to that view for each finger that we want to support. The subview and image wells should look like the following screenshot:

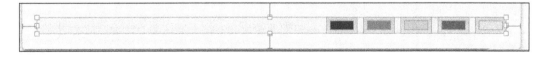

 The order of the subviews is important. Make sure to add them from left to right, starting with the black color well and ending with the white color well.

4. Add the following program code in the `BTSFingerView.h` file to define the objects we will use to reference the finder colors in our implementation:

```
// A reference to the custom view object that will
// contain the NSColorWell subviews
@property (strong) IBOutlet NSView *m_colorWellView;

// A reference to the array of NSColorWell objects
@property (strong) NSArray *m_colorWells;
```

5. Add the following program code in the `BTSFingerView.m` file to synthesize the objects we will use to reference the finder colors in our implementation:

```
// Synthesize the object that will
// store the color well information
@synthesize m_colorWellView;
@synthesize m_colorWells;
```

6. In the `.xib` file, right-click on the **Finger View** and drag to connect it to the new **Custom View** using the **Outlets** named **m_colorWellView** as shown in the following screenshot:

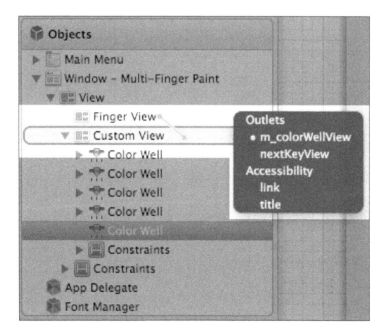

7. In `BTSFingerView.m`, implement the `awakeFromNib` method and include the program code to get the array of color well subviews:

```
// This method is automatically invoked
// when the view is created
- (void) awakeFromNib
```

```
{
    // Get the color well views
    // into an array
    m_colorWells = [m_colorWellView subviews];
}
```

8. In `BTSFingerView.m`, change the `touchesBeganWithEvent:` method to ignore
    any touches for which there is no color defined, by adding the following program
    code:

```
- (void)touchesBeganWithEvent:(NSEvent *)event
{
    // Ignore touches for which there is no color
    if ([m_activeTouches count] > ([m_colorWells count] - 1))
    {
        return;
    }
}
```

9. In the `BTSFingerView.h` file add a new `@property` for the array of active strokes.
    This array will contain a `BTSStroke` object for each finger that is touching the
    trackpad.

```
// A reference to the array of Active Strokes
@property (strong) NSMutableDictionary *m_activeStrokes;
```

10. In the `BTSFingerViewContoller.m` file, synthesize the `m_activeStrokes`
    property as follows:

```
// Synthesize the object that will
// store the currently active stokes
@synthesize m_activeStrokes;
```

11. Add the following, highlighted, program code to the `initWithFrame:` method in
    the `BTSFingerView.m` file to create the dictionary object that will be used to store
    the stroke touch objects:

```
- (id)initWithFrame:(NSRect)frame
{
    self = [super initWithFrame:frame];
    if (self) {
        // Initialization code here.

        // Create the mutable dictionary that
        // will hold the list of currently active
        // touch events
        m_activeTouches = [[NSMutableDictionary alloc] init];

        // Create the mutable dictionary that
```

```
        // will hold the list of currently active
        // strokes
        m_activeStrokes = [[NSMutableDictionary alloc] init];

        // Accept trackpad events
        [self setAcceptsTouchEvents: YES];

    }

    return self;
}
```

12. Add the program code to the `touchesBeganWithEvent:` method to create a new `BTSStroke` object that contains a single `BTSPoint` object at the location of the touch in our custom `NSView`:

```
for (NSTouch *l_touch in l_touches)
{
     [m_activeTouches setObject:l_touch forKey:l_touch.
identity];

            // Get the color for the stroke
            NSColor *l_color =
               [[m_colorWells objectAtIndex:
                  [m_activeTouches count] - 1] color];

            // Create a new stroke object with
            // the color
            BTSStroke *l_stoke =
             [[BTSStroke alloc]
               initWithWidth:2.0 /* BAD MAGIC NUMBER */
               red:[l_color redComponent]
               green:[l_color greenComponent]
               blue:[l_color blueComponent]
               alpha:[l_color alphaComponent]];

            // Add the stroke to the array of active strokes
            [m_activeStrokes setObject:l_stoke
                               forKey:l_touch.identity];

            // Create a new point at the location of the
            // finger touch.  This is done by getting the
            // normalized position (between 0 and 10 and
            // calculating the position in the view bounds
            NSPoint l_touchNP =
             [l_touch normalizedPosition];
            l_touchNP.x =
```

```
                   l_touchNP.x * self.bounds.size.width;
               l_touchNP.y =
                 l_touchNP.y * self.bounds.size.height;
               BTSPoint * l_point =
                 [[BTSPoint alloc] initWithNSPoint:l_touchNP];

               // Add the point to the stroke
               [l_stoke addPoint:l_point];
       }
```

13. Add the program code to the `touchesMovedWithEvent:` method to add more `BTSPoint` objects to the `BTSStroke` as tracked fingers move on the trackpad:

```
    for (NSTouch *l_touch in l_touches)
    {
        // Update the touch only if it is found
        // in the active touches dictionary
        if ([m_activeTouches objectForKey:l_touch.identity])
        {
            [m_activeTouches setObject:l_touch
                              forKey:l_touch.identity];

                // Retrieve the stroke for this touch
                BTSStroke *l_Line =
                  [m_activeStrokes objectForKey:l_
                  touch.identity];

                // Create a new point at the location of the
                // finger touch.  This is done by getting the
                // normalized position (between 0 and 10 and
                // calculating the position in the view
                // bounds
                NSPoint l_touchNP =
                  [l_touch normalizedPosition];
                l_touchNP.x =
                  l_touchNP.x * self.bounds.size.width;
                l_touchNP.y =
                  l_touchNP.y * self.bounds.size.height;
                BTSPoint * l_point =
                  [[BTSPoint alloc]initWithNSPoint:l_touchNP];

                // Add the point to the stroke
                [l_Line addPoint:l_point];
        }
    }
```

14. Add the program code to the `drawRect :` method to perform the actual drawing of the active strokes. This code uses core graphics to create a path for each stroke and render it in the view. The first part of the code fills the rect with the selected transparent color, so that we can see through this view to the one below, with a focus ring.

```
// Fill the view with fully transparent
// color so that we can see through it
// to whatever is below
[[NSBezierPath bezierPathWithRect:dirtyRect] fill];
```

15. Because we wanted a focus ring just around the drawing area, we need to restore the graphics context to the state it was in previously so that the focus ring is not drawn around the remaining objects.

```
// Restore the graphics content
// so that other things we draw
// don't get focus rings
[NSGraphicsContext restoreGraphicsState];

// Get the current graphics context
NSGraphicsContext *  l_GraphicsContext =
  [NSGraphicsContext currentContext];
```

16. Then we can get the graphics port and draw the active strokes using the correct color for the stroke. First, we do some basic initialization of variables that we will use for drawing:

```
// Get the low level Core Graphics context
// from the high level NSGraphicsContext
// so that we can use Core Graphics to
// draw
CGContextRef l_CGContextRef  =
  (CGContextRef) [l_GraphicsContext graphicsPort];

// We will need to reference the array of
// points in each store
NSMutableArray *l_points;

// We will need a reference to individual
// points
BTSPoint *l_point;

// We will need to know how many points
// are in each stroke
NSUInteger l_pointCount;

// We will need a reference to the
// first point in each stroke
BTSPoint * l_firsttPoint;
```

17. Once we have declared our variable references, we loop through all of our active strokes as follows:

```
// For all of the active strokes
for (BTSStroke *l_stroke in m_activeStrokes.allValues )
{
```

18. We need to set the stroke width and stroke color for each stroke as follows:

```
// Set the stroke width for line
// drawing
CGContextSetLineWidth(l_CGContextRef,
                      [l_stroke width]);


// Set the color for line drawing
CGContextSetRGBStrokeColor(l_CGContextRef,
                           [l_stroke red],
                           [l_stroke green],
                           [l_stroke blue],
                           [l_stroke alpha]);
```

19. Then, we need to get all the points and create a path from the points:

```
// Get the array of points
l_points = [l_stroke points];



// Get the number of points
l_pointCount = [l_points count];

// Get the first point
l_firsttPoint = [l_points objectAtIndex:0];

// Create a new path
CGContextBeginPath(l_CGContextRef);

// Move to the first point of the stroke
CGContextMoveToPoint(l_CGContextRef,
                     [l_firsttPoint x],
                     [l_firsttPoint y]);
```

```
    // For the remaining points
for (NSUInteger i = 1; i < l_pointCount; i++)
    {
        // note the index starts at 1
        // Get the SECOND point
    l_point = [l_points objectAtIndex:i];

        // Add a line segment to the stroke
    CGContextAddLineToPoint(l_CGContextRef,
                                [l_point x],
                                [l_point y]);
    }
```

20. Once we have created a path from the list of points, we simply draw the path and the stroke will appear in our view.

```
    // Draw the path
    CGContextDrawPath(l_CGContextRef,kCGPathStroke);

}
```

21. In both the `touchesEndedWithEvent:` and `touchesCancelledWithEvent:` methods, change the code so that when the `activeTouch` is removed the `activeStroke` is also removed as follows:

```
    // For each ended touch, remove the touch
    // from the active touches dictionary
    // using its identity as the key
    // Also remove the active stroke for
    // the touch
    for (NSTouch *l_touch in l_touches)
    {
        [m_activeTouches removeObjectForKey:l_touch.identity];
        [m_activeStrokes removeObjectForKey:l_touch.identity];
    }
```

What just happened?

We implemented the drawing code so that when fingers touch the trackpad, lines will be drawn to follow their motion. The line color will be selected from an image well based on when the finger touched the trackpad. When a finger is lifted from the trackpad the line disappears.

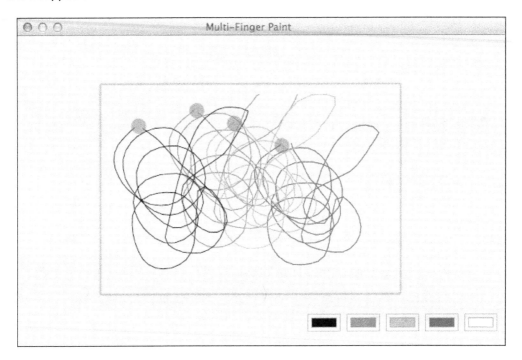

Saving strokes

Currently when we lift our finger from the trackpad, the stroke that we draw disappears. We need some way to save that stroke. One way we can do this is to create another custom view and hand the stroke to that view just before we remove it from the list of active strokes.

Time for action – saving the strokes

Similar to how we created a custom view for our finger touches, we can create a second custom view for completed strokes.

1. Create a new file in Xcode, using the **Mac OS X Cocoa Objective-C class** template, that is a subclass of NSView, and call it BTStrokeView.

2. In the .xib file, click on the **Finger View** object and select **Duplicate** from the **Edit** menu to make a copy of the **Finger View** object.

3. Select the new **Finger View**, and in the **Identity inspector**, change its **Class** to `BTSStrokeView`.

4. In the **Objects** hierarchy, drag the **Finger View** object into the original **Stroke View** object to make it a subview of the original object. The new Objects hierarchy will look as shown in the following screenshot:

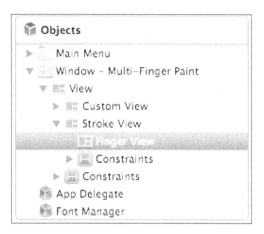

5. In the file named `BTSStrokeView.h`, add a `@property` that will be used to reference the mutable array that will hold the saved `BTSStroke` objects. We are also going to need a method to add strokes to the `m_Strokes` array so we can define the interface for that method as well.

```
#import <Foundation/Foundation.h>
#import "BTSStroke.h"

@interface BTSStrokeView : NSView

// A reference to the array of Saved Strokes
@property (strong) NSMutableArray *m_Strokes;

/**
 ** - (void) addStroke: (BTSStroke *)a_stroke
 **
 ** Add a stroke to the saved array of
 ** BTSStroke objects
 **
 ** Input: A BTSStroke object
 **
 ** Output: none
 */
- (void) addStroke: (BTSStroke *)a_stroke;

@end
```

6. In the file named BTSStrokeView.m, add the program code to synthesize the m_Strokes as follows:

```
#import "BTSStrokeView.h"

@implementation BTSStrokeView

// Synthesize the object that will
// store the saved stokes
@synthesize m_Strokes;
```

7. In the file named BTSStrokeView.m, add the program code to implement the addStroke: method:

```
- (id)initWithFrame:(NSRect)frame
{
    self = [super initWithFrame:frame];
    if (self) {
        // Initialization code here.


        // Initialize and allocate the array
        m_Strokes = [[NSMutableArray alloc] init];
    }

    return self;
}

/**
 ** - (void) addLine: (BTSStroke *)a_line
 **
 ** Add a stroke to the saved array of
 ** BTSStroke objects
 **
 ** Input: A BTSStroke object
 **
 ** Output: none
 */
- (void) addStroke: (BTSStroke *)a_stroke
{

    // Add the stroke to the array
    [m_Strokes addObject: a_stroke];
}
```

8. In the file named `BTSStrokeView.m`, add the program code to implement the `drawRect:` method. This method is almost identical to the method used in the **Finger View** except that instead of a transparent background, it draws a white background and instead of iterating (looping) over the dictionary values, it iterates over the array values. The complete method is shown in the following code snippet but the two highlighted sections are the ones that are different from the previous method:

```
- (void)drawRect:(NSRect)dirtyRect
{
    // Drawing code here.

    // color the background white
    [[NSColor whiteColor] set];

    // Fill the view with fully white color
    [[NSBezierPath bezierPathWithRect:dirtyRect] fill];

    // Get the current graphics context
    NSGraphicsContext * l_GraphicsContext =
    [NSGraphicsContext currentContext];

    // Get the low level Core Graphics context
    // from the high level NSGraphicsContext
    // so that we can use Core Graphics to
    // draw
  CGContextRef l_CGContextRef =
    (CGContextRef) [l_GraphicsContext graphicsPort];

    // We will need to reference the array of
    // points in each store
    NSMutableArray *l_points;

    // We will need a reference to individual
    // points
    BTSPoint *l_point;

    // We will need to know how many points
    // are in each stroke
    NSUInteger l_pointCount;

    // We will need a reference to the
    // first point in each stroke
    BTSPoint * l_firsttPoint;

    // For all of the saved strokes
    for (BTSStroke *l_stroke in m_Strokes )
    {
```

```objc
    // Set the stroke width for line
    // drawing
    CGContextSetLineWidth(l_CGContextRef,
                            [l_stroke width]);

    // Set the color for line drawing
    CGContextSetRGBStrokeColor(l_CGContextRef,
                                [l_stroke red],
                                [l_stroke green],
                                [l_stroke blue],
                                [l_stroke alpha]);
    // Get the array of points
    l_points = [l_stroke points];

    // Get the number of points
    l_pointCount = [l_points count];

    // Get the first point
    l_firsttPoint = [l_points objectAtIndex:0];

    // Create a new path
    CGContextBeginPath(l_CGContextRef);

    // Move to the first point of the stroke
    CGContextMoveToPoint(l_CGContextRef,
                            [l_firsttPoint x],
                            [l_firsttPoint y]);

    // For the remaining points
    for (NSUInteger i = 1; i < l_pointCount; i++)
        {
            // note the index starts at 1
            // Get the SECOND point
        l_point = [l_points objectAtIndex:i];

            // Add a line segment to the stroke
        CGContextAddLineToPoint(l_CGContextRef,
                                    [l_point x],
                                    [l_point y]);
    }

    // Draw the path
    CGContextDrawPath(l_CGContextRef,kCGPathStroke);

    }

    }
```

9. In the file named `BTSFingerView.h`, add a `#define` that we will use to add strokes to the **Stroke View** only if they contain at least two points:

```
// Define the minimum number of
// points that can be in a stroke
#define D_MIN_POINTS 2
```

10. In the file named `BTSFingerView.m`, modify the `touchesEndedWithEvent:` method to add a stroke to the **Stroke View**, and mark the **Stroke View** as it needs to be redisplayed, just before removing it from the active strokes dictionary. This is done by getting the `superview` of the **Finger View**, which will be the **Stroke View**, and invoking the `addStroke:` method on that view.

```
// For each ended touch, remove the touch
// from the active touches dictionary
// using its identity as the key
// Also remove the active stroke for
// the touch

// Get a reference to the
// stroke view object
BTSStrokeView *l_strokeView =
  (BTSStrokeView *)[self superview];

for (NSTouch *l_touch in l_touches)
{
    // If there is an active touch
    if ([m_activeTouches objectForKey:l_touch.identity])
    {
        // Get the active stroke for the touch
        BTSStroke *l_stroke =
        [m_activeStrokes
         objectForKey:l_touch.identity];

        // If the stroke has at least 2 points
        // in it add it to the stroke view
        // object
        if (l_stroke.m_points.count > D_MIN_POINTS)
        {
            [l_strokeView addStroke: l_stroke];
            [l_strokeView setNeedsDisplay:YES];
        }

        // Remove the active touch
        [m_activeTouches removeObjectForKey:l_touch.identity];

        // Remove the active stroke
        [m_activeStrokes removeObjectForKey:l_touch.identity];
    }
}
```

What just happened?

We implemented our `BTSStrokeView` object and made our `BTSFingerView` object a subview of the `BTSStrokeView` object. The `BTSStrokeView` keeps track of all the strokes that we want to be drawn but that are no longer active. Now we can use **Multi-Finger Paint** to draw a complete picture as follows:

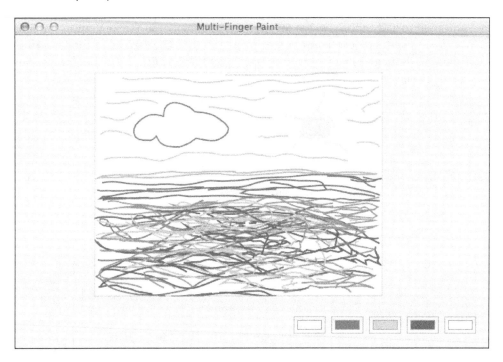

Have a go hero – implementing a Pen Down checkbox

Sometimes, we are going to want to use the touchpad to perform gestures. Because gestures would result in lines potentially being draw where we don't want them we can add a checkbox to our GUI that is used to determine if lines are to be drawn during touches.

Go ahead and implement the **Pen Down** checkbox:

1. In the `.xib` file, create a checkbox to the **Multi-Finger Paint** window, and title it `Pen Down`.
2. In the **Attributes Inspector** make sure the checkbox state is **Off**.
3. In the `BTSFingerView.h` file, add an `IBOutlet @property` for the `NSButton` and call it `m_penDownCheckbox`.
4. In the `BTSFingerView.m` file, synthesize the `m_penDownCheckbox` property.

5. In the BTSFingerView.m file, change the touchesBeganWithEvent: implementation to add an active line only if the m_penDownCheckbox state is equal to NSOnState.

6. In the BTSFingerView.m file change the touchesMovedWithEvent: implementation to add points to an active line only if the m_penDownCheckbox state is equal to NSOnState.

Once these steps are complete, we can use the mouse to check and uncheck the **Pen Down** GUI item so that we can control whether or not lines are drawn. But because we disconnect the mouse hardware from the mouse cursor when a finger is on the trackpad, it would be really nice to be able to toggle the checkbox using a keyboard event.

1. In the file named BTSFingerView.h, implement a new method with the prototype:
   - (void)keyDown:(NSEvent *)event

2. The event has a member named characters that returns an NSString, add code to examine the characters to see if the first character is equal to the *Space bar*, @" ".

3. If the first character is equal to @" ", then add code that examines the state of m_penDownCheckbox and if it is equal to NSOnState, set it to NSOffState, otherwise set it to NSOnState.

4. If the first character is not equal to @" ", pass the event to the super class to be handled.

How to receive gesture events

Gestures are combinations of touches and just like touch events, our view will automatically receive gesture events. The gesture events that we can receive are as follows:

◆ - (void)magnifyWithEvent:(NSEvent *) event
◆ - (void)rotateWithEvent:(NSEvent *)event
◆ - (void)swipeWithEvent:(NSEvent *)event
◆ - (void)beginGestureWithEvent:(NSEvent *)event
◆ - (void)endGestureWithEvent:(NSEvent *)event

Time for action – handling rotate gestures

When a gesture event is received by our view, we can take whatever action we would like to handle the event. We decide which gestures we want to handle and what we want them to do.

1. In Xcode, click on the file named `BTSFingerView.m` in the project navigator and add the following method to handle a `rotateWithEvent:` gesture:

```
/**
 ** (void) rotateWithEvent: (NSEvent *) event
 **
 ** Invoked when two fingers make a rotating
 ** gesture on the trackpad
 **
 ** Input: event - the gesture event
 **
 ** Output: none
 */

- (void) rotateWithEvent: (NSEvent *) event
{
    // If the pen is not down
    if (NSOffState == m_penDownCheckbox.state)
    {
        // Rotate the super view
        // By the amount of rotation in the
        // event
        [self.superview
         setFrameCenterRotation:
           [self.superview frameCenterRotation] + [event rotation]];
    }

}
```

What just happened?

We implemented an event handler for the `rotateWithEvent:` gesture that rotates the `superview`. Because our view is contained in the `superview`, our view will also rotate as shown in the following screenshot:

Have a go hero – implementing swipe to clear

We can use other gestures to do more complex things. For example, we could use a four-finger swipe to erase our picture.

[189]

Go ahead and implement the swipe to clear gesture:

1. In the `BTSStrokeView.h` file, add a method to the interface called `clear` that returns nothing and has no arguments.

2. In the `BTSStrokeView.m` file implement the clear method. It needs to remove all the `BTSStroke` objects from the `m_strokes` `NSMutableArray` and send the `setNeedsDisplay` message with a value of `YES` to the view.

3. In the `BTSFingerView.m` file add a method using the swipe prototype - `(void) swipeWithEvent:(NSEvent *)event`. It needs to check to make sure the pen is not down and then remove all the objects from `m_activeTouches` and `m_activeStrokes`. It can, optionally, re-attach the mouse hardware to the mouse cursor and unhide the mouse. Finally, it should send the `clear` method to the `superview`.

Once these steps are complete we can use the *four-finger* swipe gesture to clear the painting from the view.

Summary

In this chapter, we have implemented an application that uses the multi-touch trackpad to paint with our fingers. We have also implemented several multi-touch gestures to clear the painting from our view.

Specifically, we covered what is multi-touch, how to implement custom views and subviews, how to select colors from a color well and draw strokes in a custom view, how to manage the mouse cursor, and how to receive keyboard, touch, and gesture events and respond to them.

Now that we have spent some time looking at the cool multi-touch and gesture event handling and how to draw in a view, we are going to shift gears and look at another cool input device, the iSight camera. We will learn how to take still pictures with the camera, which is the topic of our next chapter.

7
Capturing Still Images – iSight iMage cApture App

This chapter will walk us through the steps needed to create a still image capture App that uses the built-in iSight camera. Apple provides a framework that has been specifically designed to provide Apps with everything they need to capture, filter, and store images that are captured from the iSight camera. We can take advantage of that framework to create a fully functional image capture App very quickly.

In this chapter, we shall learn the following:

- What is Image Kit and how does it work
- Adding framework to a project
- Browsing images
- Capturing and saving images
- Modifying the behavior of the Picture Taker
- Deleting images

What is Image Kit?

Image Kit is an Objective-C Mac OS X framework (set of interfaces and program code) that allows us to efficiently do the following:

- ◆ Browse, view, and edit images
- ◆ Browse core image filters, including previewing effects and providing controls for individual filters
- ◆ Import images, including taking a snapshot with an iSight (or other) camera
- ◆ Apply image filters

For our iSight iMage cApture App, we will be focusing on the components of Image Kit that are required to browse images and capture images from the iSight camera.

Adding framework to a project

Before we can use the Image Kit framework, we need to add the framework that provides the interface and implementation for its objects. The Image Kit framework is part of the greater 2D drawing framework called **Quartz** so to use Image Kit we need to add the Quartz framework to our project.

Time for action – creating a project and adding the Quartz framework

So the first thing that we need to do is, once again, create a new project and then add the Quartz framework to the project.

1. Create a new Xcode project with **Automatic Reference Counting** enabled and the options set as follows:

Option	Value
Product Name	`iSight iMage cApture`
Company Identifier	`com.yourdomain`
Class Prefix	Your initials (again recall we are using BTS throughout this book for consistency)

2. After Xcode creates the new project, design an icon and drag it into the **App Icon** field on the **TARGET Summary**.

3. Remember to set the **Organization** in the **Project Document** section of the **File Inspector**.

4. Select the **iSight iMage cApture TARGET** in the standard editor.

5. Select **Build Phases**.

6. Click on the disclosure triangle to reveal the items in the section titled **Link Binary With Libraries**.

7. Click on the + button.

8. Locate and click on the **Quartz.framework** and then click on the **Add** button.

9. In the project navigator, drag the **Quartz.framework** into the **Frameworks** folder.

What just happened?

We included the Quartz framework, which implements Image Kit, in our project so that our project can reference the objects implemented in the Image Kit framework. If we had not included the framework, our program would crash and the debugger would appear when we tried to run it.

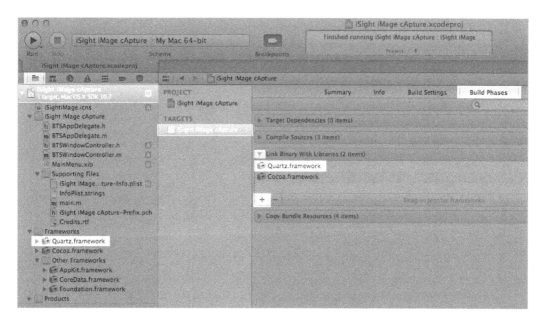

Browsing images

Before we can capture images, we need a way to browse images. Image Kit provides an Image Browser view designed specifically for this purpose.

Time for action – implementing the interface for browsing our pictures folder

The `Pictures` folder is the default location for storing images. While the App user may want to store them elsewhere, Apple wants developers to stick with the `Pictures` folder and has provided standard ways to locate and access this folder.

 App **Sandboxing**, which is required if we want to put an App in the Mac OS X App store, requires us to use the standard methods of accessing the `Pictures` folder. It is very important to use these methods and not create an App that accesses the user's filesystem in a non-standard manner by trying to write to other folders.

To begin, we will implement the interface to the browser.

1. In the project navigator, click on the file named **MainMenu.xib**.

2. In the **Object Library**, locate the **Scroll View** and drag it into the window leaving half an inch at the bottom of the window as room for us to add some buttons later.

3. In the **Objects** hierarchy, locate **Scroll View** and click on the disclosure triangle to reveal the **View** and **Scroller** objects.

4. Click on the **View** object and in the **Identity Inspector** set the **Class** of the **Custom Class** to be **IKImageBrowserView**.

5. From the **File** menu, select **New File...** and using the **Mac OS X Cocoa Objective-C class** template create a new **Class** named BTSWindowController that is a **Subclass** of NSWindowController.

6. In the **Object Library**, locate the **Object** and drag it into the **Objects** hierarchy. In the **Identity Inspector**, set the **Class** to BTSWindowController.

7. Connect the **Image Browser view** (in the Scroll View) **delegate**, **dataSource**, and **dragDestinationDelegate** to the **Window Controller**.

8. In the file named BTSWindowController.h, add the following program code to import the Quartz interface definition, define the Image Kit Browser View outlet for Interface Builder, and define a reference to the array that will hold the images to be displayed:

```
//
//  BTSWindowController.h
//  iSight iMage cApture
//
//  Created by rwiebe on 12-06-04.
//  Copyright (c) 2012 BurningThumb Software. All rights reserved.
//
```

```
#import <Cocoa/Cocoa.h>
#import <Quartz/Quartz.h>

@interface BTSWindowController : NSWindowController

// Define the references to the GUI view and
// the array that will hod the images for it
// to display
@property (strong) IBOutlet
  IKImageBrowserView *m_imageBrowser;
@property (strong) NSMutableArray *m_images;
```

9. Because we only want to present valid image types (.jpg, .png, and so on) in our Image Browser view, we need to define an array that will be used to cache valid image file extensions. We will obtain the list of valid extensions from the NSImage class but we only want to get the list one time and cache it for later use. Add the following program code to the file named BTSWindowController.h to define the array:

```
// Define a reference to an array that will cache
// valid image file extensions
@property (strong) NSArray *m_validFileExtensions;
```

> **NSArray instead of NSMutableArray**
>
> Note that we will use an NSArray and not an NSMutable array. We do this because we will not be changing the contents of the array. We will simply populate it once and reference the objects in it later. We will never add objects to or remove objects from the array.

10. Because we don't want to present hidden files, or folders, in our Image Browser view, we need to define an array that we will use to cache the file attribute keys needed to obtain the file attributes that tell us if a file directory is hidden. We will obtain the list of attributes from every file URL object but we only want to create the array of attributes one time and cache it for later use. Add the following program code to the file named BTSWindowController.h to define the array and complete the content of the .h file:

```
// Define a reference to an array that will cache
// desired file attribute keys
@property (strong) NSArray *m_fileAttributeKeys;

@end
```

11. In the file named `BTSWindowController.m`, add the following program code to synthesize the properties:

```
// Implement the accessors to the GUI view and
// the array that will hod the images for it
// to display
@synthesize m_imageBrowser;
@synthesize m_images;

// Implement the accessor for the array of
// valid image file types
@synthesize m_validFileExtensions;

// Implement the accessor for the array of
// desired image file attributes
@synthesize m_fileAttributeKeys;
```

12. While it is not yet implemented, we are going to implement a method to set up the `IKImageBrowserView`. Because we know that we are going to implement the method, we add the following program code to the `BTSWindowController.m` file to invoke the method:

```
// When the object is successfully loaded from a .xib
// file this method is automatically invoked
- (void) awakeFromNib
{
    // Setup the IKImageBrowserView
    [self setupBrowser];
}
```

It is quite common, when developing program code, to add references to methods that are not yet implemented because we believe that we will need them. While our App will not run until we implement the methods it is helpful to not have to think about the details of the implementation. Sometimes we will add a note to ourselves as a *To Do* or *To Be Done* (*TBD*) comment in the program code when we create references to the methods we plan to implement later.

13. Using the **Assistant** editor (recall that we can show the **Assistant** editor by clicking on the **Show the Assistant Editor** icon in the **Editor** icons section of Xcode's main window), connect the `m_imageBrowser` property to the **Image Browser View** as shown in the following screenshot:

14. We are going to use a custom object, `BTSImage`, so that we can use an `NSURL` object to reference our images, to wrap the images that we will display in the `IKImageBrowserView`. From the **File** menu, select **New File...** and using the **Mac OS X Cocoa Objective-C class** template create a new **Class** named `BTSImage` that is a **Subclass** of `NSObject`.

15. Add the following program code in the `BTSImage.h` file to define its properties and its only instance variable, `NSURL`, that will contain the path to the image file:

```
//
//   BTSImage.h
//   iSight iMage cApture
//
//   Created by rwiebe on 12-06-04.
//   Copyright (c) 2012 BurningThumb Software. All rights reserved.
//

#import <Foundation/Foundation.h>

@interface BTSImage : NSObject

// A reference to the file URL
@property (strong)   NSURL *m_URL;
```

16. When we create a new `BTSImage` object, we will initialize it with a URL so we need to define the interface to that method using the following program code:

```
// The interface for initializing
// a new BTSImage using a URL that
// points to the image
- (id) initWithURL: (NSURL *) a_URL;
```

17. Finally, the `BTSImage` object is going to implement the `IKImageBrowserView` protocol. It must implement all of the required methods, and will also implement one of the optional methods. Complete the definition of the `BTSImage` object interface by entering the following program code:

```
// The IKImageBrowserView dataSource protocol
// methods

// Required methods

// Returns a unique string that identifies
// the data source item.
- (NSString *) imageUID;

// Returns the representation type of the
// image to display.
- (NSString *) imageRepresentationType;
```

```
// Returns the image to display.
- (id)  imageRepresentation;


// Optional methods

// Returns the display title of the image
- (id) imageTitle;

@end
```

 Note that we have completely defined the interface to our
BTSImage object but we have not implemented any of the
methods. We have not been thinking about how we will do these
things, we have only been thinking about the things that we need
to do. Once we believe we know what we want to do then we can
get into the details of how to implement the desired behavior.

18. Add the following program code in the `BTSImage.m` file to `#import` the Quartz 2D
interface definition. We need to `#import` the Quartz interface so that references
to Image Kit interface elements will be recognized by Xcode. If we did not
`#import` the Quartz interface Xcode would report errors in our `BTSImage` object
implementation.

```
//
//  BTSImage.m
//  iSight iMage cApture
//
//  Created by rwiebe on 12-06-04.
//  Copyright (c) 2012 BurningThumb Software. All rights reserved.
//

#import <Quartz/Quartz.h>
#import "BTSImage.h"
```

19. Continue by adding the following program code to `@synthesize` the `NSURL` object
instance variable of the `BTSImage` object:

```
@implementation BTSImage

// Create the accessor methods for
// the image URL
@synthesize m_URL;
```

What just happened?

We have implemented the interface to our image browser including some stub methods that need to be coded to complete the implementation. We are halfway to our goal of having a working image browser.

Time for action – implementing the methods for browsing our Pictures folder

Now that we have defined the interface and some stub methods for browsing our `Pictures` folder, we can continue to complete the implementation by coding the methods required to implement the desired behavior.

1. When a `BTSImage` object is created, it must be initialized with an `NSURL`. We accomplish this by implementing the method named `initWithURL:` using the following program code, which simply assigns the `NSURL` passed to the method to the instance variable.

```
// Assign an NSURL to the BTSImage
// and return the BTSImage object
-  (id)initWithURL:(NSURL *)a_URL
{
    self = [super init];
    if (self)
    {
        // Initialization code here.
        m_URL = a_URL;
    }

    return self;
}
```

2. The `IKImageBrowserView` object `dataSource` protocol will invoke a method on our object to determine how we have selected to represent the image. Because we are using an `NSURL` to represent our images, we can simply return the constant `IKImageBrowserNSURLRepresentationType`, which is defined in the Image Kit interface (in fact the reason we need to import Quartz is so that this constant is recognized). Continue by entering the following program code to return the constant when the `imageRepresentationType` method is invoked.

```
#pragma mark -
#pragma mark item data source protocol

// Return the constant that indicates
// the image is represented by an
// NSURL
```

```
-  (NSString *)  imageRepresentationType
{
    return IKImageBrowserNSURLRepresentationType;
}
```

3. The IKImageBrowserView object dataSource protocol will invoke a method on our object to get a reference to our selected image representation. Because we are using an NSURL to represent our images, we can simply return the NSURL. Continue by entering the following program code to return the NSURL instance variable when the imageRepresentation method is invoked:

```
// Return the NSURL for the image
-  (id)  imageRepresentation
{
   return m_URL;
}
```

4. The IKImageBrowserView object dataSource protocol requires a unique identifier for each image. We can return anything that we want, provided it is unique to our App. Since the full path to a file is unique to the file system, it will also be unique to our App. Continue by entering the following program code to return the full path of the file when the imageUID method is invoked:

```
// Return the full path to the image
// as its unique id
-  (NSString *)  imageUID
{
    return [m_URL path];
}
```

5. The IKImageBrowserView object dataSource protocol provides an optional method so that our object can return a title, which will be displayed under the image in the Image Browser View. Again we can return anything we want as the title. Complete the implementation by entering the following program code to return just the last path component (also known as the filename) of the file when the imageTitle method is invoked:

```
// Return just the file name component
// of the path as the image title
-  (NSString *)  imageTitle
{
   return [m_URL lastPathComponent];
}

@end
```

Categories

When we want to extend the behavior of a class, we may choose to implement the new behavior in a different set of .h and .m files. We may do this to keep the size of our files small, because multiple people are working on the implementation, or we don't have the source code file and we don't want to use a subclass. The way this is done in Objective-C is through categories. **Categories** allow us to implement additional behavior on existing objects.

6. We are going to use a category to extend the behavior of our BTSWindowController object. From the **File** menu, select **New**, and then select the **File...** option.

7. Select the **Mac OS X Cocoa Objective-C** category template and click on the **Next** button.

8. For the **Category**, enter **Browser** and for the **Category on** option select **BTSWindowController**, then click on the **Next** button.

9. Click the **Create** button.

10. In the file named BTSWindowController+Browser.h, add the following program code to import the interface to BTSImage objects and expose the setupBrowser method that we invoked in the awakeFromNib method:

```
//
//   BTSWindowController+Browser.h
//   iSight iMage cApture
//
//   Created by rwiebe on 12-06-06.
//   Copyright (c) 2012 BurningThumb Software. All rights reserved.
//

#import "BTSWindowController.h"
#import "BTSImage.h"

@interface BTSWindowController (Browser)

// The method to setup the IKBrowserView
- (void) setupBrowser;

@end
```

11. In the file named `BTSWindowController+Browser.m,` add the following
program code to implement the required method for the `IKImageBrowserView`
`dataSource protocol.` These methods will return the number of images and an
individual image object. The number of images, is simply the `count of m_images`
array and a specific image is simply the object from the `m_images` array at the
requested index.

```
#pragma mark -
#pragma mark IKImageBrowserDataSource

// Implement image-browser's datasource protocol
// Our datasource representation is a simple mutable array

// Return the number of items in the array
- (NSUInteger) numberOfItemsInImageBrowser:
  (IKImageBrowserView *) a_view
{
    return [self.m_images count];
}


// Return the requested BTSImage object
- (id) imageBrowser:(IKImageBrowserView *) a_view
        itemAtIndex: (NSUInteger) a_index
{
    return [self.m_images objectAtIndex:a_index];
}
```

12. We are going to need some program code that adds individual images to our array.
In the file named `BTSWindowController+Browser.m,` add the following program
code to implement the `addImageWithURL:` methods that adds an individual image
to the `m_images array.` Note that `addImageWithURL:` obtains the attributes of
the `NSURL` object and uses an `if` statement to ensure the object does not reference
a hidden file or a directory, since we don't want to add hidden files or directories
to our image browser. If the object passes those two tests, then a new `BTSImage`
object is created with the `NSURL` added to the `m_images` array.

```
#pragma mark -
#pragma mark import images from a directory

/*
 ** - (void) addImageWithURL:(NSURL *) a_fileURL
 **
 ** Add one image URL to the array of images.
 ** Filter out images that are directories
 ** or hidden files
 **
```

```
**  Input:   A URL that points to an image
**  Output: None.
*/

- (void) addImageWithURL:(NSURL *) a_fileURL
{
    // A reference to an image
    BTSImage *l_image;

    // A reference to an error object
    NSError *err;

    // Get the file attributes
    NSDictionary *fileAttribs =
      [a_fileURL resourceValuesForKeys:self.m_fileAttributeKeys
                                error:&err];

    // For directories or hidden files, do nothing
    if (
        (YES == [[fileAttribs
                     objectForKey:NSURLIsDirectoryKey]
                 boolValue]) ||
        (YES == [[fileAttribs
                     objectForKey:NSURLIsHiddenKey]
                 boolValue])
        )
    {
        return;
    }

    // Create a BTSImage object for the URL
    l_image = [[BTSImage alloc] initWithURL:a_fileURL];

    // Add the object to the array of images
    [self.m_images addObject:l_image];

}
```

13. We are going to need some program code that looks at all the items in a directory, and adds the images to our array. In the file named `BTSWindowController+Browser.m`, add the following program code to begin the implementation of the `addImagesFromDirectory:` method:

```
/*
** - (void) addImagesFromDirectory:(NSString *) path
**
** Add all the images from a folder and its
** subfolders to the array of images.
** Filter out images that do not have supported
** file extensions (like .jpg, or .png, etc)
```

```
**
** Input:   A string that represents a file system
**          path.
** Output: None.
*/

- (void) addImagesFromDirectory:(NSString *) path
{

    // Cache a reference to the default
    // shared file manager object
    NSFileManager *l_manager =
      [NSFileManager defaultManager];

    // Create a flag that indicates if
    // a file system item is a directory
    BOOL l_isDir;

    // Ask the file manager to determine if the
    // item exists, and if it is a directory
    [l_manager fileExistsAtPath:path
                   isDirectory:&l_isDir];
```

14. Continue the implementation by looking at the path to see if it is a directory. If the path is a directory, we need to iterate over all of the items in the directory and invoke this same method on each of the items.

```
// If the item is a directory
    if (l_isDir)
    {
        // Ask the file manager for a list
        // of everything in the directory
        NSArray *l_content =
          [l_manager contentsOfDirectoryAtPath:path
                                         error:nil];
        // For each item in the directory
        for (NSString *l_path in l_content)
        {
            // Call this function again
            [self addImagesFromDirectory:
              [path stringByAppendingPathComponent:l_path]];
        }
    }
```

Recursion and iteration

This method invokes itself. When program code invokes itself, it is referred to as a **recursive** method. Some problems, such as navigating down a directory tree, lend themselves naturally to recursive methods. Contrast this with looping over the elements of an array, which is referred to as **iteration**. Often the same problem can be solved recursively, or iteratively, or using a combination of recursion and iteration and it is up to the programmer or the programming team leader to decide which method to use to solve the problem.

15. Otherwise, for items that are files, validate the file extension and add images to the array of images to be displayed. Note that the `addImagesFromDirectory:` method invokes the `addImageWithURL:` method to add individual files. Since the `addImageWithURL:` method filters out hidden files and directories the `addImagesFromDirectory:` method only needs to validate the file extension against the cached list of valid image file extension.

```
// Otherwise the item is a file
else
{
    // If the file has a supported image extension
    // like .jpg or .png etc
    if ([self.m_validFileExtensions containsObject:
        [path pathExtension]])
    {
        // Add the item to the array of images
        [self addImageWithURL:
            [NSURL fileURLWithPath:path]];
    }
}
```

16. Complete the implementation of the method by redisplaying the array of images as follows:

```
    // Redisplay the IKBrowserView
  [self.m_imageBrowser reloadData];
}
```

17. Finally, we need to implement the `setupBrowser` method that will
be called when the view is loaded from the `.xib` file. In the file named
`BTSWindowController+Browser.m`, add the following program code to begin
the implementation of the `setup` method. This method will cache the array of file
attributes used by the `addImageWithURL:` method and the array of supported
image file types used by the `addImagesFromDirectory:` method. Then it will,
if required, create the directory named iSight iMage cApture, in the users
`Pictures` folder. Finally, it will invoke the `addImagesFromDirectory:` method
to add all the images in that directory to the m_images array.

```
#pragma mark -
#pragma mark setup the IKBrowserView

/*
 ** - (void) setupBrowser
 **
 ** When the view is loaded from the .xib
 ** file, invoke this method to setup the
 ** view
 **
 ** Input:  None.
 ** Output: None.
 */

- (void) setupBrowser
{
```

18. The first thing we will do is cache some references that will be used later in the
method. This is done to make the code more efficient and compact.

```
    // Cache a reference to the default
    // NSFileManager object
    NSFileManager *l_manager =
      [NSFileManager defaultManager];

    // Cache an array of desired file system
    // attribute keys
    self.m_fileAttributeKeys =
      [[NSArray alloc] initWithObjects:
        NSURLIsDirectoryKey,
        NSURLIsHiddenKey,
        nil];

    // Cache a list of supported image file
    // extensions like .jpg, .png, etc.
    self.m_validFileExtensions =
      [NSImage imageFileTypes];
```

19. We continue by allocating the array that will store our image objects and storing the reference to it in one of our objects instance variables so that it is globally accessible by all the methods in our implementation.

```
// allocate our datasource array: will contain instances
// of BTSImage
self.m_images = [[NSMutableArray alloc] init];
```

20. Then, we customize the appearance of each image browser cell. There are a few options that we can select from and we will simply display cells with a title, which we will later provide in a delegate method.

```
// Set IKImageBrowser cell style so that the
// title is displayed
[self.m_imageBrowser setCellsStyleMask:IKCellsStyleTitled];
```

21. Next, we retrieve the path to the user's `Pictures` folder in a sandbox compliant manner, and if needed (which should only be the case the first time our App is launched) we create a subfolder in the `Pictures` folder with the name of our App.

```
// Find the Pictures folder the "correct" way
NSArray *l_paths =
  NSSearchPathForDirectoriesInDomains(NSPicturesDirectory,
                                      NSUserDomainMask,
                                      YES);

// There should be only one
NSString *l_path = [l_paths lastObject];

// Append the name of our App to the
// path to the Pictures folder
NSString *l_finalPath =
      [l_path stringByAppendingPathComponent:
      [[[NSBundle mainBundle] infoDictionary]
        objectForKey:(NSString *)kCFBundleNameKey]];

// If the directory does not exist
if (NO == [l_manager fileExistsAtPath:l_finalPath])
{
    // Create the directory
    [l_manager createDirectoryAtPath:l_finalPath
        withIntermediateDirectories: YES
                         attributes:nil
                             error: nil];
}
```

22. We complete the implementation by adding all the images from the `Pictures/ iSight iMage cApture` folder to our array of images and then redisplaying the images. The first time we run our App that folder will be empty but later, after the user has added some images, we will find things to add.

```
// Add all the images from the directory
// to the array
[self addImagesFromDirectory:l_finalPath];

// Re-display the view
[self.m_imageBrowser reloadData];
}
```

23. Finally, since the `BTSWindowController` `awakeFromNib` method invokes the `setupBrowser` method, it needs to import the browser interface. Add the following highlighted line of program code to the file named `BTSWindowController.m` to import the browser interface:

```
//
//  BTSWindowController.m
//  iSight iMage cApture
//
//  Created by rwiebe on 12-06-04.
//  Copyright (c) 2012 __MyCompanyName__. All rights reserved.
//

#import "BTSWindowController.h"
#import "BTSWindowController+Browser.h"
```

What just happened?

We implemented all of the methods needed to create an Image Kit Browser View that shows us the contents of a folder named **iSight iMage cApture** in the user's **Pictures** folder. When we run the App, the very first time, it will create that folder.

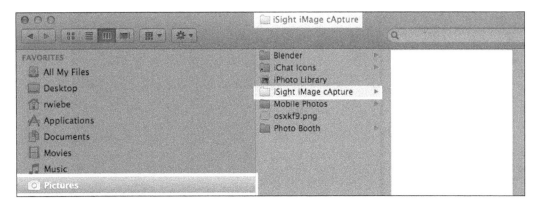

Because the folder is empty, our App will display an empty Image Browser View. This is OK.

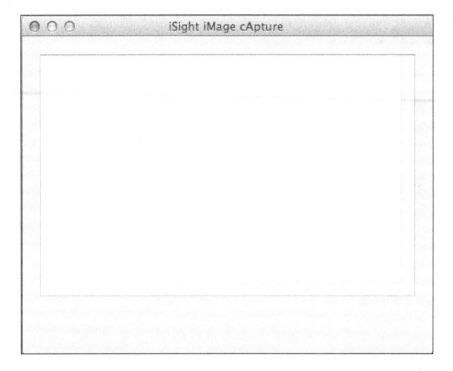

Have a go hero – placing some images in the iSight iMage cApture folder

Before we continue writing our program code, we will want to make sure that our image browser is working. Drag some images into the `iSight iMage cApture` folder and then run our App to make sure it is able to browse the images. We should see the images that we dragged into the folder appear in the image browser view.

Capturing and saving images

Now that we can browse our image folder, we need to be able to capture images. We will need the following:

- A button in our GUI that the App user will click on to begin an image capture.
- An action method that is invoked when the button is clicked in the GUI.
- A method that is automatically called when an image has been captured.

Time for action – capturing and saving images

Once more, we will use a category to organize our program code. This time our category will be used for capturing and saving still images.

1. In Xcode, click on the file named `MainmMenu.xib` in the project navigator and add a button with the name **Take Picture**.

2. We are going to use another category to extend the behavior of our `BTSWindowController` object. From the **File** menu, select **New**, and then select the **File...** option.

3. Select the **Mac OS X Cocoa Objective-C** category template and click on the **Next** button.

4. For the **Category**, select **Importer** and for the **Category on** select **BTSWindowController**, then click on the **Next** button.

5. Click the **Create** button.

6. In the file named `BTSWindowController+Importer.h`, add the following program code to expose the interface to the `takePicture:` method:

```
// The action method to capture an image
- (IBAction) takePicture:(id) sender;
```

7. In the **Assistant** editor, connect the **Take Picture** button to the `takePicture:` method by right-clicking on the button and dragging it to the method name in the file named `BTSWindowController+Importer.h`.

8. In the file named `BTSWindowController+Importer.m`, enter the following program code to display the **Picture Taker** sheet on our window:

```
#pragma mark -
#pragma mark Actions

/** - (IBAction) takePicture:(id)sender
 **
 ** This method is invoked when the Take Picture
 ** button is clicked
 **
 ** Input:  a_sender - the button object
 ** Output: none
 */

- (IBAction) takePicture:(id)a_sender
```

```
{
    // Get a reference to the didEndSelector method
    SEL l_didEndSelector =
     @selector(pictureTakerDidEnd:returnCode:contextInfo:);

    // Get a reference to the buttons window
    NSWindow *l_window = [a_sender window];

    // Get a reference to the shared Picture Taker
    // object
    IKPictureTaker *l_pictureTaker =
     [IKPictureTaker pictureTaker];


    // Display the Picture Taker sheet
    [l_pictureTaker
      beginPictureTakerSheetForWindow:l_window
        withDelegate:self
          didEndSelector:l_didEndSelector
            contextInfo:nil];
}
```

9. When we take a picture, we are going to save it as a JPG in our App's folder and we need to give this file a name. We will use the current date and time to come up with a unique name for each picture. In the `BTSWindowController+Importer.h` file, add the following to define what we will use as the string template for our filenames:

    ```
    #define D_FILENAME_TEMPLATE @"IMG%u%02u%02u%02u%02u%02u.jpg"
    ```

10. When the App user clicks on the **Cancel** or **Set** button in the **Picture Taker** sheet, the method named `pictureTakerDidEnd:returnCode:contextInfo:` will be invoked. In the file named `BTSWindowController+Importer.m`, enter the following program code to implement this `didEndSelector:` method, which will get the image from the **Picture Taker**, save it in our App's `Pictures` folder, and update the **Image Browser** to display the new image. Oddly, the most complex part of saving an image file, from a program code perspective, is obtaining the current date and time to create the filename string object that we will use to save the image. Obtaining the image data and writing it to a file requires only the few lines of the following highlighted program code:

    ```
    /** - (void) pictureTakerDidEnd:(IKPictureTaker *)a_pictureTaker
     **                  returnCode:(NSInteger)a_returnCode
     **                 contextInfo:(void  *)a_contextInfo
     **
     ** This method is invoked when the Take Picture
     ** sheet Cancel or Set button is pressed
     **
    ```

```
**  Input:   a_pictureTaker - the Picture Taker object
**           a_returnCode - The status (Cancel or OK)
**           a_contextInfo - Any object or nil
**
** Output: none
*/

- (void) pictureTakerDidEnd:(IKPictureTaker *)a_pictureTaker
              returnCode:(NSInteger)a_returnCode
              contextInfo:(void  *)a_contextInfo
{

… some code omitted here

    // Append the file name to the path
    // of our Apps folder
    l_finalPath =
        [l_finalPath stringByAppendingPathComponent: l_filename];

    // Get the image from the Picture Taker
    NSImage *l_image = [a_pictureTaker outputImage];

    // Get the image data as a TIFF file
    NSData *l_imageData = [l_image TIFFRepresentation];

    // Get a bitmap from the TIFF
    NSBitmapImageRep *l_imageRep =
    [NSBitmapImageRep imageRepWithData:l_imageData];

    // Set the jpg compression to best
    NSDictionary *l_imageProps =
     [NSDictionary dictionaryWithObject:
      [NSNumber numberWithFloat:1.0]
       forKey:NSImageCompressionFactor];

    // Convert the TIFF to a JPG
    l_imageData = [l_imageRep representationUsingType:
      NSJPEGFileType
       properties:l_imageProps];

    // Write the JPG to a file
    [l_imageData writeToFile:l_finalPath atomically:YES];

    //add it to our datasource
    [self addImageWithURL:[NSURL fileURLWithPath: l_finalPath]];

    //reflect changes
    [self.m_imageBrowser reloadData];

}
```

What just happened?

We implemented the methods needed to capture an image using the `IKPictureTaker`. Now, when we click the **Take Picture** button the Picture Taker allows us to capture an image from the iSight camera as shown in the following screenshot:

Modifying the behavior of the Picture Taker

To modify the behavior of the Picture Taker, we need to change some of its default values. The keys that are available are as follows:

- `IKPictureTakerAllowsVideoCaptureKey`: A key for allowing video capture. The associated value is an NSNumber value (BOOL) whose default value is YES.

- `IKPictureTakerAllowsFileChoosingKey`: A key for allowing the user to select a file. The associated value is an NSNumber object that contains a BOOL value whose default value is YES.

- `IKPictureTakerUpdateRecentPictureKey`: A key for allowing a recent picture to be updated. The associated value is an NSNumber object that contains a BOOL value whose default value is YES.

- `IKPictureTakerAllowsEditingKey`: A key for allowing image editing. The associated value is an NSNumber object that contains a BOOL value whose default value is `YES`.

- `IKPictureTakerShowEffectsKey`: A key for showing effects. The associated value is an NSNumber object that contains a BOOL value whose default value is NO.

- `IKPictureTakerInformationalTextKey`: A key for informational text. The associated value is an `NSString` or `NSAttributedString` object whose default value is Drag Image Here.

- `IKPictureTakerOutputImageMaxSizeKey`: A key for the maximum size of the output image. The associated value is an NSValue object (`NSSize`).

- `IKPictureTakerCropAreaSizeKey`: A key for the cropping area size. The associated value is an NSValue object (`NSSize`).

- `IKPictureTakerShowAddressBookPictureKey`: A key for showing the address book picture. The associated value is a Boolean value package as an `NSNumber` object. The default value is `NO`. If set to `YES`, the Picture Taker automatically adds the address book image for the Me user at the end of the **Recent Pictures** pop-up menu.

- `IKPictureTakerShowEmptyPictureKey`: A key for showing an empty picture. The associated value is an `NSImage` object. The default value is nil. If set to an image, the Picture Taker automatically shows an image at the end of the **Recent Pictures** pop-up menu that means "no picture".

- `IKPictureTakerRemainOpenAfterValidateKey`: A key that determines if the Picture Taker should remain open after the user selects done. This allows the application to programmatically dismiss the panel. The associated value is an `NSNumber` object that contains a BOOL value whose default value is `NO`.

Time for action – drawing our fingers

The most interesting keys are `IKPictureTakerAllowsFileChoosingKey`, `IKPictureTakerShowRecentPictureKey`, `IKPictureTakerOutputImageMaxSizeKey`, `IKPictureTakerCropAreaSizeKey`, and `IKPictureTakerShowEffectsKey`. We can use these keys to disable file selection, eliminate the recent pictures pop-up menu, allow us to take larger images, and to apply effects to those images.

1. In the `BTSWindowController+Importer.h` file, add the following defines that we will use to set the maximum size of the picture that we can take:

```
#define D_MAX_WIDTH 640
#define D_MAX_HEIGHT 480
```

2. In the `BTSWindowController+Importer.m` file, in the `takePicture:` method, add the following program code to modify the behavior of the Picture Taker:

```
// Set the maximum size
NSSize l_size = NSMakeSize(D_MAX_WIDTH, D_MAX_HEIGHT);

// Disable the file chooser
[l_pictureTaker setValue:[NSNumber numberWithBool:NO]
                  forKey:IKPictureTakerAllowsFileChoosingKey];

// Disable the recent pictures popup
[l_pictureTaker setValue:[NSNumber numberWithBool:NO]
                  forKey:IKPictureTakerShowRecentPictureKey];

// Show the effects button and apply effects
[l_pictureTaker setValue:[NSNumber numberWithBool:YES]
                  forKey:IKPictureTakerShowEffectsKey];

// Take larger pictures
[l_pictureTaker setValue:[NSValue valueWithSize:l_size]
                  forKey:IKPictureTakerOutputImageMaxSizeKey];
[l_pictureTaker setValue:[NSValue valueWithSize:l_size]
                  forKey:IKPictureTakerCropAreaSizeKey];
```

What just happened?

We modified the behavior of the Picture Taker. Now, we can take pictures that are much larger than the default and we can apply effects to those pictures as shown in the following screenshot:

Have a go hero – making more changes to the Picture Taker behavior

You can take this opportunity to try some of the other key-value pairs that can be used to change the behavior of the Picture Taker. Experiment with the different settings until you find the combination that creates the Picture Taker interface you prefer.

Deleting images

Now that we can take pictures it would be really nice if we could delete the pictures we don't want to keep.

Time for action – deleting an image

Because we have built our App around the Image Kit framework, we can trash unwanted images with a small amount of our own program code.

1. In the `BTSWindowController+Importer.m` file, in the `setupBrowser` method, add the following program code to turn animation on for the Image Browser View:

```
- (void) setupBrowser
{
    // Turn on the animation effect
    [self.m_imageBrowser setAnimates:YES];
```

2. In the `BTSWindowController+Importer.m` file, in the `IKImageBrowserDataSource` section, add the following program code to delete the selected images:

```
// Delete the selected images
- (void) imageBrowser:(IKImageBrowserView *) a_view
        removeItemsAtIndexes: (NSIndexSet *) a_indexes
{
    // Cache a reference to the default
    // NSWorkspace object
    NSWorkspace * l_workspace =
     [NSWorkspace sharedWorkspace];

    // Create an array to hold the deleted
    // objects
    NSMutableArray *l_deletedURLs =
     [[NSMutableArray alloc] init];
```

```
        // For all the selected images
        [a_indexes enumerateIndexesUsingBlock:
         ^(NSUInteger l_idx, BOOL *stop)
        {
            // Get the BTSImage object
            BTSImage *l_image = [self.m_images objectAtIndex:l_idx];

            // Get the URL for the from the BTSImage
            NSURL *l_URL = l_image.m_URL;

            // Add the URL to the list of
            // deleted URLs
            [l_deletedURLs addObject:l_URL];

        }];

        // Move the delete items to the Trash
        [l_workspace recycleURLs:l_deletedURLs completionHandler:nil];

        // Remove all the images from the array
        [self.m_images removeObjectsAtIndexes:a_indexes];
    }
```

What just happened?

We implemented the program code to move the images to the trash. Now, we can select one or more images in the Image Browser View and just press the *Delete* key to send them to trash.

Summary

In this chapter, we have implemented an application that uses Image Kit to allow us to take pictures with the iSight camera.

Specifically, we covered what is Image Kit, how to browse images (including deleting), how to take pictures and apply effects using the Picture Taker object, and how to implement our first recursive method.

Now that we have seen how easy it can be to take still images with the iSight camera, we are going to look at a somewhat more complex method of obtaining images from the camera. Specifically, we are going to look at capturing frames. An individual frame could be stored as a captured image or a series of frames can be stored, and combined with audio, as a movie. We need to use different programming interfaces to capture a series of frames and that will be the topic of our next chapter.

8

Video Recording – iSight Recorder

*In Chapter 7, On Capturing Still Images with the iSight Camera, we examined the **Image Kit** component of the Quartz framework, which includes classes focused on providing support for capturing and displaying still images. In this chapter, we will examine another framework, Quicktime Kit. Specifically, we will examine Quicktime Kit Capture, which is a subset of the QTKit framework and includes classes focused on providing support for capturing movies.*

In this chapter, we shall learn the following:

- ◆ What is Quicktime Kit Capture and how does it work?
- ◆ Previewing the video capture
- ◆ Capturing a single frame as a still image
- ◆ Previewing audio capture
- ◆ Capturing a movie to disk
- ◆ Capturing compressed movies to disk

What is Quicktime Kit Capture?

Quicktime Kit (QTKit) is an Objective-C Mac OS X framework that provides a rich set of programming interfaces for manipulating time-based media such as audio and video. With QTKit, we can perform the following tasks with time-based media:

- ◆ Play
- ◆ Edit
- ◆ Export
- ◆ Capture
- ◆ Record

For our iSight Recorder App, we will be focusing on the component of QTKit called QTKit Capture, which provides the classes we need to capture and record audio and video to Quicktime movies.

QTKit Capture, at its core, provides us with the following key classes:

- ◆ QTCaptureSession
- ◆ QTCaptureInput
- ◆ QTCaptureOutput
- ◆ QTCaptureConnection

In essence, we need to create a capture session, which will have some inputs (iSight camera, built-in microphone), some outputs (preview view, movie file), and some connections between the inputs and the outputs.

We are only going to implement single audio and video inputs with single preview and file outputs but it's important to understand that the QTKit Capture architecture is not limited to single inputs and outputs. For example, we could capture input from multiple cameras and multiple microphones in a single capture session.

Previewing the video capture

Before we can use the QTKit framework, we need to create a new Xcode project and add the **QTKit.framework** to the set of linked frameworks. Once the project has been created and the **QTKit.framework** has been added we can, very quickly, create the part of our App that will allow us to preview video capture.

Time for action – creating a project and adding the program code to preview video and audio

We are now ready to create an Xcode project and begin writing program.

1. Create a new Xcode project for a **Mac OS X Application** using the **Cocoa Application** template with **Automatic Reference Counting** enabled and the options set as follows:

Option	Value
Product Name	iSight Recorder
Company Identifier	com.yourdomain
Class Prefix	Your initials (for consistency we use BTS throughout this book)

2. After Xcode creates the new project, design an icon and drag it in to the **App Icon** field on the **TARGET Summary**.

3. Remember to set the **Organization** in the **Project Document** section of the **File inspector**.

4. Select the **iSight Recorder TARGET** in the standard editor, and in the **Build Phases** section titled **Link Binary With Libraries** add the **QTKit.framework**.

5. Remember to drag the **QTKit.framework** to the **Frameworks** folder in the project navigator.

6. In the file named MainMenu.xib, select the **iSight Recorder** window and in the **Size Inspector**, constrain its minimum size.

7. Then add the following GUI components:

- ❑ A button titled Record
- ❑ A button titled Stop
- ❑ A button titled Take Picture
- ❑ A Quicktime capture view

8. In the **Attributes Inspector**, for the **Stop** button, uncheck the **State [] Enabled** checkbox.

9. In the file named BTSAppDelegate.h use the #import directive to import the <QTKit/QTKit.h> file so that the QTKit interface objects can be referenced.

10. Then, add a new strong @property named m_QTCaptureView that will be our **Interface Builder Outlet (IBOutlet)** for the QTCaptureView object.

11. Using the **Assistant** editor, connect m_QTCaptureView outlet from the file named BTSAppDelegate.h to the capture view in the file named MainMenu.xib.

12. Then, add three new strong `@property` entries named `m_takePictureButton`, `m_stopButton`, and `m_recordButton` that will be our `IBOutlet` for the `NSbutton` objects.

13. Using the **Assistant** editor, connect the `m_takePictureButton`, `m_stopButton`, and `m_recordButton` outlets from the file named `BTSAppDelegate.h` to the respective buttons in the file named `MainMenu.xib`.

14. Remember to `@synthesize` all of these properties in the file named `BTSDelegate.m`.

15. Since we will need a capture session, a capture input device for video, and a capture input device for audio, now is a good time to add those properties to the file named `BTSAppDelegate.h`. Use the object types of `QTCaptureSession*` and `QTCaptureDeviceInput*`, and the names `m_CaptureSession`, `m_CaptureInputDevice_Video`, and `m_CaptureInputDevice_Audio`.

16. Now that our project and interface have been created, we can modify the implementation in the file named `BTSAppDelegate.m` in the method named `applicationDidFinishLaunching:`. Start by adding the following code to `@synthesize` the interface elements:

```
// Create accessors for the Capture View
@synthesize m_QTCaptureView;


// Create accessors for the session,
// audio input device and video input
// device
@synthesize m_CaptureSession;
@synthesize m_CaptureDeviceInput_Video;
@synthesize m_CaptureDeviceInput_Audio;
```

17. Typically, when we are accessing QTKit capture objects, the methods we invoke will return a status (success or failure) and a more detailed description (`NSError` object) should something go wrong. Add the following code to the `applicationDidFinishLaunching:` method to create the local references to this returned information:

```
// Define two local variables
// that will contain the results
// of various operations
BOOL l_success = NO;
NSError* l_error;
```

18. Then, add the code to allocate and initialize the capture session. When we have connected all the inputs and outputs, we can start the capture session running.

```
// Create the capture session
m_CaptureSession = [[QTCaptureSession alloc] init];
```

19. Next, we need to find and open the video input device. The program code assumes there is an iSight camera and that it will be successfully found and opened. Later we will modify the code to allow the user to select any video device for input but for now we are just going to assume everything works fine and the iSight camera is available.

```
// Find a video device
QTCaptureDevice* l_videoDevice =
 [QTCaptureDevice
  defaultInputDeviceWithMediaType:QTMediaTypeVideo];

// Open the video device
l_success = [l_videoDevice open:&l_error];
```

20. If the video device was successfully initialized, then we can connect it to the session as our video input device.

```
// Add the video device to the session as a device input
// only if it was successfully initialized
if (l_videoDevice)
{
// Allocate and initialize the video input device
m_CaptureDeviceInput_Video =
     [[QTCaptureDeviceInput alloc]
        initWithDevice:l_videoDevice];

// Add the video input device to the session
l_success = [m_CaptureSession
                  addInput:m_CaptureDeviceInput_Video
                  error:&l_error];

}
```

21. Some video capture devices also capture audio. Even though we know the current generation of iSight cameras do not capture audio, we are going to check to see if our video capture device does capture audio and only add a separate audio input if it does not. This check will future proof our program code in case future iSight cameras do capture audio and will also make it compatible with non-iSight video capture devices that include both audio and video capture.

```
// If the video device doesn't also supply audio,
// add an audio device input to the session
if (![l_videoDevice hasMediaType:QTMediaTypeSound] &&
    ![l_videoDevice hasMediaType:QTMediaTypeMuxed])
{
    // Find an audio device
```

```
QTCaptureDevice *l_audioDevice =
 [QTCaptureDevice
  defaultInputDeviceWithMediaType:QTMediaTypeSound];

// open the audio device
l_success = [l_audioDevice open:&l_error];

// Add the audio device to the session as a device
// input
// only if it was successfully initialized
if (l_success)
{
    // Allocate and initialize the audio input
    // device
    m_CaptureDeviceInput_Audio =
     [[QTCaptureDeviceInput alloc]
       initWithDevice:l_audioDevice];

    // Add the audio input device to the session
    l_success = [m_CaptureSession
                    addInput:m_CaptureDeviceInput_Audio
                       error:&l_error];

}

}
```

22. Finally, we need to set the capture session for the capture view to associate the session with the view, and then start the session running.

```
// Set the capture session for the Capture View
[m_QTCaptureView setCaptureSession:m_CaptureSession];

// Start the capture session
[m_CaptureSession startRunning];
```

What just happened?

We created a new Xcode project and implemented the program code required to preview video from our iSight camera and audio from our default audio input source (as set in the System Preferences). The capture session will display a preview of the video in the capture view as shown in the following screenshot:

Capturing a single frame as a still image

Now that we have a preview running for the video input from the iSight camera, we can look at another way of taking a still picture. This method does not use the Image Kit so we have a lot more control over what we can do with the image – that control, however, adds complexity.

Time for action – capturing a frame

When a capture session is running, we can add another output object that will be notified each time a new, uncompressed, frame is captured. The output's delegate object can do whatever it wants to do to that captured frame, for example, save it to a file.

1. Select the **iSight Recorder TARGET** in the standard editor. In the **Build Phases** section titled **Link Binary With Libraries**, add the **QuartzCore.framework**.

2. Remember to drag the **QuartzCore.framework** to the **Frameworks** folder in the project navigator.

3. In the file named BTSAppDelegate.h, add a #define for our captured image's width, height, and JPG file extension.

```
// Define the image size for pictures
#define D_BTS_SNAP_WIDTH 640
#define D_BTS_SNAP_HEIGHT 480


// Define the image type for pictures
#define D_BTS_SNAP_TYPE @"jpg"
```

4. Then add a new @property of type QTCaptureDecompressedVideoOutput. The delegate of the object referenced by this property will receive uncompressed frame data.

```
// Use this property to capture images
// from frames
@property (strong) QTCaptureDecompressedVideoOutput* m_CDVO;
```

5. Then add an action method that will be invoked when the **Take Picture** button is clicked.

```
// The action method for the Take Picture button
- (IBAction)takePicture:(id)a_sender;
```

6. Use the **Accessory** editor to connect the **Take Picture** button in the file named MainMenu.xib to the IBAction method takePicture:.

7. In the file named BTSAppDelegate.m, synthesize the m_CDVO property as follows:

```
// Create the accessors for the Capture
// Decompressed Video Output object
@synthesize m_CDVO;
```

8. Now we need to implement the `takePicture` action method.
The first thing this method will do is examine the reference to the
`QTCaptureDecompressedVideoOutput` object to see if it exists. If it
does not exist, the method will create and initialize the object so that it will
receive uncompressed frames in the size we want using a pixel format that
can be easily converted to a JPG file.

```
// The action method for the take snapshot button
- (IBAction)takePicture:(id)a_sender
{
    // If the QTCaptureDecompressedVideoOutput object
    // does not exist
    if (nil == m_CDVO)
    {
        // Create the QTCaptureDecompressedVideoOutput object
        m_CDVO = [[QTCaptureDecompressedVideoOutput alloc] init];

        // Set the frame size and pixel format to provide
        // a nice image buffer for JPG creation
        [m_CDVO setPixelBufferAttributes:
         [NSDictionary dictionaryWithObjectsAndKeys:
           [NSNumber numberWithDouble:D_BTS_SNAP_WIDTH],
           (id)kCVPixelBufferWidthKey,
           [NSNumber numberWithDouble:D_BTS_SNAP_HEIGHT],
           (id)kCVPixelBufferHeightKey,
           [NSNumber numberWithInt:kCVPixelFormatType_32ARGB],
           (id) kCVPixelBufferPixelFormatTypeKey,
            nil]];

    }
```

9. Then the capture session needs to be stopped and the output for the decompressed
frame added to the session.

```
        // Stop the capture session
        [m_CaptureSession stopRunning];

        // Add the QTCaptureDecompressedVideoOutput object
        // to the capture session
        [m_CaptureSession addOutput:m_CDVO error:nil];
```

10. Next the `BTSAppDelegate` needs to be assigned as the delegate object of the
`QTCaptureDecompressedVideoOutput` object so that the delegate method is
called when raw frames are ready.

```
        // Make ourselves the delegate so that the
        // captureOutput:didOutputVideoFrame:
        //  withSampleBuffer:fromConnection:
        // method will be invoked
        [m_CDVO setDelegate:self];
```

11. And finally, the capture session needs to be restarted:

```
// Restart the capture session
[m_CaptureSession startRunning];
```

```
}
```

12. Now that the `CaptureDecompressedVideoOutput` object has been created and the `BTSAppDelegate` object has been set as its delegate, we need to implement the delegate method that will be invoked as frames become ready:

```
// This method is automatically invoked on the
// QTCaptureDecompressedVideoOutput objects
// delegate when a frame is ready

- (void)captureOutput:(QTCaptureOutput *)captureOutput
   didOutputVideoFrame:(CVImageBufferRef)videoFrame
     withSampleBuffer:(QTSampleBuffer *)sampleBuffer
        fromConnection:(QTCaptureConnection *)connection
{
```

13. Because we only need a single decompressed frame, the first thing this method does when it is invoked is remove itself as an output from the capture session and remove the `BTSAppDelegate` object as the delegate object.

```
// We only need one frame so remove ourselves
// as the delegate and then remove the
// QTCaptureDecompressedVideoOutput from
// the session
[m_CDVO setDelegate:nil];
[m_CaptureSession removeOutput: m_CDVO];
```

14. Now that no more frames will be sent, the delegate method can process the frame that it received. The frame is converted to an `NSImage` object so that we can use the `NSImage` instance methods to manipulate the data.

```
// Create a new image representation for
// the frame
NSCIImageRep *imageRep =
 [NSCIImageRep imageRepWithCIImage:
  [CIImage imageWithCVImageBuffer:videoFrame]];

// Create an NSImage object from with the
// new image representation
NSImage *l_image = [[NSImage alloc]
                      initWithSize:[imageRep size]];
[l_image addRepresentation:imageRep];
```

15. Finally the delegate invokes another method that will be responsible for saving the image as a JPG file to disk. This method is invoked on the main program thread so that none of the objects we have created will be cleaned up while we still need references to them.

```
// Save the image on the main
// program thread, make sure we
// wait until the save is done so that
// no object disappear out from under us
[self performSelectorOnMainThread:@selector(saveImage:)
                        withObject:l_image
                    waitUntilDone:YES];


}
```

16. Of course we still need to implement the `saveImage:` method, and that is what we will do next.

```
// This method will be invoked on the
// main thread to save an image

-(void)saveImage:(NSImage*)a_image
{
```

17. The first thing that the `saveImage:` method needs to do, is convert the NSImage into raw JPG data:

```
// Get the TIFF Representation
// and convert it to raw JPG data
// using default settings
NSData *bitmapData = [a_image TIFFRepresentation];
NSBitmapImageRep *bitmapRep =
  [NSBitmapImageRep imageRepWithData:bitmapData];
NSData *imageData =
[bitmapRep representationUsingType:NSJPEGFileType
                       properties:nil];
```

18. Then the `saveImage:` method will create an accessory view so that the image can be displayed on the save dialog. The accessory view is created using the full resolution of the captured image and then it is attached to the save panel.

```
// Use the image size as the
// accessory view frame size
// and create a new NSImage view
NSRect l_frame =
 NSMakeRect(0,0,a_image.size.width,a_image.size.height);
NSImageView* l_imageView =
[[NSImageView alloc] initWithFrame:l_frame];
```

```
// Set the image for the accessory view
[l_imageView setImage:a_image];

// Create a new save panel
NSSavePanel *l_savePanel = [NSSavePanel savePanel];

// Set the image view as the save panel
// accessory view
[l_savePanel setAccessoryView:l_imageView];
```

19. The save panel is also restricted to allow saving only files that end in the .jpg extension so that our images are easy to identify in the Finder.

```
// Restrict the save panel to
// JPG files
[l_savePanel setAllowedFileTypes:
  [NSArray arrayWithObject:D_BTS_SNAP_TYPE]];
```

20. Finally the saveImage: method runs the save panel as a sheet on the **iSight Recorder** window, and if the **Save** button is clicked the image is written to disk at the path selected by the user.

```
// Begin the save panel as a sheet on the
// window
[l_savePanel beginSheetModalForWindow:_window
                    completionHandler:^(NSInteger result)
{
    // If the Save button is pressed
    if (result == NSFileHandlingPanelOKButton)
    {
        // Write the JPG data to the URL
        [imageData writeToURL: l_savePanel.URL atomically:
YES];
    }
}
];
}
```

What just happened?

We added a new output to our capture session so that our App could access a raw, uncompressed, frame of video from our iSight camera. Once our App has a single frame it can do whatever it wants with the image data and we decided to write it to a file as a JPG image. This method of taking snapshots is more complex than using the Image Capture framework but gives us much more control over the image data.

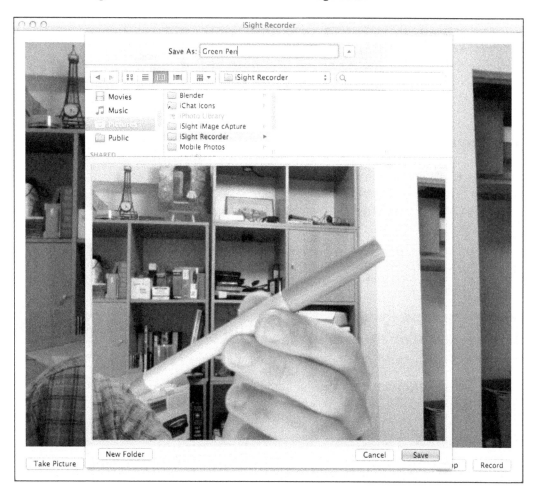

Have a go hero – skipping the first frame(s)

Sometimes, but not always, the first frame received by the `captureOutput` method does not contain the desired image data and the resulting JPG is too dark. This is an example of a race condition between the hardware and the software that can occur when we are changing the capture session configuration. One way to address the problem is to ignore the first frame received and capture the second frame for our JPG image. Another way to address the problem is to provide a countdown, similar to the 3, 2, 1 countdown provided by the Image Capture framework, prior to selecting the frame for our JPG image.

Now is a good time for us to think of a way that we could either skip the first frame, or provide a countdown prior to capturing the frame and add our frame skipping to the implementation of the program code that captures a still image.

Previewing audio capture

In addition to previewing the video that our camera is capturing, we may want to preview the audio that is being captured. In the same way as we added a video preview to our capture session, we can add an audio preview to the session.

 When previewing audio, we need to wear headphones to avoid the feedback that would occur if the microphone was to pick up the audio that was being previewed.

Time for action – capturing and saving images

In its simplest form, we can add audio preview with three lines of program code.

1. In the file named `BTSAppDelegate.m`, create the audio preview output object by adding the following program code in the method named `applicationDidFinishLaunching:`. Add it to the capture session, just prior to the line that starts the capture session:

```
// Allocate and initialize and audio preview object
QTCaptureAudioPreviewOutput* l_audioPreviewOutput =
  [[QTCaptureAudioPreviewOutput alloc] init];

// Set the preview volume
[l_audioPreviewOutput setVolume:0.5];

// Add the preview to our capture session
[m_CaptureSession addOutput:audioPreviewOutput error:nil];
```

2. Run the iSight Recorder App and say something to hear the audio preview (make sure you are wearing headphones to avoid audio feedback).

3. Obviously, we would like our App user to be able to control the volume of the audio preview rather than having it permanently set to 0.5 by our App so we need to add a slider to GUI. Use the **Attribute Inspector** to set the **Current** value of the slider to 0 and make sure that **Continuous** is enabled in the **State**, as shown in the following screenshot:

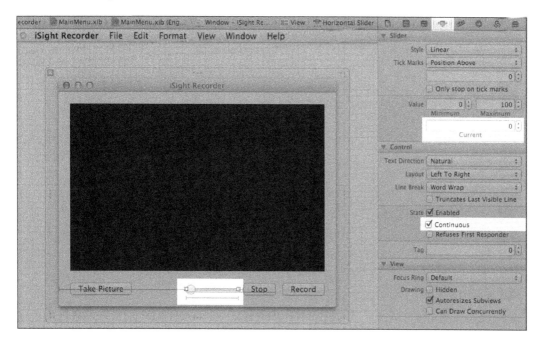

4. As with all GUI items, we need to add the property to the .h file and synthesize the property in the .m file:

```
// A reference to the volume slider in the GUI
@property (strong) IBOutlet NSSlider* m_volumeSlider;

// Create the volume slider accessor
@synthesize  m_volumeSlider;
```

5. We also need to use the Assistant editor to connect from the @property in the .h file to the GUI item in the .xib file.

6. We also need to change the local declaration of the l_audioPreviewOutput reference into a @property so that it can be accessed by different methods in our implementation. This means adding it as a @property in the .h file and using @synthesize to create accessor methods in the .m file.

> **Accessor** methods are used in Objective-C to get or set the value of an object's instance variable. Instead of directly getting or setting values, we invoke a method and the object instance returns or sets the value of the variable. We can write the program code for these methods ourselves or we can ask the compile to automatically generate the program code using synthesize.

```
// Use this property to preview audio
@property (strong) QTCaptureAudioPreviewOutput*
m_audioPreviewOutput;
```

```
// Create the audio preview accessor
@synthesize m_audioPreviewOutput;
```

7. Then we can change the program code that sets the preview volume to use the @property and the NSSlider reference.

```
// Allocate and initialize and audio preview object
m_audioPreviewOutput =
 [[QTCaptureAudioPreviewOutput alloc] init];

// Set the preview volume
[m_audioPreviewOutput setVolume:
 [self.m_volumeSlider floatValue] / 100];

// Add the preview to our capture session
[m_CaptureSession addOutput:m_audioPreviewOutput error:nil];
```

8. Of course we also need an action method that is invoked when the slider is moved in the GUI. This action method needs to be included in the .h file and the .m file:

```
// The action method for the preview volume slider
- (IBAction) setPreviewVolume: (id) a_sender;
```

```
// The action method for the preview volume slider
- (IBAction) setPreviewVolume: (id) a_sender
{
    // Set the preview volume
    [m_audioPreviewOutput setVolume:
     [self.m_volumeSlider floatValue] / 100];
}
```

9. We need to use the **Assistant** editor to connect from the slider in the .xib file to the action method in the .h file.

What just happened?

We implemented the program code required to preview the audio that will be captured by our capture session. Because previewing audio through the speakers will result in audio feedback, we made sure to have our headphones plugged in if the audio preview volume was greater than zero.

Capturing a movie to disk

Now that we have a working capture session that provides both audio and video previews it is time to capture a movie to disk. The QTKit Capture framework treats a movie file just like any other output and all we need to do to capture our movie to disk is to add a movie file output to the capture session.

Time for action – capturing a Quicktime movie

In addition to adding the movie file output, we will need to provide some GUI interaction to allow our App user to save the movie to a file of their choice once it has been captured.

1. As with all of our Apps' instance variables, we need to add the program code for the @property in the file named BTSAppDelegate.h and to @synthesize the accessor in the file named BTSAppDelegate.m.

```
// Use this property to capture a movie to disk
@property (strong) QTCaptureMovieFileOutput*
 m_CaptureMovieFileOutput;



// Create the accessors for the Capture
// Movie File Output object
@synthesize m_CaptureMovieFileOutput;
```

2. In the file named BTSAppDelegate.m to create the movie file object, add the following program code in the method named applicationDidFinishLaunching:. Add it to the capture session, just prior to the line that starts the capture session.

```
// Create the movie file output and add it to the session
m_CaptureMovieFileOutput =
 [[QTCaptureMovieFileOutput alloc] init];
l_success = [m_CaptureSession addOutput:
m_CaptureMovieFileOutput
 error:&l_error];
```

3. We also need to make the BTSAppDelegate object the delegate of the capture movie file output object so that it receives notifications when important events, like the movie recording stopping, occur.

```
// Make the BTSAppDelegate also the delegate for the
// capture movie file output object so that it receives
// a notification when movie recording stops
[m_CaptureMovieFileOutput setDelegate:self];
```

4. In the file named BTSAppDelegate.h, define the action methods for the buttons titled Stop and Record as follows:

```
// The action method for the Stop and Record buttons
- (IBAction)startRecording:(id)a_sender;
- (IBAction)stopRecording:(id)a_sender;
```

5. Use the **Assistant** editor to connect the buttons from the file named MainMenu.xib to the actions defined in the file named BTSAppDelegate.h.

6. In the file named BTSAppDelegate.h, implement the startRecording: method. Start by caching a reference to the default NSFileManager which will be used later in the method.

```
// The action method invoked when the button
// titled Record is clicked in the GUI
 - (IBAction)startRecording:(id)sender
{
    // Cache a reference to the NSFileManager
    NSFileManager* l_manager = [NSFileManager defaultManager];
```

7. Then, append the name of our App (iSight Recorder) to the NSTemporaryDirectory and create a new directory at that location. This temporary directory will be used to store movies while they are being recorded. If the App user decides to keep the recorded movie it will be moved to the location requested by the user.

```
// Append the name of our App to the
// path to the NSTemporaryDirectory folder
NSString *l_finalPath =
[NSTemporaryDirectory() stringByAppendingPathComponent:
 [[[NSBundle mainBundle] infoDictionary]
  objectForKey:(NSString *)kCFBundleNameKey]];

// If the directory does not exist
if (NO == [l_manager fileExistsAtPath:l_finalPath])
{
    // Create the directory
    [l_manager createDirectoryAtPath:l_finalPath
        withIntermediateDirectories: YES
                        attributes:nil
                             error: nil];
}
```

8. Then, use the current date and time to create a temporary filename for the movie as follows:

```
// Use the date and time to create a unique file name
NSDate *today = [NSDate date];
NSDateFormatter *dateFormat = [[NSDateFormatter alloc] init];
[dateFormat setDateFormat:@"yyyy-MM-dd hh.mm.ss"];
NSString *dateString = [dateFormat stringFromDate:today];
```

9. Now, combine the temporary folder name, and the temporary filename to create a file URL that can be used to locate the temporary movie file as follows:

```
// Build the URL to the final path in temporary items
NSURL* l_url =
  [NSURL fileURLWithPath:
    [[l_finalPath stringByAppendingPathComponent:dateString]
     stringByAppendingPathExtension:@"mov"]];
```

10. Once we have a valid file URL, we can assign it to the capture movie file output object and movie recording will automatically begin.

```
// When the output URL is set to a path, recording starts
[m_CaptureMovieFileOutput recordToOutputFileURL:l_url];
```

11. Because we only want the App user to be able to stop the movie recording, we complete the method implementation by disabling the buttons titled **Take Picture** and **Record**, and enabling the **Stop** button.

```
// Reset the button states
[self.m_recordButton setEnabled:NO];
[self.m_stopButton setEnabled:YES];
[self.m_takePictureButton setEnabled:NO];

}
```

12. Now we need to implement the `stopRecording:` action method. This is trivial – we simply assign the output file as nil and movie recording will automatically stop.

```
// The action method invoked when the button
// titled Stop is clicked in the GUI
 - (IBAction)stopRecording:(id)sender
{
    // When the output file is set to nil, recording stops
    [m_CaptureMovieFileOutput recordToOutputFileURL:nil];
}
```

13. Because the `BTSAppDelegate` was made the delegate for the `QTCaptureMovieFileOutput` object the `captureOutput:captureOutput di dFinishRecordingToOutputFileAtURL:forConnections: dueToError:` method will be automatically invoked when the movie recording stops. We need to implement that method. The first thing that it needs to do is invoke another method, which we will implement next, that saves the recorded movie.

```
// Do something with the QuickTime movie
// in the temporary items folder
- (void)captureOutput:(QTCaptureFileOutput *)a_captureOutput
        didFinishRecordingToOutputFileAtURL:(NSURL *)a_
outputFileURL
        forConnections:(NSArray *)a_connections
           dueToError:(NSError *)a_error
{
    // Preform the save on the main thread
    [self performSelectorOnMainThread:@selector(saveMovie:)
                           withObject:a_outputFileURL
                        waitUntilDone:YES];
```

14. Because we want the App user to be able to take a still picture or record another movie, we complete the method implementation by enabling the buttons titled **Take Picture** and **Record**, and disabling the **Stop** button.

```
    // Reset the button states
    [self.m_recordButton setEnabled:YES];
    [self.m_stopButton setEnabled:NO];
    [self.m_takePictureButton setEnabled:YES];


}
```

15. Finally, we need to implement the method named `saveMovie:` which will either move the recorded movie to the location of the App user's choice, or delete the temporary movie if the App user decides not to keep it. The first thing we need to do is cache a reference to the default `NSFileManager` object as it will be used later in the method implementation.

```
// This method will be invoked on the
// main thread to save a movie
-(void)saveMovie:(NSURL*)a_url
{
    // Cache a reference to the NSFileManager
    NSFileManager* l_manager = [NSFileManager defaultManager];
```

16. Then we will create a new save panel and restrict it to saving MOV file types as follows:

```
// Create a new save panel
NSSavePanel *l_savePanel = [NSSavePanel savePanel];

// Restrict the save panel to
// MOV files
[l_savePanel setAllowedFileTypes:
 [NSArray arrayWithObject:@"mov"]];
```

17. Once the restricted save panel is created we will run it on the Apps window and it will wait for the user to either cancel or save the recorded movie file.

```
// Begin the save panel as a sheet on the
// window
[l_savePanel beginSheetModalForWindow:_window
                completionHandler:^(NSInteger result)
   {
```

18. If the **Save** button is clicked, the temporary movie file is moved to the permanent location selected by the App user.

```
    // If the Save button is pressed
    if (result == NSFileHandlingPanelOKButton)
    {
        // Write the JPG data to the URL
        [l_manager moveItemAtURL:a_url toURL:[l_savePanel
URL] error:nil];
    }
```

19. If anything other than the **Save** button is clicked, the temporary movie file is deleted.

```
    else
    {
        [l_manager removeItemAtURL:a_url error:nil];
    }
   }
  ];
}
```

What just happened?

We implemented the program code required to save a movie to disk. If we open the saved movie in Quicktime Player and look at the **Movie Inspector** window, we can see that both the audio and video are being saved in the camera's native, uncompressed format. The result will be very large movie files.

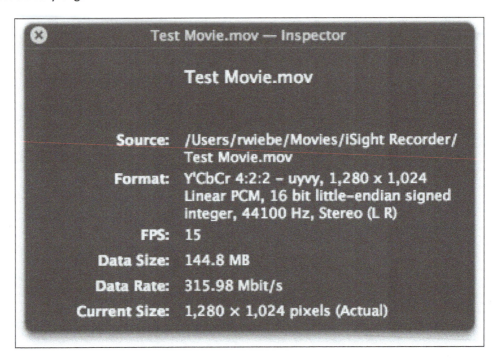

Have a go hero – replacing literals with symbols

The program code to save movie files contains some hard coded string literals such as @"mov" and @"yyyy-MM-dd hh.mm.ss". While this works, it is poor programming style to leave literal values in code. Any time we see a literal left in our code we should go back and replace it with a symbol. This is a good time to go through our code and use #define to create symbolic names for these literal values and replace the literal values in the program code with the newly defined symbols.

Capturing compressed movies to disk

Now that we have a working movie file output connected to our session and can capture a movie to a disk file, we will want to change the format of the saved movie from the native format of the camera to a standard compressed format. QTKit provides an object, `QTCompressionOptions`, to help us implement automatic compression during movie capture.

Time for action – saving a compressed movie

We are going to add two new pop-up menus to our App that will allow the user to select the audio and video compression methods that will be used when a movie file output is connected to our capture session. We will also add a checkbox that is used to enable or disable the selected compression options.

1. In the file named `MainMenu.xib`, select the **iSight Recorder** window.

2. In the **Size Inspector**, change the **Height** to `400` and the **Minimum Size Constraint Height** to `400`.

3. Add a checkbox titled **Compress** and two pop-up buttons below the buttons titled **Stop** and **Record**. It should look similar to the following screenshot:

4. In the file named `BTSAppDelegate.h`, add a new `@property` items of type `NSButton*` and name it `m_compressButton`.

5. Add two more properties of type `NSPopUpButton*` and name them `m_audioCompressionPopup` and `m_videoCompressionPopup`.

6. Use the **Assistant** editor to connect the newly defined properties from the `.h` file to the buttons in the `.xib` file.

7. In the file named `BTSAppDelegate.h`, `@synthesize` the accessors for the new button properties.

8. Then add the following program code to define the methods we will use to implement the menus:

```
// The methods for the compression menus
- (IBAction)compressButtonAction:(id)a_sender;
- (void) populateMenus;
```

9. Using the Assistant editor, connect from the checkbox titled **Compress** in the .xib file to the method named `compressButtonAction` in the .h file.

10. We are going to use Cocoa bindings to manage the content of the pop-up button menus. Cocoa bindings provide a convenient way to manage the content of menus when that content is provided using objects in an NSArray object. The first thing we need to do is add an NSArrayController object to the .xib file for each of the pop-up buttons.

11. Once the **Array Controller** objects have been added in the .xib file, we can use the **Identity Inspector** to name them **Video Compression Array Controller** and **Audio Compression Array Controller** respectively. It will look similar to the following screenshot:

12. Select the first pop-up button in the GUI and select the **Bindings Inspector**.

13. Click on the disclosure triangle beside the **Content Values** binding.

14. Tick the **Bind to:** checkbox and select **Video Compression Array Controller** from the pop-up menu.

15. In the **Model Key Path** field, enter **localizedDisplayName** as shown in the following screenshot:

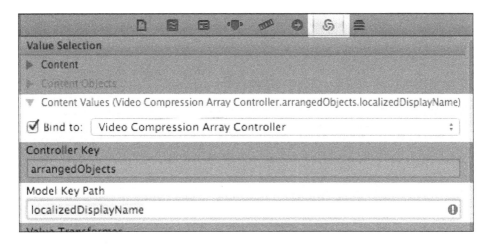

16. Click on the disclosure triangle beside the **Selected Index** binding.

17. Tick the **Bind to:** checkbox and select **Video Compression Array Controller** from the pop-up menu.

18. In the **Controller Key** field, enter `selectionIndex` as shown in the following screenshot:

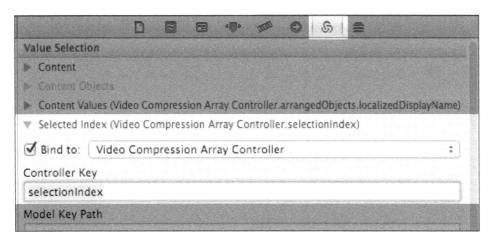

19. Repeat the process for the second pop-up button in the GUI, binding the attributes to the **Audio Compression Array Controller**.

20. In the file named `BTSAppDelegate.h`, add two new `@property` items of type `NSArrayController*` and name them `m_videoCompressionArrayController` and `m_audioCompressionArrayController` respectively.

21. Using the **Assistant** editor, make a connection from each of the new properties in the `.h` file to their respective `NSArrayController` objects in the `.xib` file.

22. Remember to `@synthesize` the array controller objects in the file named `BTSAppDelegate.m`.

23. In the file named `BTSAppDelegate.m`, in the method named `applicationDidFinishLaunching:` add the following code to invoke the method that will populate the pop-up button menus.

```
// Populate the compression format menus
[self populateMenus];
```

24. Now that we are invoking the method that populates the pop-up button menus, and they have been bound to the array controllers in the GUI, all we need to do is implement the method to populate the array controllers and our pop-up buttons will work. The QTKit framework will automatically provide us with the identifiers that we need for both video and audio compression. All of the different compression options that we ask for will be returned to us as an `NSArray` of `NSString` objects so the first thing we need to do is create a local variable to store the references the `NSArray` that will be returned.

```
#pragma mark -
#pragma mark - Set movie file compression

// The method that will populate the video and
// audio compression PopUp button menus
- (void) populateMenus
{
    // A reference to the array of returned
    // compression options
    NSArray* l_optionsIdentifiers;
```

25. Next, we need to ask the QTKit framework to give us all the identifiers for the video compression options that are available.

```
// Retrieve all the video compression
// options identifiers
l_optionsIdentifiers =
 [QTCompressionOptions
  compressionOptionsIdentifiersForMediaType:
  QTMediaTypeVideo];
```

26. Now that we have the list of identifiers, we can use them to retrieve the actual QTCompressionOptions objects. It is these QTCompressionOptions objects, that we will add to the video compression array controller.

```
// Add each video option to the video
// compression array controller
for (NSString* l_optionID in l_optionsIdentifiers)
{
    [m_videoCompressionArrayController
      addObject:
        [QTCompressionOptions
          compressionOptionsWithIdentifier:l_optionID]];
}
```

27. Then we repeat the process to retrieve the audio compression option identifiers and use the identifiers to add the actual QTCompressionOptions objects to the audio compression array controller.

```
// Retrieve all the audio compression
// options identifiers
l_optionsIdentifiers =
  [QTCompressionOptions
    compressionOptionsIdentifiersForMediaType:
      QTMediaTypeSound];

// Add each audio option to the audio
// compression array controller
for (NSString* l_optionID in l_optionsIdentifiers)
{
    [m_audioCompressionArrayController
      addObject:
        [QTCompressionOptions
          compressionOptionsWithIdentifier:l_optionID]];
}
```

28. Once the array controllers are populated, we want to select the first option (if we don't select the first option, the pop-up buttons will display the last option added and things will look a bit strange in our GUI).

```
// Select the first option for video and audio
[m_videoCompressionArrayController setSelectionIndex:0];
[m_audioCompressionArrayController setSelectionIndex:0];
```

29. Our App needs to take action when the user selects a compression option in the GUI. We can determine when a pop-up menu value changes by using key-value observing but first we need to define the key that we want to observe as a symbol in the file named `BTSAppDelegate.h`.

```
#define kBTS_SelectionIndex @"selectionIndex"
```

30. Once the key is defined, we complete the method implementation by using key-value observing to register our `BTSAppDelegate` object with both the audio and video array controllers using the `kBTS_SelectionIndex` property. This will result in the array controller objects invoking the method `observeValueForKeyPath:ofObject:change;context` on our `BTSAppDelegate` object whenever the PopUp button menu selections change.

```
// Use Key-value observing  to monitor the state
// of the selected video compression option
[m_videoCompressionArrayController
 addObserver:self
   forKeyPath: kBTS_SelectionIndex
     options:NSKeyValueObservingOptionNew
     context:nil];

// Use Key-value observing  to monitor the state
// of the selected audio compression option
[m_audioCompressionArrayController
 addObserver:self
   forKeyPath: kBTS_SelectionIndex
     options:NSKeyValueObservingOptionNew
     context:nil];

}
```

 Both bindings and key-value observing technologies are core components of the Mac OS X technology that provide us with very powerful mechanisms to link App components together using very little program code.

31. Since we are using key-value observing, we need to implement the method that will be called when an observed property changes. In this case, we know that the only observed properties are the compression options so we can simply invoke another method (which we will implement shortly) to attach the selected options to our capture session if the compression checkbox is enabled.

```
// The method that will be invoked when an
// observed value changes for the @"selectionIndex" key
- (void) observeValueForKeyPath:(NSString *)keyPath
```

```
                    ofObject:(id)object
                      change:(NSDictionary *)change
                     context:(void *)context
{

    // Is compression enabled
    if (NSOnState == [m_compressButton state])
    {
        // Invoke the method to set the video
        // and audio compression options
        [self setCaptureOptions];
    }

}
```

32. In addition to using key-value observing to determine what compression options have been selected, we need to implement the action method that will be invoked when the **[] Compress** checkbox changes in our GUI. Since this method will invoke the same `setCaptureOptions` method, we will implement it before we implement that method. This method will also invoke another new method, `clearCaptureOptions`, if compression is turned off.

```
// The action method that is invoked when the Compress
// checkbox value changes
- (IBAction)compressButtonAction:(id)a_sender
{
    // If compression is enabled
    if (NSOnState == [m_compressButton state])
    {
        // Set the compression options
        [self setCaptureOptions];
    }
    // Otherwise
    else
    {
        // Turn off compression
        [self clearCaptureOptions];
    }
}
```

33. Now we can implement the methods that do the actual work of clearing and setting the compression options on our capture setting. First, we will implement the method to clear the compression options. Clearing the options is achieved by setting the compression object on all of the connection objects to nothing, or `nil`.

```
// This method is invoked to clear any compression
// that may have been enabled on a capture session
-(void) clearCaptureOptions
{
    // Get the list of capture connections for the file output
    NSArray* l_connections = [m_CaptureMovieFileOutput
connections];

    // Stop the capture session
    [m_CaptureSession stopRunning];

    // For each of the connections
    for (QTCaptureConnection* l_connection in l_connections)
    {
        // Set the compression option to nil, which
        // turns compression off
        [m_CaptureMovieFileOutput
         setCompressionOptions:nil
         forConnection:l_connection];
    }

    // Restart the capture session
    [m_CaptureSession startRunning];

}
```

34. Finally, we complete the implementation with the `setCaptureOptions` method implementation. This method also iterates over all of the connections but this time it inspects the type of each connection and performs a different action depending on the type of the connection.

```
// This method is invoked to set any compression
// that may have been enabled on a caputure session
- (void) setCaptureOptions
{
    // Get the list of capture connections for the file output
    NSArray* l_connections = [m_CaptureMovieFileOutput
connections];

    // Stop the capture session
    [m_CaptureSession stopRunning];
```

```
    // For each of the connections
    for (QTCaptureConnection* l_connection in l_connections)
    {
        // Get the media type of the connection
        NSString *l_mediaType = [l_connection mediaType];
```

35. For video connections, the video compression options are set and for audio connections the audio compression options are set.

```
        // Is it video
        if (YES == [QTMediaTypcVideo isEqual: l_mediaType])
        {
            // Assign the selected video compression options
            [m_CaptureMovieFileOutput
             setCompressionOptions:
              [[m_videoCompressionArrayController
                selectedObjects] lastObject]
             forConnection:l_connection];
        }
        // Is it audio
        else if (YES == [QTMediaTypeSound isEqual: l_mediaType])
        {
            // Assign the selected audio compression options
            [m_CaptureMovieFileOutput
             setCompressionOptions:
              [[m_audioCompressionArrayController
                selectedObjects] lastObject]
             forConnection:l_connection];
        }

    }
```

36. The method implementation completes, as before, by restarting the capture session.

```
    // Restart the capture session
    [m_CaptureSession startRunning];

}
```

37. There is one other small thing that we can do to "fine tune" the user interface and that is to disable the compression GUI elements in `startRecording:` method and to enable them in the `stopRecording:` method.

What just happened?

We implemented the program code required to manage not only which compression options we will use but also whether or not compression is turned on. This allows us to turn compression on or off without the need to change the compression settings. We also obtained the list of compression options programmatically so that if they change in the future (for example, if Apple adds new compression options) we do not need to change our program code. Now when we turn on compression and capture a movie file we can see that it is much smaller and that it is, indeed, using the compression options that were selected in the GUI.

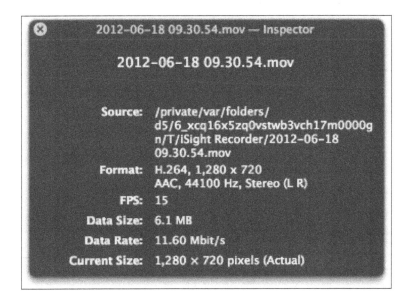

Summary

In this chapter, we have implemented an application that uses Quicktime Kit to capture still images and movies.

Specifically, we covered what Quicktime Kit is and how to capture audio and video previews. We also learned how to capture both still images and movie files. Finally, we looked at how to apply compression options to both the audio and video of captured movie files.

Now that we have seen how much control we have using Quicktime Kit and how easy it is to add connections to a capture session, we want to continue to explore the concept of video recording but this time as a full-screen App. We will see how to put an App into full-screen mode and explore how we may change the user's interaction with the App when it is in full-screen mode, and that will be the topic of our next chapter.

9

Video Recording – Full Screen iSight Recorder

In this chapter, we are going to continue exploring the iSight Recorder App by converting it to support full screen. There are several ways that an App can be modified to support full screen and depending on the method we choose we will also want to modify components of our user interface to provide a good full screen experience.

In this chapter, we shall learn the following:

- What is full screen mode?
- Enabling full screen mode
- Disabling auto layout
- Modifying our user interface to take advantage of full screen mode
- Customizing the full screen window size
- Customizing the full screen animation

What is the full screen mode?

Full Screen mode is a standardized protocol provided by Apple, introduced in Mac OS X 10.7, to support Apps that want to make use of the entire display rather than windows on the display. When an App enters full screen mode, the protocol automatically creates a new space for it and resizes the desired window or view to occupy the complete display. Historically, Apps that wanted this kind of interface have had to do all of the implementation in detail and different App developers have selected different mechanisms to achieve the full screen mode experience. By providing a standardized mechanism, Apple has recognized that there is a place for full screen Apps and they are encouraging App developers that have used non-standard implementation to migrate to the new standardized protocol for full screen.

Enabling the full screen mode

With some experience, you will find that most problems in software development have multiple solutions. Often, it's not that one way is better or worse than the other, they are just different ways of doing a similar thing.

Enabling the full screen mode on an Apps main window is one of those things that can be done programmatically (that is in code) or in the `.xib` file. At first glance, it would appear that both methods work equally well, but there is one major difference. If we enable full screen mode in program code, rather than in the `.xib` file, then the App will not launch in full screen even if the user quits while in full screen mode. We may or may not want that subtle difference in behavior, but we do need to be aware of it and make the correct choice for our needs.

Time for action – enabling full screen mode in iSight Recorder

We are now yet ready to enable the full screen mode for our iSight Recorder.

1. Open the **iSight Recorder** project in Xcode.
2. Select the `MainMenu.xib` file.
3. Select the `iSight Recorder` window.

4. In the **Attributes Inspector**, locate the **Full Screen** option and change the pop-up menu value from **Unsupported** to **Primary** as shown in the following screenshot:

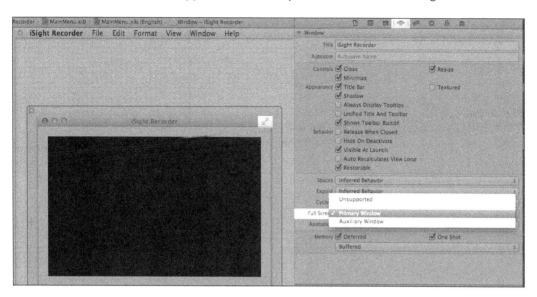

5. Click on the **Run** button to launch the **iSight Recorder** App.

6. Click on the full screen icon in the window drag bar to put the App into full screen mode. The following screenshot shows the full screen icon:

7. Quit the App.

8. Launch it again. Notice that this time it did launch in full screen, and then quit the App.

9. Modify the `.xib` file and set the **Full Screen** pop up back to **Unsupported**.

10. Select the file named `BTSAppDelegate.m` and in the method named `applicationDidFinishLaunching:` add the following program code:

```
- (void)applicationDidFinishLaunching:(NSNotification *)
aNotification
{
    // Insert code here to initialize your application

    // This App window supports Full Screen
    [_window setCollectionBehavior:
     NSWindowCollectionBehaviorFullScreenPrimary];
```

11. Click on the **Run** button to launch the **iSight Recorder** App.

12. Click on the full screen icon in the window drag bar to put the App into full screen mode.

13. Quit the **iSight Recorder** App.

14. Launch it again, and note that it did not launch in the full screen mode.

What just happened?

We modified the **iSight Recorder** App window to support full screen both in the .xib file and in the App Delegate. We noticed the subtle, but important difference between the two methods of enabling full screen mode support on a window. Because we always want our App to launch in a window and not the full screen mode, we will enable full screen mode in our App's program code and not in the .xib file.

Disabling auto layout

Mac OS X 10.7 introduced a new feature, called **Auto Layout**, that manages how our GUI items interact. While Auto Layout is powerful, it introduces an extra level of semantic complexity when we programmatically add and remove views from our windows. By default, Xcode always enables Auto Layout. To eliminate the semantic complexity of Auto Layout, since we don't need it, we can disable Auto Layout for our project and Xcode will revert to using **Autosizing**.

Time for action – using the traditional layout model

When we turn off Auto Layout in Xcode, we will need to configure our GUI elements using Autosizing layout.

1. Select the file named MainMenu.xib.

2. Select the **iSight Recorder** window.

3. In the **File Inspector**, disable the **Use Auto Layout** item, as shown in the following screenshot:

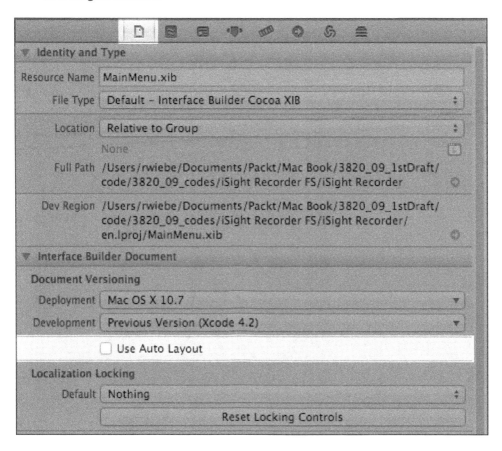

4. In the .xib file, select all of the GUI elements below the **Quicktime Capture View**.

5. From the **Editor** menu, select **Embed In**, and then select **Custom View**. This will take all of our buttons and sliders and embed them in a subview.

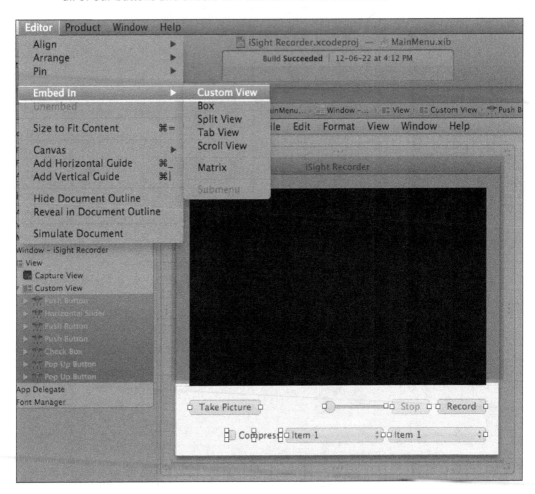

6. Because we are using **Autosizing**, we need to make some adjustments to the **Autosizing** properties of our GUI items in the **Size Inspector**. Select the Quicktime **Preview View** and then, using the **Size Inspector**, select all of the bars and arrows in the **Autosizing** box, as shown in the following screenshot:

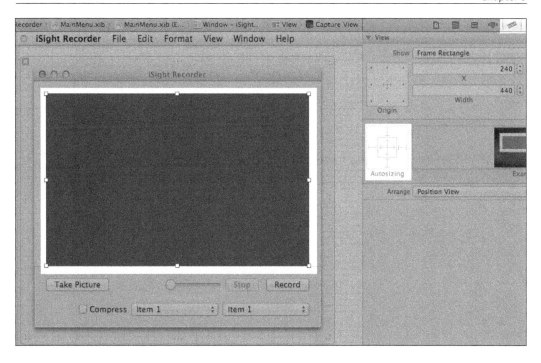

7. Select the custom view that contains all of the GUI controls and set its Autosizing attributes to match the following screenshot. This will change the **Autosizing** so that the view expands and contracts along the bottom of the window.

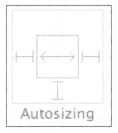

8. To keep the **Take Picture** button pinned to the top-left side of the **Custom View**, set its Autosizing attributes as shown in the following screenshot:

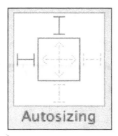

9. And finally, to pin the remaining GUI controls to the bottom-right side of the **Custom View**, set their Autosizing element as shown in the following screenshot:

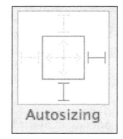

10. Use the `@property` and `@synthesize` directives to create a new `NSView` property named `m_controlsView` so that we can access the new custom view from our program code. Remember to include the `IBOutlet keyword` so that we can connect the program code to the object in the `.xib` file.

11. Use the **Assistant** editor to create a connection from `m_controlsView` in the `.h` file to the **Custom View** in the `.xib` file.

12. Click on the **Run** button and when the **iSight Recorder** launches, resize the window to make sure all of the controls behave as expected.

13. Click on the full screen icon in the **iSight Recorder** window to enter the full screen mode; the controls should all be in the correct place.

14. Press the *Esc* key on the keyboard to exit the full screen mode; the controls should all remain in the correct place.

What just happened?

We disabled Auto Layout on the `MainMenu.xib` file and configured our GUI elements using Autosizing. We did this because the semantics of using Auto Layout are much more complex (and powerful) than Autosizing but since we don't need the power provided by Auto Layout we prefer the simplicity of Autosizing. Reverting to Autosizing allows us to focus on the full screen aspect of our App rather than on the semantic complexity of Auto Layout.

Modifying our user interface to take advantage of full screen

Currently, when we enter full screen, our App's main window scales to fill the screen, the dock is hidden, and the menu bar auto hides. This accomplishes the first goal of full screen Apps which is to bring a single App into focus for the user. But we can make a few other user interface changes that will really enhance the full screen experience provided by our App. The first thing we can do is take the capture view and have it fill the screen so that the image being captured by the camera is the focus of attention. The second thing we can do is move our GUI buttons and sliders into a HUD window that floats on top of the capture view.

Time for action – refining how we enter and exit full screen

Refining the user interface is the part of App development where art takes over from science and everyone will have an opinion. These changes are an example of what can be done but are by no means meant to be the only possible solution. We are going to begin by moving our controls and animating the transition in to and out of full screen.

1. In the file named `MainMenu.xib`, add a HUD window that we will use to display our controls floating over the full screen view.

2. The HUD window should match the size needed to hold the controls subview. The easiest way to accomplish that is to do the following:
   - Select the subview in our main window
   - Copy it
   - Select the HUD window
   - Paste the subview into the HUD window
   - Resize the window to match the size of the subview
   - Delete the copy of the subview from the HUD window

3. Alternatively, we can select the HUD window and use the **Size Inspector** to set its **Width** and **Height** to `480` and `100` respectively.

4. In the **Size Inspector**, enable the **Minimum** and **Maximum** size constraints so that the window is not resizable.

5. In the **Attributes Inspector**, under the **Controls** section, disable **Close**.

6. It is very important that we don't allow the App user to close this window because it is configured to be released when it is closed which would result in our GUI Controls Custom Subview also being released, and a program crash when we exit from the full screen mode.

7. In the **Attributes Inspector**, change the Window title from `Window` to `Controls`.

8. As we do with every GUI element, we need to add `IBOutlet @property` in our `.h` file to create a reference to the item, the `@synthesize` in our `.m` file to generate the accessor methods, and use the **Assistant** editor to draw the connection between the code and the `.xib` file. Do that now for the HUD window and name the reference `m_HUDWindow`.

9. Because we are going to be implementing methods invoked as part of the `NSWindowDelegate` protocol, we need to change our App interface to tell Xcode (otherwise it will report warnings when we implement our methods). In the file named `BTSAppDelegate.h`, change the `@interface` declaration to include the `NSWindowDelegate` protocol as shown in the following code snippet:

```
@interface BTSAppDelegate : NSObject <NSApplicationDelegate,
                                      NSWindowDelegate>
```

10. We could edit the `.xib` file to indicate that our App is the window delegate but we can also do that in our program code. This is an example of how there are two equally correct methods of doing the same thing and how we choose to do it comes down to the preference of the App developer. In the file named `BTSAppDelegate.m`, in the method named `applicationDidFinishLaunching:`, add the following program code, to establish the relationship that our App is the delegate of its main window:

```
// This App is going to implement Full Screen methods
// so it need to be the window delegate
[_window setDelegate:self];
```

11. Because our `BTSAppDelegate.h` file is getting large, we are going to create a new file that is a category on `BTSAppDelegate`. This will allow us to implement the methods for the full screen mode in a separate file. From the **File** menu, select **New**, and then select the **File...** option.

12. For the template, under **Mac OS X**, select **Cocoa**, and then select **Objective-C category**.

13. Name the **Category** as `WindowDelegate` and make it a category on `BTSAppDelegate`.

14. Create the file and we should now have the files
`BTSAppDelegate+WindowDelegate.h` and
`BTSAppDelegate+WindowDelegate.m` visible in the project navigator.

15. Because instance variables cannot be created in category interfaces, we need to add the variables needed by the category in the file named `BTSAppDelegate.h` as follows:

```
// Our App handles the NSWindowDelegate protocol to
// support Full Screen
@interface BTSAppDelegate : NSObject <NSApplicationDelegate,
                                      NSWindowDelegate>

// ----- Reader challenge, skip one frame
{
    BOOL m_skipOneFrame;

    // The window delegate needs to remember
    // windowFrame and bounds rectangles
    NSRect m_windowFrame;
    NSRect m_viewBounds;
    NSRect m_viewFrame;

    // The window delegate needs to remember
    // controls view Frame and Bounds
    NSRect m_controlsViewBounds;
    NSRect m_controlsViewFrame;

}
```

16. Now in the file named `BTSAppDelegate+WindowDelegate.m`, add the code to hide the HUD window when the `.xib` file is loaded. We are going to hide and show the HUD window by fading it between fully transparent and fully visible, so hiding it is accomplished by fading it to fully transparent in the method named `awakeFromNib`.

```
// Initialize a few values when the nib has been loaded
- (void) awakeFromNib
{
    // Since the App always starts in windowed mode, it is
    // safe to always hide the HUD window by making it
    // transparent
    [self.m_HUDWindow setAlphaValue:0];

}
```

17. Now we can implement the program code that modifies the view frames and boundaries when the App is about to enter the full screen mode. This is done in the method named `windowWillEnterFullScreen` which is automatically invoked at that time.

```
// This method is automatically invoked on the
// WindowDelegate object when the window is preparing
// to enter full screen
- (void)windowWillEnterFullScreen:(NSNotification *)notification
{
```

18. The first thing the App needs to do is save the window frame and the Capture View frame, as well as the bounds of the Capture View so that they can be restored when the App exits the full screen mode:

```
// Save the current settings for the window and view
// frames and boundaries so that we can restore them later
m_windowFrame = [self.window frame];
m_viewFrame = [self.m_QTCaptureView frame];
m_viewBounds = [self.m_QTCaptureView bounds];
```

19. Similarly, the frame and bounds of the custom view that contains the GUI controls needs to be saved so that it can be restored later.

```
// Save the current frame and bounds of the custom view
// that contains the GUI so that we can restore them
//later
m_controlsViewFrame = [self.m_controlsView frame];
m_controlsViewBounds = [self.m_controlsView bounds];
```

20. Then we need to adjust the frame and the bounds of the Capture View so that the view completely covers the window. This will result in the view completely filling the screen when the App has entered the full screen mode.

```
// Scale the capture view frame up to fill the window
[self.m_QTCaptureView
  setFrame:NSMakeRect(0,
                      0,
                      m_windowFrame.size.width,
                      m_windowFrame.size.height)];

// Scale the capture view bounds up to fill the window
[self.m_QTCaptureView
  setBounds:NSMakeRect(0,
                       0,
                       m_windowFrame.size.width,
                       m_windowFrame.size.height)];
```

21. Finally, since there is no longer any room to display the capture controls in the main window, we need to remove the subview that contains the controls from the main window and add it to the HUD window.

```
// Remove the controls from the main window
[self.m_controlsView removeFromSuperview];

// Add the controls to the HUD window
[[self.m_HUDWindow contentView]
 addSubview:self.m_controlsView];

}
```

22. At this point, the views have been resized and moved but the HUD window is still invisible because we set its alpha value to 0. We can take advantage of another delegate method, named windowDidEnterFullScreen:, to change the alpha value to 1 which will result in the HUD window becoming visible.

```
// This method is automatically invoked on the
// WindowDelegate object when the window has
// entered full screen
- (void)windowDidEnterFullScreen:(NSNotification *)notification
{
    // Show the HUD Window
    [self.m_HUDWindow setAlphaValue:1];

}
```

23. Now, when our App enters full screen everything works as we would like and it's time to implement the program code that will reverse the process when the App exits full screen. There are two more delegate methods, named windowWillExitFullScreen: and windowDidExitFullScreen:, that we can use. First, we need to hide the HUD window when the App is preparing to exit the full screen mode.

```
// This method is automatically invoked on the
// WindowDelegate object when the window is preparing
// to exit full screen
- (void)windowWillExitFullScreen:(NSNotification *)notification
{
    // Hide the HUD Window
    [self.m_HUDWindow setAlphaValue:0];
}
```

24. Finally, once the App is completely out of the full screen mode, we need to restore the views to their original states.

```
// This method is automatically invoked on the
// WindowDelegate object when the window has
// exited full screen
- (void)windowDidExitFullScreen:(NSNotification *)notification
{
```

25. First, we remove the custom view that contains our controls from the HUD window, resize the view using the save frame and bounds, and add it back to the main window as follows:

```
// Remove the controls from the HUD Window
[self.m_controlsView removeFromSuperview];

// Restore the custom view to its original size
[self.m_controlsView setFrame:m_controlsViewFrame];
[self.m_controlsView setBounds:m_controlsViewBounds];

// Add the controls to the main window
[self.window.contentView addSubview:self.m_controlsView];
```

26. Then, we restore the Capture View to its original location and size as follows:

```
// Restore the Capture View to its original size
[self.m_QTCaptureView setFrame:m_viewFrame];
[self.m_QTCaptureView setBounds:m_viewBounds];
```

27. Finally, rather than have the controls just appear on the main window we start a short animation to fade the controls in as follows:

```
// Hide the Controls
[self.m_controlsView setAlphaValue:0];

// Start an animation to cause the controls to fade in
[[self.m_controlsView animator] setAlphaValue:1.0];



}
```

What just happened?

We completed the first part of our interface refinement by managing the transitions in to and out of the full screen mode. We did this by implementing the program code needed to move our App's buttons and sliders between the main App window and a HUD style window. We also scaled the Quicktime Capture View to the desired size depending on whether or not our App is in the full screen mode.

Time for action – refining text colors

The next part of the interface that we want to change is the color of the text for the checkbox. While the text looks fine in a standard window, it is difficult to read black text on the black background of a HUD window. While the NSButton object does not contain its own method for setting text color, we can use what we have learned about Categories to create our own method.

1. The first thing that we need to do is create a new file using the **Objective-C category** template. We will call our category TextColor and it will be a category on **NSButton**. Do that now. The result should be that two new files, named NSButton+TextColor.h and NSButton+TextColor.m, will be created and displayed in the project navigator.

2. In the file named NSButton+TextColor.h, add the following program code to declare the interface method that can be invoked on an NSButton to set its text color.

```
@interface NSButton (TextColor)

// The method to set the text color
- (void)setTextColor:(NSColor *)textColor;


@end
```

3. In the file named NSButton+TextColor.m, add the following program code to implement the setTextColor: method.

```
// This method applies the passed color
// to the attributed title string
- (void)setTextColor:(NSColor *)a_Color
{
```

4. Start the implementation by making a mutable copy of the buttons attributed title.

```
// Create a mutable copy of the title
NSMutableAttributedString *l_attrTitle =
[[self attributedTitle] mutableCopy];
```

5. Continue by determining the length of the title string and applying the new font color to the entire title.

```
// Create a range corresponding to the length
// of the attributed string
NSRange l_range =
 NSMakeRange(0, [l_attrTitle length]);

// Add a foreground color attribute to the
// attributed string using the provided color
[l_attrTitle
 addAttribute:NSForegroundColorAttributeName
        value:a_Color
        range:l_range];
```

6. Complete the implementation by setting the new title string.

```
// Set the title
[self setAttributedTitle:l_attrTitle];
}
```

> **Categories can be added to any object**
>
> We can create categories on any object, regardless of whether or not we have the program source code that implements the object. This means we can extend the behavior of any object provided by any framework.

7. To use our new category we need to import its interface definition in the file named BTSAppDelegate+WindowDelegate.m so that the window delegate knows about the new method named setTitleColor:.

```
//  Created by rwiebe on 12-06-22.

//  Copyright (c) 2012 BurningThumb Software. All rights reserved.

//


#import "BTSAppDelegate+WindowDelegate.h"

#import "NSButton+TextColor.h"


@implementation BTSAppDelegate (WindowDelegate)
```

8. Then, in the method named `windowWillEnterFullScreen:`, we need to add one line of program code to change the text color to white.

```
// Change the checkbox text color to white
[self.m_compressButton setTextColor:[NSColor whiteColor]];
```

9. In the method named `windowDidExitFullScreen:`, we need to add one line of program code to change the text color to the default control text color.

```
// Restore the checkbox text color
[self.m_compressButton setTextColor:[NSColor
controlTextColor]];
```

What just happened?

We added a Category to the `NSButton` class so that we could set the color of the text displayed by an `NSButton` object.

Time for action – refining controls using fading

For some categories of full screen Apps, we may want components of the GUI to simply fade away if the mouse is not moved. We can do this in our iSight Recorder App by using a custom subview to monitor mouse moved events.

1. First, we need to create a new file that uses the **Mac OS X Objective-C class** template.

2. We can refer to the new class as **BTSViewController** and make it a subclass of **NSView**.

3. After we create the class files we need to assign it, in the `.xib` file, to the **Custom Class** of the content view of the iSight Recorder window.

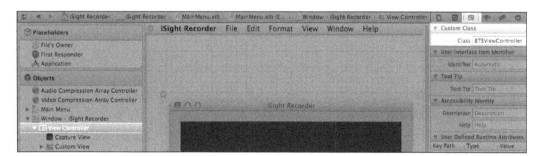

Receiving mouseMoved events

The conditions under which a view receives mouseMoved events are that the window accepts mouseMoved events and that the view accepts first responder. It is a simple set of conditions but since by default neither condition is true, the program code required to enable a view to receive mouseMoved events eludes many programmers.

4. We can use the acceptsFirstResponder method in our NSView subclass to satisfy both the conditions required for the view to receive mouse-moved events. It simply needs to invoke setAcceptsMouseMovedEvents:YES on its window, and return YES.

```
// The view MUST return YES if it wants
// mouseMoved events
- (BOOL)acceptsFirstResponder
{

    return YES;
}
```

5. Now that our view will receive the mouse-moved events whenever the window accepts them, we can complete the implementation of the subclass by having it forwarding mouse-moved events to the App delegate, as shown in the following program code. It will be the responsibility of the App delegate to know what to do with these events.

```
// This method is invoke automatically whenever the
// mouse moves
- (void)mouseMoved: (NSEvent*)a_event
{
    // Just forward the event to the App Delegate
    // It knows what to do when the mouse moves
    [[NSApp delegate] mouseMoved:a_event];
}
```

6. In the App Delegate, we are going to use an NSTimer object to determine if the GUI Controls window can fade out. So we need to add a new #define and @property to the file named BTSAppDelegate.h.

```
// Define how long to wait for mouse movement
#define D_BTS_FADE_TIME 10

// Use this property to manage the timer object
@property (strong) NSTimer* m_fadeTimer;
```

7. Remember to `@synthesize` the `m_fadeTimer` accessor methods in file named `BTSAppDelegate.m`.

8. In our `WindowDelegate`, we are going to implement a method, named `handleFadeEvent`, that knows what to do when the mouse is moved so for now we (having faith that it will "do the right thing") will invoke it as needed. The first place that it is needed is in the `windowDidEnterFullScreen:` method. We need to change this method so that the view will receive mouse-moved events and we also need to invoke our `handleFadeEvent` because we want to start the fade time as soon as we enter the full screen mode. The method needs to be changed as shown in the following code snippet:

```
- (void)windowDidEnterFullScreen:(NSNotification *)notification
{
    // Show the HUD Window
    [self.m_HUDWindow setAlphaValue:1];

    // When in full screen the mouse needs to be tracked
    // so we enable acceptance of mouse moved events
    [self.window setAcceptsMouseMovedEvents:YES];

    // Showing the HUD Window is a Fade event so we
    // handle it here
    [self handleFadeEvent];

}
```

9. When we exit from the full screen mode, we don't need a mouse-moved event. So in the `windowWillExitFullScreen:` method, we can add the following line of code to disable the forwarding of mouse-moved events:

```
    // When not in full screen the mouse does not need to be
    // tracked
    [self.window setAcceptsMouseMovedEvents:NO];
```

10. Whenever the user clicks on the GUI Controls HUD window it will become the key window and effectively be pinned. It will not fade. When the user clicks back on the full screen window, the full screen window will become key and it will need to start tracking mouse-moved events again. The window delegate will be notified when this happens and it needs to handle this click just like a mouse-moved event.

```
// This method is invoked automatically whenever our
// window becomes the key window
- (void)windowDidBecomeKey:(NSNotification *)notification
{
    // Just handle the event
    [self handleFadeEvent];
}
```

11. The window delegates implementation of `mouseMoved:` is similarly trivial, it just invokes the `handleFadeEvent` method.

```
// This method is invoked by our custom NSView subclass
// whenever it receives a mouse moved event
- (void)mouseMoved: (NSEvent*)a_event
{
    // Just handle the event
    [self handleFadeEvent];
}
```

12. Next, we can implement the `handleFadeEvent` method.

```
// This is invoked when:
// -- The window becomes full screen
// -- The window becomes key
// -- The mouse moves
- (void) handleFadeEvent
{
```

13. The first thing it does is cancel any timer that may already be running because it is going to, if needed, start a new timer.

```
// If a timer is running, cancel it
if (self.m_fadeTimer)
{
    [self.m_fadeTimer invalidate];
    self.m_fadeTimer = NULL;
}
```

14. Next, it checks to see if the window is in the full screen mode. If the window is not in full screen nothing else needs to happen.

```
// If its a Full Screen window
if ( self.window.styleMask & NSFullScreenWindowMask)
{
```

15. Since the window is in the full screen mode, and a fade event occurred, the HUD window should be visible so its alpha is set to `1.0`.

```
// Display the controls
[self.m_HUDWindow setAlphaValue:1];
```

16. Since the HUD window is visible, and the window is in the full screen mode, a timer is started. When the timer counts down to zero it will invoke the method named `handleTimer:`, which will, in turn, fade out the HUD Controls window.

```
// Start a fade timer
self.m_fadeTimer =
[NSTimer scheduledTimerWithTimeInterval:D_BTS_FADE_TIME
```

```
                            target:self
                             selector:@selector(handleTimer:)
                              userInfo:nil
                              repeats:NO];
        }
    }
```

17. Finally, we implement the `handleTimer:`, method. Very simply put, if the Capture View window is key, then the HUD control window will fade out.

```
// If the NSTimer object counts down to zero then this
// method will be invoked
- (void) handleTimer: (id) a_object
{
    // If the GUI Controls window was clicked it will be key
    // so we don't want it to fade
    if (self.window.isKeyWindow)
    {
        // If the GUI controls window was not clicked the
        // capture view will be key so fade the Controls out
        [[self.m_HUDWindow animator] setAlphaValue:0];
    }

}
```

What just happened?

We tracked mouse-moved events and used them in conjunction with an NSTimer object to fade the HUD Controls window in and out based on the movement of the mouse. We have now completed the interface refinements that we wanted to make.

Have a go hero – implementing a textColor getter for NSButton

Typically, when we implement a setter, like `setTextColor:`, we also implement the getter, like `textColor`. In the case of an attributed string each character could, in theory, be a different color so a getter that just returned a single color would need to be some kind of compromise, for example, it could return the color of just the first character in the range. Think about how you may go about developing the `textColor` getter for the `TextColor` category on `NSButton` and implement it now. Remember to do the following:

- Add the method definition to the interface file
- Think about what to return if the button has no title or the title is blank
- Figure out how to use the `fontAttributesInRange:` method to get the attributes for just the first character of the attributed string

Customizing the full screen window size

The standard, default, full screen animation scales the window up to fill the screen. We may decide that, in order to give our full screen App some depth, we don't want to fill the entire screen.

Time for action – adding a full screen window that has depth

If the size of the full screen window is less than the size of the screen then a background pattern will be visible and the full screen window will cast a shadow. The result is a full screen App with a window that still provides an illusion of depth.

1. The first thing we need to do is create a `#define` that specifies the size of the border around our window.

```
// Define the size of the border around the window
#define BTS_WINDOW_BORDER 100
```

2. It's also a good idea to define a minimum size that is acceptable.

```
// Define the minimum acceptable size
#define BTS_MIN_WIDTH 320
#define BTS_MIN_HEIGHT 240
```

3. Then we need to override the window delegate method `window:willUseFullScreenContentSize:proposedSize` and have it return our calculated window size.

```
- (NSSize)window:(NSWindow *)window willUseFullScreenContentSize:(NSSize)proposedSize
{
```

4. The window size that we want to use is the proposed size plus the defined border.

```
// calculate the desired window size
NSSize l_windowSize =
 NSMakeSize(proposedSize.width -  BTS_WINDOW_BORDER ,
           proposedSize.height - BTS_WINDOW_BORDER );
```

5. It is possible, though unlikely, that the size we calculate is smaller than the minimum size. If that does turn out to be the case then we will return the smaller of the minimum size and the proposed size (just in case the proposed size was even smaller).

```
// If the desired size is smaller than the
// minimum acceptable size use minimum acceptable
// size bounded by the proposed size
if ((l_windowSize.width < BTS_MIN_WIDTH ) ||
    (l_windowSize.height < BTS_MIN_HEIGHT))
{
    l_windowSize =
     NSMakeSize(MIN(BTS_MIN_WIDTH,  proposedSize.width),
               MIN(BTS_MIN_HEIGHT, proposedSize.height));
}
```

6. And finally, we just return the calculated value, which we expect to be the screen size minus the border size.

```
// Return the result.
return l_windowSize;
}
```

What just happened?

We created a window that does not fill the entire screen when the App enters the full screen mode. Instead there will be a border around the window and a shadow in the border space. This adds depth to our full screen App.

Have a go hero – playing with the border define

Change the value of the D_BTS_WINDOW_BORDER define, use some very large values, some very small values, even some negative values and put the App into the full screen mode to see how it behaves with various border sizes.

Does the program behave correctly for all the values that you try?

Customizing the full screen animation

If we do nothing at all, the system will scale our window up as it moves it to its own space for full screen display. If we like, we can create our own animation to move the window in sync with the system animation.

To create our own full screen animation, we need to implement four methods in our window delegate as follows:

- ◆ `customWindowsToEnterFullScreenForWindow:`
- ◆ `window:startCustomAnimationToEnterFullScreenWithDuration:`
- ◆ `customWindowsToExitFullScreenForWindow:`
- ◆ `window:startCustomAnimationToExitFullScreenWithDuration:`

Time for action – customizing the full screen animation

We are now ready to implement the program code that customizes the full screen animation.

1. The first thing we can do is implement the methods that return the list of windows to be animated. It's important to understand that it is acceptable to animate more than one window into full screen, which is why the methods return an NSArray of NSWindow objects. Having said that, in our iSight Recorder App, we will only be animating a single window so we simply return an NSArray that contains the single window object.

```
// Return the list of windows in the custom animation for
// entering full screen
- (NSArray *)customWindowsToEnterFullScreenForWindow:
  (NSWindow *)a_window
{
    // Just our window
    return [NSArray arrayWithObjects:a_window, nil];
}
```

```
// Return the list of windows in the custom animation for
// exiting full screen
- (NSArray *)customWindowsToExitFullScreenForWindow:
  (NSWindow *)a_window
{
    // Just our window
    return [NSArray arrayWithObjects:a_window, nil];
}
```

2. Now, we need to implement the delegate method to animate the transition to enter the full screen mode.

```
// This method is automatically invoked to allow us to
// Synchronize out custom animation with the system animation
- (void)window:(NSWindow *)a_window
        startCustomAnimationToEnterFullScreenWithDuration:
          (NSTimeInterval)a_duration
{
```

3. First we save the window frame so that the method to exit from the full screen mode can restore the original frame.

```
// Save the window frame so that it can be restored later
m_windowFrame = self.window.frame;
```

4. Then we update the window style mask to indicate the window is in full screen. We do this so that when we test to see if the window is in the full screen mode we get the correct result.

```
// Make sure the window style mask includes the
// full screen bit
[a_window setStyleMask:([a_window styleMask] |
                        NSFullScreenWindowMask)];
```

5. Now we get the windows screen. It is possible there are multiple monitors attached to the Mac and we want the animation to occur on the screen for this window.

```
// Get the first screen
NSScreen *l_screen = self.window.screen;
```

6. Then we calculate the final frame size and position on the screen.

```
// The final, full screen frame
NSRect l_finalFrame;

// Invoke the delegate to get the custom frame size
l_finalFrame.size =
 [self window:a_window
       willUseFullScreenContentSize:l_screen.frame.size];
```

```
// Calculate the origin as half the difference between
// the window frame and the screen frame
l_finalFrame.origin.x +=
  floor((NSWidth(l_screen.frame) -
         NSWidth(l_finalFrame)) / 2);

l_finalFrame.origin.y +=
  floor((NSHeight(l_screen.frame) -
         NSHeight(l_finalFrame)) / 2);
```

7. And we calculate center frame for the window which will be used during the first half of the animation.

```
// The center frame for the window is used during
// the 1st half of the fullscreen animation and is
// the window at its original size but moved to the
// center of its eventual full screen frame.
NSRect l_centerWindowFrame = [a_window frame];

l_centerWindowFrame.origin.x =
  l_finalFrame.size.width / 2 -
  l_centerWindowFrame.size.width / 2;

l_centerWindowFrame.origin.y =
  l_finalFrame.size.height / 2 -
  l_centerWindowFrame.size.height / 2;
```

8. We also need to make a slight adjustment to our custom animation, making it just slightly shorter than the system animation with which it is being synchronized to avoid a flash that will otherwise occur at the end of the animation. In the file named BTSAppDelegate+WindowDelegate.h, create the following two defines:

```
// Define the number of custom animation steps
#define D_BTS_DURATION_ADJUSTMENT 0.1
#define D_BTS_ANIMATION_STEPS 2
```

9. Now, back in the file named BTSAppDelegate+WindowDelegate.m, continue implementing the program code as follows:

```
// Our animation must be slightly shorter than
// the system animation to avoid a black flash
// at the end of the animation -- seems like a bug
a_duration -= D_BTS_DURATION_ADJUSTMENT;

// Our animation will be broken into two steps.
```

10. Finally, we can begin the animation steps as follows:

```
[NSAnimationContext
 runAnimationGroup:^(NSAnimationContext *l_context)
{
```

11. The first step is to move the window to the center of the screen.

```
// First, we move the window to the center
// of the screen
[l_context setDuration:a_duration / D BTS_ANIMATION_
STEPS];
[[a_window animator]
  setFrame:l_centerWindowFrame display:YES];



}
```

12. When the first step completes, we can start the second step as follows:

```
completionHandler:^
{
```

13. The second step, which completes the implementation of the method, is to scale the frame to its full size.

```
[NSAnimationContext
 runAnimationGroup:^(NSAnimationContext *l_context)
 {
// and then we enlarge it its full size.
[l_context setDuration:a_duration/ D_BTS_ANIMATION_
STEPS];
  [[a_window animator] setFrame:l_finalFrame
display:YES];


}
   completionHandler:^
   {
   }
 ];
}
];
}
```

14. Now, we need to reverse the process and implement the delegate method to animate the transition to exit the full screen mode:

```
// This method is automatically invoked to allow us to
// Synchronize out custom animation with the system animation
- (void) window:(NSWindow *)window
      startCustomAnimationToExitFullScreenWithDuration:
        (NSTimeInterval)duration
{
```

15. First, we update the window style mask to indicate the window is not in the full screen mode. Note the ~ character in front of the literal named NSFullScreenWindowMask indicates not. We do this so that when we test to see if the window is in the full screen mode we get the correct result.

```
// Make sure the window style mask does not
// include full screen bit
[window setStyleMask:([window styleMask] &
                      ~NSFullScreenWindowMask)];
```

16. Then we calculate the centered frame based on the window's original size, which was saved by the custom animation to enter the full screen mode.

```
// The center frame for the window is used during
// the 1st half of the fullscreen animation and is
// the window at its original size but moved to the
// center of its eventual full screen frame.
NSRect l_centerWindowFrame = m_windowFrame;
l_centerWindowFrame.origin.x =
 window.frame.size.width / 2 -
 m_windowFrame.size.width / 2;

l_centerWindowFrame.origin.y =
 window.frame.size.height / 2 -
 m_windowFrame.size.height / 2;
```

17. Finally, we can begin the animation steps as follows:

```
// Our animation will be broken into two stages.
[NSAnimationContext
 runAnimationGroup:^(NSAnimationContext *context)
 {
```

18. The first step will scale the window down to the original size that was saved by the custom animation step to enter the full screen mode.

```
// First, we'll restore the window to its original size
// while centering it
[context setDuration:duration / D_BTS_ANIMATION_STEPS];
[[window animator]
```

```
            setFrame:l_centerWindowFrame display:YES];

    }
        completionHandler:^
        {
            [NSAnimationContext
             runAnimationGroup:^(NSAnimationContext *context)
             {
```

19. The second step, which completes the implementation of the method, will move the window back to the original position that was saved by the custom animation step to enter the full screen mode.

```
                // And then we'll move it back to its initial
                // position.
                [context setDuration:duration / D_BTS_ANIMATION_
STEPS];

                [[window animator]
                 setFrame:m_windowFrame display:YES];


            }
                completionHandler:^
                {
                }
            ];


        }
    ];
}
```

What just happened?

We implemented the window delegate methods needed to show our custom animation to enter and exit the full screen mode.

Have a go hero – creating your own custom animation

The custom animation can be anything that we would like it to be. The position and size of the window and even the number of animation steps can change. Make some changes to the custom animation and run the App to see what kind of custom animation you can come up with.

Summary

In this chapter, we have converted a window based App to a full screen App, including adding a custom animation for entering and exiting the full screen mode.

Specifically, we covered what is full screen and how it can be enabled for an App window, how to use Autosizing instead of Auto Layout to control the relationships between GUI items, how we may modify our Apps interface when the App user enters the full screen mode, and how to customize the full screen window size and animation.

Of course after we develop our App and we find it useful we may decide that we want to share our App. We can give copies to our friends, we can post copies on the Internet, but the best way to distribute a Mac App is through Apple's Mac App store. And how to share our App will be the topic of the next chapter.

10
Sharing Our App with Others – Becoming a Mac Developer

In this chapter, we are going to examine what it means to become a registered Mac App developer. We will look at the developer program, its costs and benefits, and how we can take advantage of the program to place our App in the Mac App store so that we can share it with the world.

In this chapter we shall learn the following:

- What is the Mac developer program?
- What are the benefits of joining the Mac developer program?
- Step by step developer program sign up
- What are the additional developer tools?
- What is code signing?
- What is Gatekeeper?
- Signing an App with a Developer ID

What is the Mac developer program?

The Mac developer program is a paid program that anyone who wants to develop and distribute Mac Apps can sign up for on the Apple website. For a nominal annual fee, membership in the program entitles us to a variety of services provided directly by Apple Inc. that are designed to help us develop and distribute Mac Apps.

 The Mac developer program is not the same as the iOS developer program. Developers who want to develop Apps for Apple's mobile platform need to sign up for the iOS developer program. If we want to develop and distribute software for both the Mac and iOS then we would need to sign up for both developer programs.

What are the benefits of joining the Mac developer program?

When we register as a Mac developer, which is free, we automatically get access to some great resources, which include the following:

◆ Access to Development Videos, including World Wide Developer Conferences sessions.

◆ Access to the Mac OS X Developer Library.

◆ Access to the Apple bug reporter system.

◆ Access to pre-release (beta) software.

◆ The opportunity to join a paid developer program.

It only makes sense to join a paid developer program if the benefits out weigh the costs (which can be as low as $99/year). The benefits we get by joining the Mac developer program are as follows:

❑ Access to developer forums

❑ Code level technical support

❑ Access to iCloud services

❑ A developer ID for Gatekeeper

❑ The ability to distribute our App through the Mac App store

Access to Development Videos, including World Wide Developer Conferences sessions

Apple produces many developer level videos, but the best of these are the videos of the World Wide Developer Conference sessions. Access to these session videos is an excellent developer benefit.

Access to the Mac OS X Developer Library

The Mac OS X Developer Library includes articles, guides, references, technical notes, sample code, and more. It is an essential resource for Mac OS X App development.

Access to the Apple bug reporter system

Whenever we are dealing with pre-release software, we are going to find problems. When we find problems, we can report them to Apple and have them fixed. But there is more to the bug reporter system than that. We may find bugs in the shipping version of Mac OS X, or in an App (like Safari) that is developed by Apple. We can report those bugs using the bug reporter and Apple may issue an interim fix to correct the problem. Finally, we can use the bug reporter system to request enhancements – we may have a great idea but we need the Mac OS to provide something for us to help bring our idea to market. We can log in to the bug reporter system and explain what we need and why, potentially influencing the direction of Mac OS X itself.

Access to pre-release (beta) software

The Mac Dev Center provides us with access to unreleased Apple software. This includes, but is not limited to, the next release of Mac OS X, the next release of Mac OS X Server, the next release of the Xcode developer tools, the next release of Safari, the next release of Java, and various developer and debugging tools. This access allows us to develop Apps that take advantage of new Mac OS features before they are publicly released so that as soon as Apple release the Mac OS, our Apps are ready to go.

The opportunity to join a paid developer program

By joining one of Apple's paid developer programs, we can receive even more benefits from the Apple developer team.

Access to developer forums

Because we have access to beta software, we will be under nondisclosure, which means we cannot discuss the software in public forums. Apple have private, developer only forums, where we can discuss any issues that we may be having with other developers who may have a solution for our problem. Of course, we can discuss anything with other developers on these forums, not just items under non-disclosure, and so they are a truly valuable resource for programmers of all experience levels.

Code level technical support

Sometimes we hit a problem with our code that we just cannot figure out. It could be a bug, it could be that the documentation is not clear, or it could be that we have not understood something completely. With code level technical support we can send our program code to Apple and they will have a technical support engineer to look at our code and help us overcome the problem.

Access to iCloud services

If we want to develop an App that takes advantage of any iCloud services, we must join the Mac (or iOS) developer program. There is no other option.

A developer ID for gatekeeper

If we want to develop an App and distribute it outside of the App store, while still providing our App users with a sense of security, we can use our developer ID with gatekeeper. Provided we have signed our App with our gatekeeper developer ID folks can download it and install it with confidence.

The ability to distribute our App through the Mac App store

If we want to distribute an App through the Mac App store, we must join the Mac developer program. There is no other option.

Step by step developer program sign up

Now that we know the benefits of joining the Mac developer program, let's get started.

Time for action – joining the Mac developer program

Joining the Mac developer program is easy and free – just follow the given steps:

1. Launch Safari.

2. Go to the URL `http://developer.apple.com/`.

3. Select the **Mac Dev Center** option.

4. Click on the **Register** button.

5. If you have an Apple ID (iTunes login, iCloud login, Apple online store account, and so on) click on the **Sign In** button, otherwise click on the **Create an Apple ID** button.

> **Business Developers Note**
>
> If you intend to enroll in a paid Developer Program for business purposes, you may prefer to create a new Apple ID that is dedicated to your business transactions and used for accounting purposes with Apple. If your Apple ID is associated with an existing iTunes Connect account, please create a new Apple ID to avoid accounting and reporting issues.

6. Click the **Continue** button.

> If you need to create an Apple ID follow the steps required to do so – they are not shown here. It is assumed at this point that you have a valid Apple ID.

7. Complete your **Personal Profile** and click the **Continue** button.

8. Complete your **Professional Profile** and click the **Continue** button.

9. Click on the checkbox to agree to the terms of the Legal agreement and click on the **I Agree** button.

10. Verify your e-mail address.

11. The final webpage will display indicating that we have successfully joined the Mac App developer program. Click the **Continue** button.

What just happened?

We successfully registered as a Mac App developer and joined the Mac developer program. This is how your screen looks after you log in:

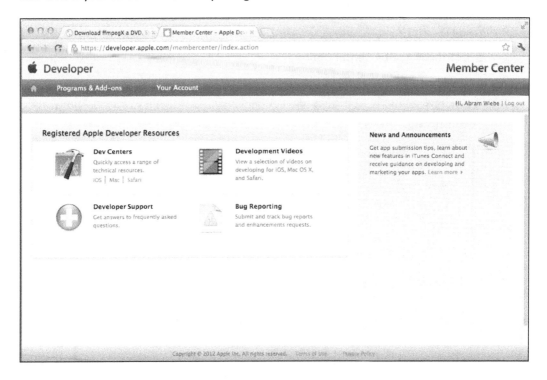

More developer tools

The primary developer tool that we will use is Xcode, which includes some additional bundled developer tools:

- **Instruments**
- **File Merge**
- **Open GL ES Performance Detective**
- **Application Loader**

Time for action – accessing the online developer tools

In addition to the bundled tools, there is a menu item called **More Developer Tools**, which will take us to the member only developer website.

1. Launch Xcode.

2. From the **Xcode** menu, select **Open Developer Tools** then select **More Developer Tools...** as shown in the following screenshot:

3. If you are not already logged in, log in to the Member site when the webpage is presented.

4. Explore the additional developer tools that are available to registered developers.

What just happened?

We discovered that there are many other developer tools that are available, including Command Line tools, Dashcode tools, Graphics tools, Hardware tools, and more, for registered developers.

What is code signing?

Code signing is about identifying who created code and resources and that they have not been modified by an unauthorized third party—nothing more and nothing less.

The code signing mechanism wraps executable images and resources, using a cryptographic seal, so that they can be reliably recognized, and any modifications made after the items are sealed can be detected.

Since code is signed, and it could be signed by anybody, the code signing mechanism also needs some way to know who signed the code.

In a nutshell, the code signing mechanism takes our developer identity (which resides in our Keychain), combines it with our final App code bundle, and produces signed code. The important thing about signed code is that it does not change. It is this signed code that we deliver to the end user. We can deliver the signed code to the end user via the Mac App store, via direct download, on a USB dongle, on a CD or DVD. The method of delivery is not important, it is only the fact the signed code does not change that is important.

On the end user's machine, when the App tries to run, it is first fed to the code signing verification component of Mac OS X. The verification component checks to ensure the code has not changed since it was signed. In addition, it checks to ensure the code was signed by us, and not by someone else.

For use with the Mac App store, Apple already provides us with ID certificates. These IDs are supposed to be restricted to Apps that ship via the App store.

In addition, Apple has created new Developer ID certificates that are intended for use outside of the Mac App store. These new Developer IDs are separate and distinct from the Mac App store IDs.

So the fundamental difference is? With the App Store IDs, we submit signed Apps to Apple, they verify them and re-sign them with their App store identity and then distribute them via the App store. With Developer IDs, we sign our Apps with our developer ID and distribute them any way we want. If we choose to distribute the same App using both mechanisms, Mac OS X is smart enough to recognize that it is the same App.

What is Gatekeeper?

Gatekeeper is a new system service available in Mac OS X 10.8 and later. Gatekeeper looks at downloaded programs to determine if they have been signed by a known developer identity and then either tells the user that the program was downloaded and makes sure they want to run it (if it was signed with a known developer ID) or tells the user that the program is from an unknown developer and does not provide the option to run it.

The only way a user of Mac OS X 10.8 will be able to run an App that is not signed, or that is signed by an unknown developer, is to turn the Gatekeeper off. Since it is unlikely that users will turn Gatekeeper off, if we want to share our App with others we need to sign it with a known Developer ID. Provided we are a member of the developer program, Apple will provide us with a Developer ID so that we can distribute trusted Apps outside of the App store.

Finally, if an App is modified (hacked or corrupted) after it has been signed, Gatekeeper will tell the user that the program is damaged and suggest they move it to the Trash. There will be no way for the user to run an App that has been modified after it has been signed.

Signing an App with a Developer ID

The first thing that we need to do is join the Mac OS X developer program and pay the annual fee. We will need to renew our membership each year in order to maintain the validity of our Developer ID.

Once we have joined the Mac OS X developer program, everything will become automatic provided we use Xcode 4.3 or later. Xcode will automatically manage our obtaining, renewing, and code signing with our Developer ID.

Time for action – signing an App with our Developer ID

Now, we can look at the steps needed to sign our App using our Developer ID:

1. If you have not joined the Mac App developer program, do so now.

2. Launch Xcode and create a new project using the Mac OS X Cocoa Application template.

3. Name the new App `DeveloperIDTest`.

4. From the **Product** menu, select **Build For**, and then select **Archiving**.

5. From the **Product** menu, select **Archive**.

6. In the **Organizer – Archives** window, click on the **Distribute...**button as shown in the following screenshot:

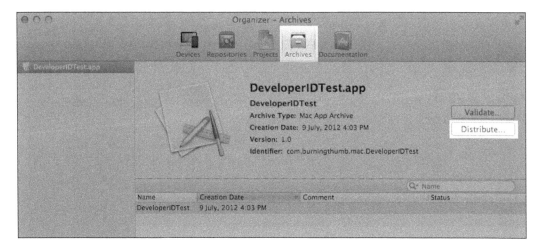

7. For the **Method of Distribution**, select **Export Developer ID-signed Application** and click on the **Next** button as shown in the following screenshot:

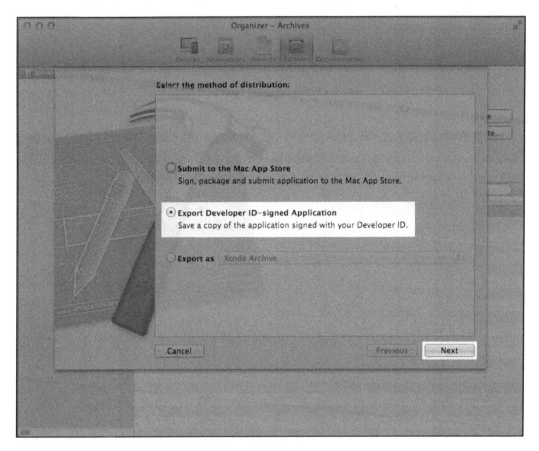

8. Select the Developer ID with which you wish to sign in the App and click on the **Next** button.

9. When prompted to enter your keychain password for codesign, enter your **Password** and click on the **OK** button as shown in the following screenshot:

10. Optionally, rename your App and click on the **Save** button.

What just happened?

We created a new App and archived it using our Developer ID. We can now distribute the App using any direct method that we prefer (or any combination of methods) and Gatekeeper will recognize and allow the App to be installed. If we look inside the App package, we can see it does include the **_CodeSignature** folder and the **CodeResources** as shown in the following screenshot:

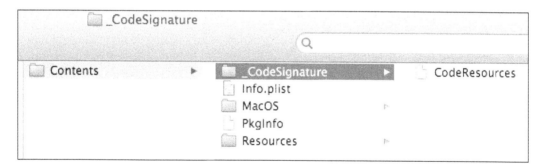

Summary

In this chapter, we have examined how to become a Mac App developer and how to code sign our App so that we can share it with users outside of the Mac App store.

Specifically, we covered what the Mac developer program is and how to join it, what additional developer tools are available to Mac developer program members, and what is code signing and how to code sign our App so that Gatekeeper will allow users to run it.

This is the final topic covered in this book. We have taken a journey from an entry level App that performs basic arithmetic through sophisticated Apps that access the Internet and cloud services, all the way to a full-screen video capture App. We have included important information on how we can share our App seamlessly with others. It has been quite a journey and we have learned a lot. But in the world of App programming there is never an end, there is only a continuous path of learning and expanding our knowledge to produce more powerful Apps as our expertise grows.

So, we end this chapter with the knowledge that our journey into App design has just begun.

Enjoy the journey!

Index

Symbols

2D drawing
  performing, in custom view 171, 172
32 bit
  to 64 bit, transitions 54
64 bit
  from 32 bit, transition 54
.app extension 16
#define compiler directive 70
@end keyword 24
.framework extension 16
.h extension 16
.h implementation, preference pane project
  customizing 69
@implementation keyword 24
#import 199
.m extension 16
.m implementation, preference pane project
  customizing 72
.pch extension 16
.plist extension 16
.prefPane extension 57
@property 234
@property declaration 62, 127
@property entries 222
@property keyword 63
.rtf extension 16
.strings extension 16
@synthesize 234
@synthesize directive 258
@synthisze definition 24

@sythesize keyword 63
.tiff extension 57

A

Accessory editor 226
active strokes
  drawing 172, 173
Add Category toolbar item 142
addImagesFromDirectory: method 204, 206
addImageWithURL: method 203, 206
Add Key toolbar item 141
addStroke: method 182, 185
App
  signing, with Developer ID 289-291
App Delegate
  connecting, to GUI 88, 125, 126
App Delegate object 30, 31
App Icon 17
Apple bug reporter system, Mac
    developer program
  access to 283
applicaitonDidFinishLaunching:
    method 222, 235
Application Programming Interfaces (APIs) 8
App, paid developer program
  distributing, through Mac App store 284
Array Controller object 242
audio capture
  previewing 232
auto layout
  about 254
  traditional layout model, using 254-258

Thank you for buying
Mac Application Development by Example
Beginner's Guide

About Packt Publishing

Packt, pronounced 'packed', published its first book "Mastering phpMyAdmin for Effective MySQL Management" in April 2004 and subsequently continued to specialize in publishing highly focused books on specific technologies and solutions.

Our books and publications share the experiences of your fellow IT professionals in adapting and customizing today's systems, applications, and frameworks. Our solution-based books give you the knowledge and power to customize the software and technologies you're using to get the job done. Packt books are more specific and less general than the IT books you have seen in the past. Our unique business model allows us to bring you more focused information, giving you more of what you need to know, and less of what you don't.

Packt is a modern, yet unique publishing company, which focuses on producing quality, cutting-edge books for communities of developers, administrators, and newbies alike. For more information, please visit our website: www.PacktPub.com.

Writing for Packt

We welcome all inquiries from people who are interested in authoring. Book proposals should be sent to author@packtpub.com. If your book idea is still at an early stage and you would like to discuss it first before writing a formal book proposal, contact us; one of our commissioning editors will get in touch with you.

We're not just looking for published authors; if you have strong technical skills but no writing experience, our experienced editors can help you develop a writing career, or simply get some additional reward for your expertise.

Xcode 4 iOS Development
Beginner's Guide

ISBN: 978-1-849691-30-7   Paperback: 432 pages

Use the powerful Xcode 4 suite of tools to build applications for the iPhone and iPad from scratch

1. Learn how to use Xcode 4 to build simple, yet powerful applications with ease

2. Each chapter builds on what you have learned already

3. Learn to add audio and video playback to your applications

4. Plentiful step-by-step examples, images, and diagrams to get you up to speed in no time with helpful hints along the way

Unity iOS Game Development
Beginner's Guide

ISBN: 978-1-849690-40-9   Paperback: 314 pages

Develop iOS games from concept to cash flow using Unity

1. Dive straight into game development with no previous Unity or iOS experience

2. Work through the entire lifecycle of developing games for iOS

3. Add multiplayer, input controls, debugging, in app and micro payments to your game

4. Implement the different business models that will enable you to make money on iOS games

Please check **www.PacktPub.com** for information on our titles

Corona SDK Mobile Game Development: Beginner's Guide

ISBN: 978-1-849691-88-8   Paperback:408 pages

Create monetized games for iOS and Android with minimum cost and code

1. Build once and deploy your games to both iOS and Android

2. Create commercially successful games by applying several monetization techniques and tools

3. Create three fun games and integrate them with social networks such as Twitter and Facebook

Unity iOS Essentials

ISBN: 978-1-849691-82-6   Paperback: 358 pages

Develop high performance, fun iOS games using Unity 3D

1. Learn key strategies and follow practical guidelines for creating Unity 3D games for iOS devices.

2. Learn how to plan your game levels to optimize performance on iOS devices using advanced game concepts.

3. Full of tips, scripts, shaders, and complete Unity 3D projects to guide you through game creation on iOS from start to finish.

Please check **www.PacktPub.com** for information on our titles

www.ingramcontent.com/pod-product-compliance
Lightning Source LLC
LaVergne TN
LVHW062307060326
832902LV00013B/2082